Teaching
Business Ethics for
Effective Learning

Teaching Business Ethics for Effective Learning

RONALD R. SIMS

QUORUM BOOKS
Westport, Connecticut • London

Library of Congress Cataloging-in-Publication Data

Sims, Ronald R.
    Teaching business ethics for effective learning / Ronald R. Sims.
        p. cm.
    Includes bibliographical references and index.
    ISBN 1–56720–482–1 (alk. paper)
    1. Business ethics—Study and teaching.   I. Title.
HF5387.S572   2002
174'.4'071—dc21   2001048805

British Library Cataloguing in Publication Data is available.

Library of Congress Catalog Card Number: 2001048805
ISBN: 1–56720–482–1

First published in 2002

Quorum Books, 88 Post Road West, Westport, CT 06881
An imprint of Greenwood Publishing Group, Inc.
www.quorumbooks.com

Printed in the United States of America

The paper used in this book complies with the
Permanent Paper Standard issued by the National
Information Standards Organization (Z39.48–1984).

10 9 8 7 6 5 4 3 2 1

Contents

Preface

I am celebrating my twentieth anniversary as a college teacher by completing this book. My intention in writing *Teaching Business Ethics for Effective Learning* provides one business ethics teacher's views on how to meet the challenge of teaching business ethics. The book does not include a list of cases or other materials that the reader can use in the classroom, but instead speaks to some important process issues that must be addressed if we are to increase our effectiveness in the classroom. The importance of getting all key stakeholders to come to agreement on the goals or purposes of teaching business ethics, along with outcomes assessment, are offered as two of the critical components for any successful business ethics teaching effort. Experiential learning theory is introduced as the foundation for various steps of the process of teaching business ethics, beginning with curriculum planning and moving into the classroom to build a climate conducive to learning and teaching business ethics.

The book is intended for anyone interested in teaching business ethics and especially those who already value a classroom environment based on open dialogue and experiential learning and those who are interested in learning more about such an environment. I do hope the readers find the book worthy of being one of the many voices on how we can improve our ability to teach or help others learn about ethics.

Once again a very, very special thanks goes to Herrington Bryce, who continues to serve as a colleague, mentor, and valued friend. The administrative support of Larry Pulley, Dean of the School of Business Administration at the College of William & Mary, is also acknowledged. I am also indebted to Eric Valentine, Publisher at Quorum Books.

My thanks and appreciation as usual also goes out to my wife, Serbrenia, and the rest of our gang, Nandi, Dangaia, Sieya, and Kani. I appreciate your tolerating the many evening, morning, afternoon, and weekend hours that I had to spend trying to write this book. A special "keep movin' forward" goes out to Ronald, Jr., Marchet, Vellice, Shelley, and Sharisse.

Teaching Business Ethics for Effective Learning

Chapter 1

Teaching Business Ethics
for Effective Learning

Fable: The Rabbit and the Goat

A Goat once approached a peanut stand that was kept by a Rabbit, purchased five cents worth of peanuts, laid down a dime, and received a punched nickel in change. In a few days the Goat came back, called for another pint of peanuts, and offered the same nickel in payment; but in the meantime had stopped the hole in it with a peg.

"I can't take that nickel," said the rabbit.

"This is the very nickel you gave me in change a few days ago," replied the Goat.

"I know it is," continued the Rabbit. "But I made no attempt to deceive you about it. When you took the coin the hole was wide open, and you could see it for yourself. In working that mutilated coin off on you I simply showed my business sagacity; but now you bring it back with the hole stopped up and try to pass it, with a clear intent to deceive. That is fraud. My dear Goat, I'm afraid the grand jury will get after you if you are not more careful about little things of this sort."

MORAL: This fable teaches that the moral quality of a business often depends upon the view you take of it.

This fable appeared in the October 8, 1885 edition of *Life* magazine and I included it in a 1991 *Journal of Business Ethics* article (see Sims & Sims, 1991). I believe it is still an excellent example of the need for the inclusion of ethics teaching in business curricula at colleges and universities. There are still everyday experiences like those of the "Rabbit and the Goat," and unfortunately some of our current and former business students take on the Rabbit's role with ease. As a result of such activities, many advocates of ethics teaching have called for increasing ethics teaching in business schools.

And given the number of business degrees awarded, I believe that such calls are appropriate. Clearly, business schools interface with a large portion of our future leaders and occupy a strategic position from which to make a contribution to their ethical and moral development. Therefore, a major premise of this book is that business schools must accept more responsibility for decreasing the number of "Rabbits" we award degrees. And this means that business schools must increase ethics teaching in their curricula.

Passion, hope, doubt, fear, exhilaration, weariness, colleagueship, loneliness, hollow victories, glorious defeats, and, above all, the certainties of surprise and ambiguity—how can one capture the reality of teaching business ethics in a single word or phrase? This book is my effort to provide responses to what I and others believe are some very central questions that must be addressed by business schools and those responsible for undertaking the challenge of actually teaching business ethics. Challenges that can be deeply emotive and bafflingly chaotic. Among these questions are "Can we *teach* ethics?" and "*should* we teach ethics?" Feldman and Thompson (1990), believing that we can and should teach business ethics, identified five questions to be asked of teachers of business ethics. These include: (1) *Who* should teach business ethics? (2) *What* should be taught in a business ethics course? (3) *Where* should business ethics be placed in the curriculum? (4) *When* should business ethics be taught to students? and (5) *How* should ethics material be delivered in the classroom? (Shannon & Berl, 1997). (Note: Gilbert [1992] offers the following questions as important to answer in teaching business ethics: What, Why, Who, Where, and When). I would add another question to Feldman and Thompson (1990): (6) *How* do we assess the impact teaching business ethics has on students? My answers to these questions and the accompanying discussion of related issues are based on personal experiences in teaching in general and teaching business ethics is particular.

Before beginning to provide answers to the questions above and exploring in more detail issues related to teaching business ethics, I will offer a brief background and historical look at reasons for the new emphasis on ethical coursework.

SOME HISTORY AND BACKGROUND ON BUSINESS ETHICS EDUCATION

The academic study of ethics is at least 2,300 years old. Questions of right and wrong were discussed at length by both Plato and Aristotle during the classical period in Athens and have been treated by Western philosophers since then. In Oriental philosophy, such discussions first appeared even earlier.

By comparison, business ethics is a very young field. With the publication of *The Education of American Businessmen* (Pierson, 1959) and *Higher Education for Business* (Gordon & Howell, 1959), emphasis was placed on the need for higher education in business to go beyond vocational training and specifically for business education to include the external environment of organizations. Pierson observed that an

important influence shaping the work of business schools is the increasing attention being given to the social responsibilities of business enterprises. Formal standards embodied in law and governmental regulations are but one aspect of this development. Even more pervasive are the informal rules and obligations which the community expects business to meet, whether they involve dealings at national, state, or local levels. No one would argue that there is a clear and precise code of conduct applicable to business in its relations with representatives of government, unions, suppliers, stockholders, rival firms, and the like, but the norms within which employers operate are nonetheless real. (p. 92)

Gordon and Howell stated that "business education must be concerned not only with competence but also with responsibility, not only with skills but also have an obligation to do what they can to develop a 'sense of social responsibility' and a high standard of business ethics in their graduates" (p. 111).

Weber (1990) suggested that in response to the new emphasis on the role of business education, there was growth in courses in business and society and in business ethics. Additionally, the emphasis on ethical coursework in the 1960s and early 1970s was a result of the belief by many people that a general moral and ethical decline in society has occurred since the 1960s. It was reported that between 1966 and 1975, the percentage of the public professing confidence in Congress had dropped from 42 percent to 13 percent; in major corporate presidents from 55 percent to 19 percent; in doctors from 72 percent to 43 percent; and in lawyers from 46 percent to 16 percent (Bok, 1976). To compound this decrease in public confidence of society's leaders, Dr. George Gallup, Jr., in 1979 predicted that Americans would face an enormous moral crisis during the 1980s unless something is done to halt society's moral decline (Hysom & Bolce, 1983).

Clearly, the number of "business ethics" and "business and society" courses, the provision of regular conferences, the growing number of textbooks on these topics, and the founding of numerous centers demonstrated a commitment to increasing the teaching and research of business ethics. Yet, as suggested by Powers and Vogel (1980), these activities, like philosophy, were "remote from the traditional intellectual center of gravity of business education" (p. 59). As Derek Bok (1986) explains:

[F]ew influential voices from our schools of management speak out on issues of corporate responsibility or the role of free enterprise, even though many prominent executives believe that public attitudes about the corporation's place in society will have a decisive influence on the future of American business. Corporate leaders sometimes complain that academic critics have a bias against business, citing authors such as John Kenneth Galbraith, Charles Lindblom, and Robert Heilbroner. Yet the wonder is not that critics of business exist, but that so few members of the leading management faculties are willing or able to contribute significantly to the debate. (p. 99)

In his 1988 annual report to Harvard University's board of trustees, Derek Bok said that universities have failed to take seriously their responsibility to instill a sense of ethics in college students. Bok felt that colleges and universities must help students develop moral and ethical standards that they are unlikely to get elsewhere (Bok, 1988).

The corporate community also voiced the need for ethics teaching on the college level in the late 1980s. Arthur Andersen & Company, a major public-accounting firm, implemented an ethics study program and the firm committed to spending $5 million over a five-year period to develop case studies on ethics for business schools. Arthur Andersen & Company of Chicago also provided free training to college professors who were interested in teaching case studies that deal with ethical dilemmas in the areas of accounting, finance, marketing, and management. In return, the college professors were expected to sponsor a series of conferences on ethics for faculty members, students, business executives, and company clients (Evangelauf, 1988). Sheppard (1988) also noted the surge of interest in college courses and executive development programs in the "new" field of business ethics, more properly called "business applied ethics."

In order to better understand the increasing need for ethics in today's business schools, one must be familiar with the history of ethics and the teaching of values in the American college system. In the early years of American colleges, most college seniors were required to take a course in ethics often taught by the college president. The course primarily focused on the prevailing values of the day and applied them to social problems and personal dilemmas. This culminating experience of moral philosophy in the undergraduate curriculum later gave way to the first signs of increasing specialization of the disciplines. Courses on practical ethics disappeared, leaving classes in theory or metaethics that were consistent with the new belief that learning should be wholly scientific and value-free. By the middle of the twentieth century, instruction in ethics had become confined almost exclusively to the department of philosophy and religion (Bok, 1986; Sloan, 1980).

In the recent past, business schools have been accused of never showing an interest in providing lectures and courses on moral conduct or surveys of ethical theory. A study by the Ethics Center reported on CNN News noted that, "In 1988 eighty-nine percent of MBA schools include ethics in their curriculum and twenty-one percent offer separate courses. This is up from sixteen percent in 1978." Additionally, Porter and McKibbin (1988) found that the area of societal trends and the environment of the organization was still underdeveloped. Sims and Sims (1991) suggested that still, too many of them have simply ignored moral education altogether. But others, like the Harvard Business School, began to offer classes concerning ethics and personal responsibility. Some business schools approached the subject by attempting to weave moral issues throughout a variety of courses and problems taught in the case method format in the regular curriculum. In this approach it was emphasized that ethical questions are not isolated problems but an integral part of the daily life and experience of the business student. According to Sims and Sims (1991), even with this approach business schools could expect only limited success in helping students learn to reason more carefully about moral issues and respond to ethical questions. In most business schools the professors had so much ground to cover in their own fields that they could not be expected or would rarely take the time to incorporate material on moral or ethical issues into their courses.

During the 1980s and most of the 1990s it appeared that in most business schools the faculty did not have a knowledge of ethics or the writings of moral philosophers that would allow them to teach ethics. Efforts to divide the responsibility for teaching ethics among a large number of faculty members often resulted in many of them giving minimal attention to the moral problems. The faculty members in all likelihood concentrated on other aspects of the course materials that they felt more comfortable teaching. During the late 1980s and early 1990s I found that students without exception felt that moral issues were seldom touched on in their courses, and when they were, were treated as afterthoughts or digressions. In addition, many of my colleagues admitted that moral issues were included in cases that focused on corporate bribes in the international arena, false advertising, and production methods, but not explicitly.

The business classes that included some mention of ethical issues, particularly at the graduate level, generally proceeded by case discussion rather than lecturing, which is often the case in undergraduate classes. In some instances the professors presented their own views on the ethical issues, if only to demonstrate that it is possible to make carefully reasoned choices about ethical dilemmas. However, they were less concerned with presenting solutions than with carrying on an active discussion in an effort to encourage students to perceive ethical issues, wrestle with the competing arguments, discover weaknesses in their own position, and ultimately reach thoughtfully reasoned conclusions.

Current Trends and Expectations

Today's business school graduates are expected to meet the ethical and socially responsible needs of corporations and take on the role of leaders and managers in devising and executing ethical programs. Given such expectations corporations and business schools have increasingly recognized that ethical behavior does not develop without knowledgeable, committed supporters at all levels. But where are these employees, managers, and leaders being educated and trained? And does that education and training sufficiently prepare them for roles in ethical, responsible companies? The propensity to reason through decisions with an ethical framework and to act based on these principles is becoming a more valued skill in corporate cultures, where "successful careers depend on business conduct as well as financial results. . . . [E]thical reasoning and the instincts to make sound ethical choices are viewed as indispensable elements in a manager's education" (Berenbeim, 1999, p. 11). Dennis Bakke, CEO of AES, goes so far as to argue that he would rather hire people who are "evangelical" about the company's values (integrity, social responsibility) than people who have good technical skills (Wetlaufer, 1999).

It is estimated that 240,000 to 250,000 undergraduate and 100,000 graduate students received degrees in business in 1999 and 2000 (Klusmann, 2000). Klusmann also noted that most of the Masters in Business Administration (MBA) graduates are not familiar with, nor are they comfortable with, the ethical and socially aware needs of many companies—including those companies that recruit and hire MBAs on their campuses. This failing at business schools is particularly disconcerting given the strong ethics components in other professional schools including medicine, law, and government (Stark, 1993).

Businesses are facing increasing amounts of pressure to perform ethically and responsibly; moreover, there is a compelling business reason to behave within these bounds. Thus, it is inherent that, when hiring, managers want to bring in new, fresh business undergraduates and MBAs with their innovative ideas, but companies also want to hire students who understand their business and corporate culture. The Conference Board found that 82 percent of companies surveyed thought that mandatory ethics programs in business schools were a good idea (Berenbeim, 1999). Today's organizations need employees who know how to think their way through difficult situations and often make decisions between what is essentially "right and right." In order to do this effectively, students need to practice this type of analysis in a safe, learning environment. When they need managers, many of these top corporate citizens (as ranked by *Business Ethics* magazine) do their recruiting and hiring through MBA programs—at the College of William & Mary as well as other top business schools. These companies include IBM, Amgen, Hewlett-Packard, Honeywell, Dell Computer, Merck,

Compaq, 3M, and Baxter International (Johannsson, 2001). To be the best employee or leader possible in corporations such as these, students should be able to relate to ethical policies and should understand the background and impetus for companies' commitment to ethical behavior and reasons for adopting ethical codes of conduct. But this type of training is not yet fully integrated in business school curricula.

The importance of ethics often comes to business school students from their external speakers. Last year, Jim McGlothlin, CEO and chairman of the United Company, and Chip Mason, co-founder of the Legg-Mason investing firm, both spoke extensively about the need for corporate ethics during visits to the Graduate School of Business at the College of William & Mary. McGlothlin's company is a large coal producer in Virginia, so his labor force is blue-collar, but he drove home the significance of communicating the goals and values of management to workers at all levels. And although Chip Mason operates in the vastly different world of finance, he also emphasized the importance of "not getting chalk on [your] shoes" (a reference to ball players going out of bounds and getting chalk on their footwear) (Vosburgh, 2001). Mason does not want his employees to cross any ethical lines, so he advises all of them against getting chalk on their shoes and attributes the striking success of Legg-Mason to honest, ethical hard work (in addition to the then rapidly growing stock market).

But despite these corporate leaders promulgating the necessity of ethics in business life, business schools are still devoting an inadequate amount of resources to the matter. Business schools seem to be falling into the "smart talk trap": they are speaking long and loud about the need for ethics, yet there is a "knowing-doing" gap that is illustrated through the lack of familiarity with ethical frameworks among MBA graduates (Pfeffer & Sutton, 1999, p. 135).

One wonders if there has been any real change today in the belief that while current attempts to teach ethics in business schools have their virtues, they are still often regarded with indifference or outright skepticism by many members of the academic community. Many academics still believe that their subjects are governed by their own internal laws and values. And, as noted by The Hastings Center (1980) more than two decades ago, often these individuals see the teaching of ethics in departments other than religion or philosophy as a way of smuggling "external values" and purposes into the autonomous life of their disciplines. Thus, students who would be learning mathematics, physics, or business, for example, are sidetracked into archaic and useless discussion of ethical issues.

What accounts for these attitudes is that many skeptics question the value of trying to teach students to reason about moral issues. According to these skeptics, courses that teach ethics may bring students to perceive more of the arguments and complexities that arise in moral issues, but this new-found sophistication will simply leave them more confused than ever and quite unable to reach any satisfactory moral conclusions. As early as 1976, Derek Bok pointed out that other skeptics conceded that ethics courses can help students reason more carefully about ethical problems (Bok, 1976). But these critics argued that moral development had less to do with reasoning than with acquiring proper moral values and achieving the strength of character to put these values into practice. Since such matters are not easily taught in a classroom, they questioned whether a course on ethics could accomplish anything of real importance. This point of view comes out clearly in the statement of one business school spokesman in explaining why there were no courses on ethics in the curriculum: "On the subject of ethics, we feel that either you have them or you don't" (Bok, 1976).

At the time of Bok's article, and today, there is clearly some force to this argument. It has been my experience that professors who teach business ethics as part of their cases in class do not seek to persuade students to accept some preferred moral values. In fact, most of us would be uneasy if they did, since such an effort would have overtones of indoctrination, which conflicts with our notions of intellectual freedom. As for building character, business schools can only make a limited contribution, and what they accomplish will probably depend more on what goes on outside the classroom than on the curriculum itself. For example, most of the sources that transmit moral standards are churches, families, and local communities, and they all have a greater influence on the business student than any ethics course in a business school. However, if a business school expects to impact the moral values of its students, it must first start offering more ethics courses.

Business changes far more rapidly than education does. Many think of business as being a "ready, fire, aim" institution while education is a "ready, aim . . . aim again . . . reload . . . aim again . . . fire" establishment. So, it is not a surprise that business schools are not keeping up with their main customers. However, they need to improve their current offerings. Organizations need employees who can operate in a complex, global community, but do so with integrity. With 350,000 new business graduates each year, corporations are clearly hiring their employees or managers and future leaders, but many are not prepared for their new demanding positions and thus are likely to take on the role of the "Rabbit" from our earlier fable.

Further evidence that business is trying to spur change at business schools can be seen in recent donations. The Pennsylvania State University Smeal School of Business was given $5 million to endow an ethics institute, and the school already has a program to support research and lectures in business ethics—also from a donation ("Graduate promises $5 million," 2000). Marymount University in Arlington, Virginia, announced plans to work with GEICO insurance company to establish a program to help small and mid-sized businesses introduce ethics programs into their companies

("GEICO and Marymount University," 2000). Another unusual example of business schools needing more ethics was illustrated when Exide Corporation settled a fraud case with the attorney general's office of Florida for $2.85 million; the attorney general gave the University of South Florida's Business School half of the settlement to endow a chair in business ethics ("USF, ethics program," 1999).

TEACHING BUSINESS ETHICS: SHOULD WE? CAN WE?

Should we teach business ethics? Can we teach it? As you may suspect, this book would not have been written if the answer to either question were "No." Additionally, it would be safe to surmise that financial and other resource commitments by companies like Arthur Andersen & Company in the late 1980s and the more recent partnership between GEICO and Marymount University are clear indications that there are those who believe we should and can teach business ethics, that the moral development of students can be enhanced through the education process. Sims and Sims (1991) argued that ethics should be and can be taught. Others suggest that there is strong support for the inclusion of ethics in business and accounting curricula (Alam, 1999; Brinkmann & Sims, 2001).

While few doubt that ethics are learned, many are not convinced that ethics can be taught. Dissenters from both the business and academic communities have raised serious questions about whether ethics can or should be taught (Trevino & Nelson, 1999). For example, some question whether teaching ethics is possible, arguing that it is too late to start ethics education at the university or college level because students come to a higher education institution with firmly set values and are not likely to change those values. More specifically, some critics argue that ethics courses cannot be effective because values are formed early in our lives and, according to Miller and Miller (1976), " 'honesty' " is not a course to be taught." Felix Rohatyn, a noted New York investment banker, said that ethics can't be taught past the age of 10. Lester Thurow, former dean of the Massachusetts Institute of Technology's Sloan School of Management, echoed this view when he stated that business schools can do little if students haven't already learned ethics from families, clergy, previous schools, or employers (Trevino & Nelson, 1999).

There is some research that supports the view that ethics can't be taught. For example, Martin (1981–1982) found that two ethics courses offered by the philosophy department did not significantly impact the students' ability to correctly assess the ethics scenarios presented to them. Similarly, others failed to find any significant impact resulting from students enrolled in a business ethics course. However, other recent research has found that ethics courses have a significant impact on students' ethical sensitivity and reasoning skills (Carlson & Burke, 1998; Weber and Glyptis, 2000) and that moral behavior can be developed from a thorough understanding of ethical concepts and dilemmas and reinfored by awareness of ethical issues (Sims & Sims, 1991). Despite these recent findings it is intriguing that many are still not convinced that ethics can be taught. Perhaps this tension, encountered when ethics is incorporated into the business curriculum, can be reframed to open the way for constructive discussion if the question is rephrased as: "If ethics can be taught to business students, then what should be the goals of teaching business ethics?"

THE GOALS OR OUTCOMES OF TEACHING BUSINESS ETHICS

As evidenced by the discussion thus far, the importance of teaching ethics in business schools and higher education has been discussed for years. And of course, the debate continues surrounding the extent to which applied business ethics courses should dominate business school curriculums. However, I believe that many educators accept the need for higher education and business schools to help develop a sense of moral judgement and obligation in students. I think this acceptance is especially important given that more than ever before, business students are turning towards careers that they hope will ensure financial success and added responsibilities. With the drive for financial success, added responsibilities, and time constraints, these future employees may not have, or want to take the time to logically develop, an ethical norm. One must hope that they will be able to recognize ethical dilemmas and make decisions based upon sound ethical principles.

For our purposes, moral judgement is action oriented. Therefore, business students should participate in experiential learning exercises that require them to ask themselves: What is the right thing to do, or what is the wrong thing to do? Experiential learning exercises that expect students to respond to moral questions that are personal in nature and involve interpersonal relations require normative responses to determine the appropriate course of action. In this age of moral relativism, business school curricula should provide students with continuous experience in examining the underlying moral issues. What are a manager's or an employee's responsibilities or obligations to an organization, a work group, themselves, their family, and the society? And what will be the possible consequences of a particular action if they make an immoral decision and knowingly harm others?

Increasing business schools' responsibilities to incorporate applied business ethics courses as part of their curriculum will require students to think about the bedrock of moral action: personal values and the meaning of abstract terms such as responsibility, negligence, blame, reward, happiness, respect, truthfulness, moral integrity, honesty, courage, loyalty, disgrace, and consideration of other human beings. Students must understand that norms of individual conduct are determined by values, which constitute the basic axioms under which individuals live. And values are formed within a framework of human relationships. Basic business values such as treating the customer with respect and manufacturing products that are safe and of high quality constitute an ideology that fortifies personal moral conduct and is fortified by personal ethics. As noted above, there are those who feel taking required courses in applied business ethics may be extreme. But I strongly feel that our future society leaders should be required to understand and recognize ethical issues. In my view, it does seem plausible to suppose that students in business schools who are required to take courses that look at moral behavior will become more alert in perceiving ethical issues, more aware of the reasons underlying moral principles, and more equipped to reason carefully in applying these principles to concrete business situations.

When people think of the goals of teaching business ethics, they should be thinking of outcomes. This means that the teacher should begin the process of any business ethics education effort—whether a single exercise or activity, a class, a module, or a whole course—by asking what the students ought to be able to do, or do better, when they finish it that they could not do, or do as well, when they began. This is the first step in teaching business ethics, and this outcomes-focused approach is the driving force behind everything in the ethics education effort (i.e., curriculum design and outcomes assessment).

The approach to teaching business ethics highlighted throughout this book is one that is concerned with the ethics teacher asking how she or he will know whether students have accomplished the outcome aimed at in the activity, class, module, or course. Clearly, how one will assess whether or not the goals or purpose of teaching business ethics were achieved is a decision that, in my experience, is not standard practice. Unfortunately, it has been my experience that far too many responsible for teaching business ethics first focus on what ethical material will be taught and what books will be used, then they teach these materials, and subsequently they design the outcomes assessment instruments to match what has been taught. They look at the teaching business ethics outcomes, if at all, only when the course or class is over and the course is being evaluated, usually by end of term student surveys. While that approach may be effective for many, it makes no sense at all if one is really committed to designing coherent business ethics teaching efforts. A basic premise of this book is that all key stakeholders must begin by agreeing on the goals, purposes, and outcomes if they want to proceed coherently and efficiently in ethics education. Business ethics instructors must begin by asking what the students ought to be able to do better when they finish the ethics activity, class, module, or course that they could not do, or do as well, when they began.

CONCLUSION

In talking with colleagues over the years, I have found that many of them agree that courses in applied business ethics should become an integral part of the business school curriculum. However, concerns arise about what the goals of teaching business ethics should be, who among the business faculty is qualified to teach them, what should be taught in the courses, when should the courses be taught, and how the impact of such efforts should be assessed. Experience shows us that poor instruction can harm any class. Sheppard points out that morality appears to be esoteric and qualitative in nature, that it has no substantial relation to objective and quantitative performance. In addition, understanding the meaning of ethics or morality requires the distasteful reworking of long-forgotten classroom studies. What could Socrates, Plato, and Aristotle possibly teach us about the world of business in the twentieth century? (Sheppard, 1988). Sims and Sims (1991) noted that "We are sure that a gap in philosophical knowledge exists between business school faculty and those in the religion and philosophy departments. However, feel comfortable with it or not, business schools must increase their emphasis upon teaching ethics" (p. 213). And if this book fulfills its intended purpose then the ideas offered here will help move the process of teaching business ethics a little forward.

REFERENCES

Alam, K.F. 1999. Ethics and accounting education. *Teaching Business Ethics* 2: 261–272.

Berenbeim, R.E. 1999. *Global corporate ethics practices: A developing consensus.* New York: The Conference Board.

Bok, D.C. 1976. Can ethics be taught? *Change* 8: 26–30.

Bok, D.C. 1986. *Higher learning.* Cambridge, MA: Harvard University Press.

Bok, D.C. 1988. Bok says students need colleges' help on ethics. *The Chronicle of Higher Education* (April 20): 42.

Brinkmann, J., & Sims, R.R. 2001. Stakeholder-sensitive business ethics teaching, *Teaching Business Ethics* 5: 171–193.

Burke, E. 1990. Teaching public administration ethically: Insights from NASPAA IVC.3. Paper presented at the National Conference on Teaching Administration, Tempa, FL, February 15–17.

Carlson, P.J., & Burke, F. 1998. Lessons learned from ethics in the classroom exploring student growth in flexibility, complexity and comprehension. *Journal of Business Ethics* 17: 1179–1187.

Evangelauf, J. 1988. Ethics-studies program planned. *The Chronicle of Higher Education* (May 4): A2.

Feldman, H.D., & Thompson, R.C. 1990. Teaching business ethics: A challenge for business education in the 1990s. *Journal of Marketing Education* (Summer): 10–12.

GEICO and Marymount University launch applied business ethics program with $30,000 from GEICO. 2000. *PR Newswire* (February 9): 2.

Gilbert, J.T. 1992. Teaching business ethics: What, why, who, where, and when. *Journal of Education for Business* 68(1): 5–8.

Gordon, R.A., & Howell, J.E. 1959. *Higher education for business*. New York: Columbia University Press.

Graduate promises $5 million for Penn State ethics program. 2000. *Centre Daily News* (March 4): 1.

The Hastings Center. 1980. *The teaching of ethics in higher education*. Hastings-on-Hudson, NY: The Institute of Society, Ethics and Life Sciences.

Hysom, J., & Bolce, W.J. 1983. *Business and its environment*. St. Paul, MN: West Publishing Co.

Johannson, P. 2001. The 100 best corporate citizens for 2001. *Business Ethics* (March–April): 2–3.

Klusmann, T. 2000. MBA: Making business accountable. *Business Ethics* (May–June): 3–4.

Martin, T.R. 1981–1982. Do courses in ethics improve the ethical judgment of students? *Business and Society* 20(2) and 21(1): 17–26.

Miller, M.S., & Miller, A.E. 1976. It's too late for ethics courses in business schools. *Business and Society Review* (Spring): 39–42.

Pfeffer, J., & Sutton, R.I. 1999. The smart talk trap. *Harvard Business Review* (May–June): 134–142.

Pierson, F.C. 1959. *The education of American businessmen*. New York: McGraw-Hill.

Porter, L.W., & McKibbin, L.E. 1988. *Management education and development: Drift or thrust into the 21st century?* New York: McGraw-Hill.

Powers, C.W., & Vogel, D. 1980. *Ethics in the education of business managers*. Hastings-on-Hudson, NY: The Hastings Center.

The rabbit and the goat. 1885. *Life* (October 8): 208.

Shannon, J.R., & Berl, R.L. 1997. Are we teaching ethics in marketing: A survey of students' attitudes and perceptions. *Journal of Business Ethics* 16: 1059–1075.

Sheppard, C.S. 1988. The ethical maze: Perspectives on business leadership and ethics. *William & Mary Business Review* (Spring): 26–31.

Sims, R.R., & Sims, S.J. 1991. Increasing applied business ethics courses in business school curricula. *Journal of Business Ethics* 10: 211–219.

Sloan, D. 1980. *Education and values*. New York: Teachers College Press.

Stark, A. 1993. What's the matter with business ethics? *Harvard Business Review* (May–June): 38–48.

Trevino, L.K., & Nelson, K.A. 1999. *Managing business ethics* (2nd ed). New York: John Wiley & Sons.

USF ethics program gets jump start. 1999. *The Tampa Tribune* (June 8): 1.

Vosburgh, L. 2001. *Corporate ethics, social responsibility, and business schools*. Independent study project, College of William & Mary (Spring), Williamsburg, VA.

Weber, J. 1990. Measuring the impact of teaching ethics to future managers: A review, assessment, and recommendations. *Journal of Business Ethics* 8: 183–190.

Weber, J., & Glyptis, S.M. 2000. Measuring the impact of a business ethics course and community service experience on students' values and opinions. *Teaching Business Ethics* 4: 341–358.

Wetlaufer, S. 1999. Organizing for empowerment: An interview with Roger Sant and Dennis Bakke. *Harvard Business Review* (January–February): 111–123.

Chapter 2

What Should Be Taught in Business Ethics Efforts?

INTRODUCTION

Like many teachers, I have had my doubts about my effectiveness. In my darkest moments as a full-time business teacher, and more recently as a part-time business ethics teacher, I often struggle with and have doubts that teaching business ethics is possible, and wonder if it may be too late for students to learn business ethics by the time I encounter them during their junior or senior year of college. In spite of the fact that teaching business ethics has never been high on the radar screen in the business schools I have worked in, and despite my own questioning as to whether or not teaching business ethics efforts make more than minor contributions to students' ethical or moral action, I find myself always coming back to the fundamental belief that ethics can be taught and learned by students. But teaching and learning can only occur if there is agreement by the key stakeholders on the goals of business ethics education efforts.

This chapter first discusses the importance of agreement among key stakeholders on the goals of teaching business ethics and offers a brief review of the goals of teaching business ethics as suggested by a number of writers and researchers. Next, we turn to a detailed discussion of a seven-objective component model based on the underlying premise that students should not be indoctrinated but rather forced to work with their own attitudes. The chapter then focuses on the findings of a review of two dozen different syllabi from various business ethics teaching efforts to categorize the goals of teaching business ethics.

AGREEMENT ON THE OBJECTIVES OF TEACHING BUSINESS ETHICS

Many faculty and other stakeholders attempting to articulate the goals or purposes undergirding business ethics teaching efforts are entering into territory that heretofore has been relatively unexplored. The fact that there exists a range of beliefs about the nature, function, and goals of ethics in personal, professional, and social life is a particularly relevant challenge. In a similar vein, it has been suggested that those involved in "the *teaching* of ethics" (Callahan, 1980, p. 61; emphasis added) face an added difficulty, since even as the concept of "ethics" has multiple meanings so also does the idea of "teaching." Callahan notes:

The very phrase "the teaching of ethics" has a variety of connotations in our culture, and so for that matter does the term "ethics." One can never be certain just what people hear when they encounter the notion of "teaching ethics": for some, it means instructing people not to break the law or to abide by some legal or professional code; for others, it means an attempt to improve moral character or to instill certain virtues; for still others, it primarily means imparting special skills in the handling of moral argumentation. Moreover, clarity is by no means guaranteed by the standard method of simply stipulating one's own definitions or viewpoints. Someone who was once "taught ethics" by harsh and repressive methods of gross indoctrination may have trouble understanding "the teaching of ethics" in any more benign sense, however carefully one may point out other possibilities. (p. 61)

In spite of the lack of agreement on what is meant by "teaching and ethics" or "teaching ethics" those responsible for teaching business ethics must agree on their goals and objectives.

The goals of teaching business ethics are important to address (see e.g., Gilbert, 1992; Alam, 1999). Agreement about educational goals is not an easy task (Pace, 1984, pp. 12–14, 17). In discussing college and university educational goals in general, Turnbull (1985, p. 24) notes that "beyond the area of basic skills there lies an immense realm of disagreement about collegiate goals . . . [I]t is essential to realize that the purposes of higher education are a matter of fundamental debate." With this in mind, it is critical that business school faculty do not overlook the need to build consensus regarding the goals of teaching business ethics. These goals should reflect the values of the business school and institution.

This process of building consensus is similar to the development of a common mission statement. Business school faculties have widely acknowledged that their responsibility to students, society, and prospective employers is not limited to preparing graduates to be astute managers, analytical financial executives, or creative manipulators of large amounts of money or data. The educational mission also includes the development of intellectual capacities for ethical discernment, analysis, judgement, and reflection.

THE GOALS OF TEACHING BUSINESS ETHICS: A BRIEF REVIEW

It is one thing to acknowledge the limitations of formal learning in business schools and quite another to deny that courses which emphasize ethical reading and discussion have any effect in developing ethical principles and moral character. Those who teach business ethics efforts that, for example, emphasize and encourage students to define moral values more carefully and to understand more fully the reasons that underlie and justify different precepts do have their supporters. Douglas Sloan (1980) looked at the history of the teaching of ethics in the American undergraduate curriculum from 1879 to 1976 and emphasized that Americans have primarily looked to education for the creation of common social values. In addition, the college was considered to have a special and leading role to perform in the shaping of societal ethics and national goals and values, and therefore it should be the logical location for ethics and values teaching.

Researchers at The Hastings Center reported in 1980 that the primary purpose of courses in ethics ought to be to provide students with those concepts and analytical skills that will enable them to grapple with broad ethical theory in attempting to resolve both personal and professional dilemmas, as well as to reflect on the moral issues facing the larger society (1980). In addition, The Hastings Center report stressed that all students should have the opportunity for a systematic exposure to ethics. Since ethical problems arise in almost all areas and domains of human activity, they should be dealt with in the university, at least to some extent, in all disciplines in the curriculum.

Sheppard (1988) pointed out that teaching performs the valuable service of conveying information, and while ethics or moral judgement cannot be taught, students can be made sensitive to them. Business courses in ethics may not only enhance a student's moral awareness but also help to achieve a greater common understanding of many everyday questions.

Over the years, external pressure seems to be the main motive for introducing ethics courses in some business schools, particularly pressure to introduce ethics so that graduates might *behave* better in their professional lives. In other business schools, the essential motive has been to grapple with some very specific moral issues in the professional field (e.g., whistle-blowing or insider trading) in order to see if some of them can be resolved. In other instances, the main motive has simply been to introduce different disciplinary and methodological perspectives into business schools dominated by heavy technical (quantitative) components. The motives for introducing ethics courses into the undergraduate curriculum are no less varied:

"sensitizing" students, teaching them intellectual skills, and helping them with personal problems. Thus it appears that many business schools look to courses in ethics to serve different functions, ranging from character improvement to the development of skills in problem resolution to a desire to expand student horizons to a desire to satisfy external critics (The Hastings Center, 1980).

Over the past decade, what has been the goal of teaching business ethics? Sims and Sims (1991) suggest that, first, business schools could help students become more alert in discovering the moral issues that arise in their work lives. By repeatedly asking students to identify moral problems and define the issues at stake, courses in applied business ethics should sharpen and refine the moral perception of students so that they can avoid the following pitfalls: failing to act morally simply because they are unaware of the ethical problems that lie hidden in the work situations they confront and failing to discover a moral problem until they have gotten too deeply enmeshed to extricate themselves.

A second accomplishment would be helping students develop their capacity for moral reasoning by learning to sort out all of the arguments that bear upon moral problems and apply them to concrete work situations. Well-taught applied business ethics courses can demonstrate that moral issues can be discussed as rigorously as many other problems considered in the classroom. Finally, teaching applied business ethics will help students grapple with moral issues and clarify their moral aspirations in a setting where no serious personal consequences are at stake. By considering a series of ethical problems, students can be encouraged to define their identity and establish the level of integrity at which they want to lead their professional lives. Students may set higher ethical standards for themselves if they first encounter the moral problems of the work world in the classroom instead of waiting to confront them at a point in their careers when they must take moral risks in their organizations. In reality, teaching applied business ethics to students provides guidance and impetus for future managerial leadership (Sims & Sims, 1991).

In sum, Sims and Sims argued that the general purpose of teaching ethics ought to be that of encouraging the moral imagination, developing skills in the identification and analysis of moral issues (including a sense of moral obligation and personal responsibility), and learning to cope with moral dilemma. They concluded that

it does seem plausible to suppose that students in business schools who are required to take courses which look at moral behavior will become more alert in perceiving ethical issues, more aware of the reasons underlying moral principles, and more equipped to reason carefully in applying these principles to concrete business situations. (p. 48)

Kracher (1999) recently noted that although there is a lack of current, comprehensive data about course goals *used* by business ethicists today, a recent survey shows that professors mention ethical decision making as a priority more than any other subject area in business ethics (Pincus, 1996). Business ethicists tend to address cognitive goals and focus on teaching students the tools and skills the need to be able to make ethical decisions in business. Kracher suggests that a business ethics course must prepare students for ethical business *action*.

According to Alam (1999), the overall objectives of teaching ethics to accounting students is not to persuade them to be ethical but to make them aware of the ethical issues in accounting practice, to enhance their analytical skills, and to develop a sense of moral obligation. Geary and Sims (1994) adapted the following goals from Callahan (1980) and Loeb (1988):

1. Relate business education to the moral issues.
2. Recognize issues in business that have ethical implications.
3. Develop "a sense of moral obligation" or responsibility.
4. Develop the abilities needed to deal with ethical conflicts or dilemmas.
5. Learn to deal with the uncertainties of the business professions.
6. "Set the stage" for a change in ethical behavior.
7. Appreciate and understand the history and composition of all aspects of business ethics and their relationship to the general field of ethics.

In addition to a common understanding of the goals of teaching business ethics, the faculty must also develop a plan to make their goals operational. A major requirement of ethics education in business must be to cover what Gandz and Hayes (1988) refer to as macro, molar, and micro issues. This means that in teaching business ethics, faculty must cover traditional "business and society" issues as well as the resolution of moral dilemmas.

McDonald and Dunleavy (1995), Gandz and Hayes (1998), and LeClair (1999) have recommended the following goals for business ethics and social responsibility courses:

1. To increase students' awareness of the ethical, legal, and social dimensions of business decision making.
2. To legitimize ethical issues as a necessary aspect of business decision making.
3. To develop students' analytical skills for resolving ethical issues.
4. To expose students to the complexity of ethical decision making in business organizations.

Other researchers (Carlson & Burke, 1998) classified a number of teaching goals that are closely aligned with those business schools that have chosen to focus on business ethics competencies. The 12 goals of ethics education most often stated by instructors are:

1. To develop an awareness of ethical issues and problems.
2. To build analytical skills in ethical decision making.
3. To cultivate an attitude of moral obligation and personal responsibility in pursuing a career.
4. To stimulate the moral imagination.

According to Carson and Burke (1998), these first four goals show that educators agree that building conceptual models and giving students a basis for reasoning in an ethical dilemma are most important. Four mid-range goals taken from Dennis (1987) (see also Burke, 1990) are discretionary power, cultivating moral character, a knowledge of Western tradition, and professional standards. The last four goals are:

9. To build capacity to deal with ambiguity and differences of opinion.
10. To convey knowledge of democratic values and the obligations of public administrators operating in the framework of the U.S. Constitution.
11. To develop practical understanding of the constraints on and expectations of administrators—knowledge of codes of ethics, conflict of interest statutes, organizational norms and rules, and so on.
12. To develop skills in managing ethics by influencing organizational culture and bureaucratic norms, modeling ethical conduct as a leader.

It is important to note that these items increase in complexity of assimilation and understanding as one moves from the first item to the last.

More recently, Brinkman and Sims (2001) proposed the following goals for teaching business ethics. I use these as the primary goals of my business ethics teaching efforts and will be discussing them in more detail in the next section:

1. Knowing thyself, your own moral values and thresholds.
2. Learning to see moral issues, conflicts, and responsibilities.
3. Learning to identify the specific moral aspects of a situation.
4. Learning to share moral understanding.
5. Learning how to handle moral issues and conflicts.
6. Acquiring moral courage.
7. Acquiring a critical attitude toward the business school curriculum and its disciplines.

GOALS: WHY GO WHERE?

Brinkmann and Sims (2001) recently noted that goals have to do with justification and perspectives—such as why business schools should teach business ethics and why students should learn something about business ethics. Justification and perspectives can serve as criteria for an important distinction between two goal levels with different functions. *Purposes*, or end-goals, have mainly an outside-world perspective and refer to intended, often promised positive functions that a business curriculum should have for societies and labor markets. Such ideals and purposes of a program are not easily disagreed with or falsified and are quite often formulated as a rather uncritical justification of the benefits of business education as such. *Objectives* refer to specific goal states, with an emphasis on internal perspectives and justification towards internal stakeholders. Objectives are used to formulate realistically what students can be expected to learn when attending any business ethics education effort. Objectives are what are measured and measurable by given exams and curriculum evaluation procedures. Ideally, objectives should be realistic operationalizations of idealistic end goals. They should contribute to the keeping of end-goal promises made by a business school. In practice, purpose or mission statements typically appear in public relations (PR) and marketing materials for business school programs, presented in glossy brochures and on homepages, without significant impact on practical school life. Objectives on the other hand live their own lives on the course level (competing with perceived exams agendas as shadow objectives).

The following two quotations give an idea of how faculty could rediscover and reacquire its role as idealistic and self-conscious academics, if necessary, at the expense of rhetorics and PR staff, and how one could formulate end goals that almost ask for course-level or program-level operationalization:

Managers should consider themselves as professionals for societally responsive, strategically effective and operatively efficient allocation of scarce resources in complex organizations with a division of labor. They should not consider themselves as promoters of a given and partial interest orientation. Future-minded and socially responsible management does not require any non-economic business ethics as a moral counterpart of business rationality, but a moral-philosophically enlightened concept of business rationality. (Ulrich, 1987; author's translation)

Business ethics as a teaching subject works with a vision of an enlightened, holistic and long-range thinking, empathetic and responsible business professional, who has the civil courage to follow up such thoughts in practice. (Brinkmann, 1998)

Such considerations can be formulated as the following proposition (cf. for similar thoughts Brinkmann & Sims, 2001): "Business school end-goal or mission statements regarding moral responsibility development are 'empty rhetorics' which can create distancing rather than loyalty unless such statements have been discussed properly among faculty and students, not least in an operational perspective" (p. 174).

Before addressing the more specific teaching business ethics objectives, an additional proposition can be offered that builds a bridge to the end-goal formulations quoted above and that makes the background assumptions more explicit and open for discussion (Brinkmann & Sims, 2001):

The intention of business ethics teaching should not be to teach students certain attitudes or even moralism, but to further awareness and critical examination of the students' pre-existing attitudes. As a result of such self-examination, the students should acquire a more critically-reflected, mature and holistic understanding of their professional role, of business activity and of the interdependence between business activity and the natural environment.

In other words, it is more the *moral reflectedness* of attitudes than specific culturally desirable moral attitudes. With such an overarching concern, James Rest's four-component model of moral behavior determination seems useful as theory reference and as a point of departure (see Rest & Narvaez 1994), with some minor modifications and additions. Business ethics should invite holistic reflection (with moral reflection as one dimension among others).

Given the underlying premise that students should not be indoctrinated but forced to work with their own attitudes, the following seven-objective component model seems useful (see Figure 2.1).

All these components are interdependent in various ways but can be sorted and addressed in a fruitful order. On the following pages, each objective component is elaborated and justified further, not the least as an invitation to a discussion, component by component, among the various stakeholders (i.e., colleagues and students) involved.

Objective 1: Knowing Thyself, Your Own Moral Values and Thresholds

As early as possible in the business program students should get help assessing their own values, moral attitudes and moral thresholds using qualitative or quantitative instruments (cf., e.g., Ferrell & Fraedrich, 1994, pp. 316–328) in order to ensure that any ethics exposure is on the students' own premises rather than a form of superficial indoctrination with politically correct values and standpoints. Such a test tries to create moral self-awareness[1] and once those types of questions have been asked, guarantees increased interest for the moral dimension of business throughout the following courses. As a result of self-reflection through such tests, some stu-

Figure 2.1
Seven Goal Components

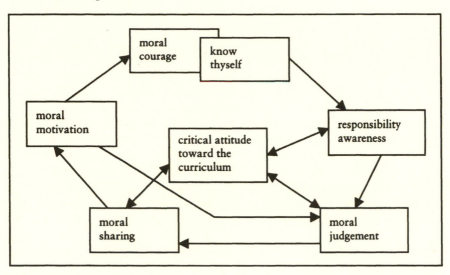

dents might become more self-critical and feel a need to be able to score better on such tests in the future, while others might very well react with ego-defense, since they feel threatened by dissonance. Such effects have to be taken into account together with other working conditions (Chapter 3 discusses working conditions in more detail).

Objective 2: Learning to See Moral Issues, Conflicts, and Responsibilities

While students tend to see the importance of their values and thresholds in private life situations, this is less sure in business and professional situations which seem clearly dominated by other dimensions: profit, quality, competition, and survival in markets. A moral responsibility awareness component is similar to what Rest suggests to call *moral sensitivity*: "the awareness of how our actions affect other people. It involves being aware of different possible lines of action and how each line of action could *affect* (emphasis added) the parties concerned. It involves imaginatively constructing possible scenarios, and knowing cause-consequence chains of events in the real world; it involves empathy and role-taking skills" (Rest & Narváez, 1994, p. 23). The main point is to develop moral imagination as a condition of a sense of moral obligation and personal responsibility (Ciulla, 1991; Sims & Sims, 1991) (i.e., seeing one's responsibility or co-responsibility for potential damage to others) and carry out a good enough analysis of consequences, in advance. Such an approach is in keeping with Kolb's (1982) suggestion that the process of student development and education in university education should include an emphasis on the appropriate ways to think and behave in our interactions with others.

Objective 3: Learning to Identify the Specific Moral Aspects of a Situation

Once one is aware of one's *own* values and of *others* as potential victims and that a given situation seems threatening to oneself, to others, or both, one needs to judge *explicitly* the *fairness* of different alternatives. This again requires a set of concepts and criteria, tools for labelling things, for comparing and ranking of alternatives. Here the most traditional part of ethics training is addressed as business students develop skills in the identification and analysis of moral issues: learning a language and methodology for problem identification, not the least for being able to formulate one's own moral standing and one's responsibilities towards others. Rest identifies this as the traditional *moral judgement* component on which L. Kohlberg's moral maturity development research has focused. This is judgement regarding "which line of action is more morally justifiable [which alternative is just, or right]. Deficiency [in this component] comes from overly simplistic ways of justifying choices of moral action." (Rest & Narváez, 1994, p. 24). Or formulated as a discussion proposition:

Knowledge of key terms and of the most important schools of thought is an important objective. Such knowledge, however, should not be isolated from the key terms' function as useful critical tools. Learning the words and rhetorics is relatively easy and not very controversial. The correct words without critical enlightenment can be worse, however, than no words at all.

Objective 4: Learning to Share Moral Understanding

This component is an addition to the Rest catalog. We are skeptical about the highly individualistic ethics conception in the Western, or at least the Anglo-Saxon, tradition, with the individual fighting an integrity conflict against others. On the contrary, business students should be invited to share moral issues with others rather than keeping them to themselves. There are a number of good reasons for such an objective: two individuals usually see more than one does, and others can function as a corrective and help with simulating action chains and with sharing responsibility. The following quotation formulates the point rather well:

Managers need . . . a space to interact with other managers in order to discuss and persuade each other on important issues. It is also important to act with other managers so as not to be atomized and isolated from the institution they are trying to serve. . . . [Otherwise,] there is a strong tendency to be concerned only with private security and private interests. This not only makes managers ineffective as citizens but also makes them more susceptible to explicit and implicit coercion, immoral ideologies and immoral ideal type behaviors. The act of working with other managers helps establish a place in the institution, a political space which makes opinions significant and actions effective. (Nielsen, 1984, pp. 158–159)

Objective 5: Learning How to Handle Moral Issues and Conflicts

At first sight, this objective seems most important and tests in a way if the previous four objective components are realized sufficiently. However, one should not start with this objective right away, even if case teaching approaches and many moral conflict handling checklists in the literature (see below) seem to suggest that. Two important sub-objectives become clear if one looks at Rest's *moral motivation* component: really being *willing* to apply moral understanding in specific moral conflict situations and not forgetting that the most interesting conflict can be between moral and *other* considerations. "Hitler . . . set aside moral considerations in pursuit of other values. . . . The Reich was more important than other values. Another value completely compromised moral values. [This component] has to do with the importance given to moral values in competition with other values, . . . when other values such as self-actualization or protecting one's organization replace concern for doing what is right" (Rest & Narváez, 1994, p. 24).

Objective 6: Acquiring Moral Courage

Rest calls this the *moral character* component, involving "ego strength, perseverance, backbone, toughness, strength of conviction, and courage" (Rest & Narváez, 1994, p. 24). Moral character or courage has to do with the individual self-confirmation effect of proper moral conflict handling and the consistency of feeling, thinking, and acting on the individual level. Nielsen (1984) seems to think of such an attitude when he suggests extending the widely accepted political citizen role model to business life, to corporate or institution citizenship as a moral right and duty: cultivating "the courage to think and judge independently as oneself as a basis for acting civically and courageously with other managers . . . as to resist the immoral 'ideal type' behaviors" (p. 160). In the psychological literature, development of such courage is referred to as "armoring," whereby individuals go through a process of psychological strengthening to develop a protective armor that will buffer them from the unsavory elements of the outside world.[2] Through armoring, business students would develop a certain amount of resiliency in order to comfortably resist external pressures to act immorally.

Objective 7: Acquiring a Critical Attitude Toward the Business School Curriculum and Its Disciplines

Perhaps business ethics teaching pays too much attention to bad practice in the business world and too little attention to theory in the business school world. Additionally, perhaps business school professors have more freedom and carry even more responsibility for their student output, and hence for the moral climate in business, than businesses and their employees, working under day-to-day bottom-line pressure.

It has been said that business ethics is mainly taught by all the other courses (Etzioni, 1991). If this is so, the critical potential (and moral responsibilities) of business ethics in relation to all the other business school courses deserves the status of an additional objective. As for business ethics in general, the question here is how much (or how radical) criticism one should invite. Honest convictions and honest intentions of the critics are probably a better rule of thumb than being liked by them. Contributing to internal self-criticism of the different business disciplines is probably more valuable than top-down criticism, which can even be counterproductive. The objectives for teaching business ethics presented above can be summarized in the following two propositions:

1. Furthering of critically reflected understanding should focus on six different, though interdependent, moral attitude components: self-conception, sensitivity, judgement, sharing, motivation, and courage.
2. Business students should not wait to apply what they have learned until after completing school. Practice should start in the business ethics teaching effort (i.e., experiential learning exercises, etc.) and other business courses, with asking the critical questions that the students have learned one can ask.

As suggested in a review of the goals discussed above, what should be taught in business ethics efforts depends on the educational philosophy of the business school and the business ethics teachers. As will be discussed in the next section, I found further support for this view and a simple way of categorizing the goals of teaching business ethics in a review of a number of colleagues' business ethics syllabi.

CATEGORIZING THE GOALS OF BUSINESS ETHICS TEACHING EFFORTS

One way of categorizing the goals, objectives, or purposes of teaching business ethics is to view them as falling in one of three categories I identified in a review of the goals and objectives listed in 24 different business ethics teaching efforts (i.e., 16 syllabi from business ethics courses and objectives from eight business ethics workshops): (1) focus on developing students' theoretical knowledge base, (2) focus on analyzing issues facing people in business situations, and (3) an equal focus on theory and practice. The first category is cognitive in its orientation, with the goal of developing and nurturing ethical knowledge in students. The second category focuses on issues—usually problems—arising in everyday business situations and encourages students to consider the ethical commitments and reasoning processes that might assist in addressing troubling business situations. The last category usually finds one half of the teaching time focused on ethical theories and the other half on using concepts in addressing ethical dilemmas. More will be said about these three categories in our discussion of pedagogical approaches to teaching business ethics in Chapters 7 and 8.

WHEN SHOULD STUDENTS BE TAUGHT BUSINESS ETHICS? IMPLICATIONS FOR GOALS

Deciding when business ethics should be taught to students is an important consideration in reaching agreement on the purposes or goals of teaching business ethics. To answer this question one must take into consideration the differences between undergraduate and graduate students before designing courses (or the curriculum) for teaching business ethics (The Hastings Center, 1980; Sims & Sims, 1991).

Sims and Sims noted more than a decade ago that students should have at least one well-organized, reasonably long course in ethics at the undergraduate level. Otherwise, they will not be able to grasp the seriousness and complexity of the subject or acquire the tools for dealing with ethical problems. An important aspect of The Hastings Center report (1980) was the special emphasis on teaching ethics at different levels of education. The suggestions on reasons (goals) why professional schools introduce ethics courses into their curricula and their distinction between curricula for undergraduate versus graduate levels of education was noted as being of special importance to business schools in increasing applied business ethics courses (Sims & Sims, 1991).

As suggested earlier in this book, one would have to agree that external pressure may be the main motive for introducing ethics courses in some business schools, particularly pressure to introduce ethics in order that graduates might *behave* better in their professional lives. In other business schools, the essential motive may be that of grappling with some very specific moral issues in the professional field (e.g., whistleblowing or insider trading, etc.) in order to see if some of them can be resolved. In yet other business schools, the main motive may be simply that of introducing different disciplinary and methodological perspectives into curricula dominated by heavy technical (quantitative) components. The motives for introducing business ethics courses into the undergraduate curriculum are no less varied: "sensitizing" students, teaching them analytical or critical thinking skills, and helping them learn how to address personal ethical problems they confront in their daily lives. It appears that it is still true today as it was two decades ago when The Hastings Center (1980) released its report that many business schools look to courses in ethics to serve different functions, ranging from character improvement to the development of skills in problem resolution to a desire to expand student horizons to a desire to satisfy external critics.

Undergraduate and Graduate Students Are Different

An important premise for me in teaching business ethics is that there are differences between undergraduate and graduate students and these differences must be taken into consideration in discussing the purpose or goals of teaching business ethics. Addressing this issue is an important component to designing business ethics education efforts that "start where the students are." The primary issue here is just *when* students should be exposed to or take ethics courses. This view is in line with an important aspect of The Hastings Center report's (1980) special emphasis on teaching ethics at different levels of education and Sims and Sims's (1991) suggestion that undergraduate and graduate students should be exposed to different kinds of business ethics teaching.

Based on research to date, graduate and undergraduate students are indeed different (i.e., maturity, work experience, etc.) and deserve a curriculum tailored for their specific situation. Teaching business ethics should start and focus on where the students are or on the kinds of jobs they will have and decisions they will have to make, since the actual work experiences of undergraduates and graduates will be different once they complete their education. This view is similar to results from research by Mathison (1988) in which he stresses the importance of teaching business ethics that addresses students' concerns and starts where they are. As I and others see it, starting where students are means integrating business ethics teaching into a sufficient number of other undergraduate business courses and postponing separate business ethics teaching to the graduate level, as an elective or mandatory topic. Before briefly discussing these two suggestions, the next few paragraphs provide a brief summary of what I believe business ethics teaching efforts could and should focus on for undergraduates and graduates, separately and as a whole.

Undergraduate Students. In most instances, undergraduate students enter business school as sophomores and juniors with little exposure to moral or ethical issues in business. In other words, they have less maturity and work experience compared to their graduate counterparts. With an eye to the background of the undergraduate student, faculty should include in the undergraduate curriculum a variety of experiences that assist in students' moral development (e.g., increasing students' self-knowledge and helping them to assess their own moral values, attitudes, and thresholds) (see, for example, Brinkmann and Sims, 2001; Ferrell and Fraedrich, 1994). The purpose is to try to create moral self-awareness[3] and to create increased interest for the moral dimension of business throughout ensuing courses.

Graduate Students. The emphasis on increased self-knowledge for undergraduates does not deny the fact that such a focus would also be an important objective for teaching business ethics to graduate students. However, the graduate business curriculum should focus on the kinds of moral problems the students will encounter as professionals and managers. This means that graduate students should learn to more fully understand the reasons that support their ethical principles and how to put those principles into practice in real world work situations. Graduate students should have at least one well-organized elective or mandatory business ethics course. Such a course would allow students to grasp the seriousness and complexity of business ethics and acquire the tools for dealing with ethical problems. In short, graduate students must be taught that learning about ethics is important in gaining competence in functional areas and in understanding the relationship between their day-to-day work and the broader values of their organization and the needs of society.

Undergraduate and Graduate Students Alike. An important objective for both undergraduate and graduate business ethics teaching efforts should be the furthering of critically reflected understanding that focuses on the six interdependent moral objective components introduced earlier in this chapter: self-knowledge or conception (as discussed previously), sensitivity, judgement, sharing, motivation, and moral courage.

As noted earlier, the moral sensitivity objective is focused on students' learning to see moral issues, conflicts, and responsibilities. This involves being aware of different possible lines of action and how each line of action could *affect* the parties concerned. The main point is to develop moral imagination as a condition of a sense of moral obligation and personal responsibility.

The judgement objective concerns how students learn to identify the specific moral aspects of a situation. The judgement aspect emphasizes the point that once one is aware of one's *own* values and of *others* as potential victims and that a given situation seems threatening to oneself, to others, or both, one needs to judge explicitly the fairness of different alternatives. Here students develop skills in the identification and analysis of moral issues.

It is also important for both undergraduate and graduate business students to learn to share moral understanding. This component suggests that students should be invited to share moral issues with others rather than keeping them to themselves. Such sharing provides the opportunity for students to discuss their moral issues with others. It also helps with simulating action chains and with sharing responsibility.

The moral motivation component tests if the previous four components (self-knowledge, sensitivity, judgement, and sharing) are sufficiently realized. This component helps students learn how to handle moral issues and conflicts while recognizing their inevitable competition with other values that will surface throughout their work lives.

Acquiring moral character or courage has to do with the individual self-confirmation effect of proper moral conflict handling and the consistency of feeling, thinking, and acting on the individual level. Both undergraduate and graduate students must learn how to develop a certain amount of resiliency to comfortably resist external pressures to act immorally.

As suggested above, business ethics teaching efforts must be responsive to the differences between undergraduate and graduate students. Sims and Sims (1991) offer the following suggestions on what should be the focus of undergraduate and graduate teaching of ethics in business schools given differences between the two groups: Undergraduate business ethics teaching should:

• Assist students in the formation of their personal values and moral ideas.
• Introduce them to the broad range of moral problems facing their society and world.
• Provide them contact with important ethical theories and moral traditions.
• Give them the opportunity to wrestle with problems of applied business ethics, whether personal or professional.

Graduate teaching of ethics in MBA programs ought to:

• Prepare future graduates to understand the kinds of moral issues they are likely to confront in their chosen functional areas.
• Introduce them to the moral ideas of their functional areas.
• Assist them in understanding the relationship between their functional work and that of the broader values and needs of the society.

CONCLUSION

The ultimate success of teaching business ethics depends on the extent to which key stakeholders can come to agreement on the purposes and objectives of teaching business ethics. Without such agreement as a starting point, it is unlikely that ethics will be taught and that students will learn. There are a variety of views on what the goals of teaching business ethics should actually be, and this chapter adds to the ideas already in existence. Once agreement is reached on the goals of any business ethics teaching effort, it is then just as important that the key stakeholders continue an open and participative process of identifying the obstacles or barriers to teaching business ethics. And that is the focus of the next chapter. More specifically, the next chapter discusses some of the working conditions that business ethics teachers and students, along with other key stakeholders, must grapple with and find strategies to minimize the impact of as many of the obstacles as possible.

NOTES

1. Cf. King (1999) about including biases of solving instead of understanding problems.

2. The term *armor* has been used in the psychotherapy literature to describe an adaptive mechanism for coping with racial oppression. See, for example, B. Greene, "African-American Women," in L. Comas-Diaz & B. Greene (eds.), *Women of Color: Integrating Ethnic and Gender Identities in Psychotherapy* (New York: Guilford Press, 1994), pp. 10–29 and J. Faulkner, "Women in Interracial Relationships," *Women and Therapy* 2(1983): 193–203.

3. Cf. also King (1999) about including biases of solving instead of understanding problems.

REFERENCES

Alam, K.F. 1999. Ethics and accounting education. *Teaching Business Ethics* 2: 261–272.

Brinkmann, J. 1998. Teaching business and environment ethics. In C.J. Schultz & J. Schroeder (eds.), *Redoubling Efforts*. Proceedings of the 23rd Macromarketing Conference, University of Rhode Island, West Greenwich, RI, pp. 188–206.

Brinkmann, J., & Sims, R.R. 2001. Stakeholder-sensitive business ethics teaching. *Teaching Business Ethics* 5: 171–193.

Burke, E. 1990. Teaching public administration ethically: Insights from NASPAA IVC.3. Paper presented at the National Conference on Teaching Administration, Tampa, FL, February 15–17.

Callahan, D. 1980. Goals in the teaching of ethics. In D. Callahan & S. Bok (eds.), *Ethics teaching in higher education*. New York: Plenum Press, pp. 61–80.

Carlson, P.J., & Burke, F. 1998. Lessons learned from ethics in the classroom exploring student growth in flexibility, complexity and comprehension. *Journal of Business Ethics* 17: 1179–1187.

Ciulla, J.B. 1991. Business ethics as moral imagination. In R.E. Freeman (ed.), *Business ethics: The state of the art*. New York: Oxford University Press, pp. 212–220.

Dennis, A. 1987. Teaching ethics in public administration: An analysis of goals, ethical standards, and approaches to ethical decision-making. Doctoral dissertation, University of Southern California.

Etzioni, A. 1991. Reflections on teaching business ethics. *Business Ethics Quarterly* 1: 355–365.

Ferrell, O.C., & Fraedrich, J. 1994. *Business ethics* (2nd ed.). Boston: Houghton Mifflin.

Gandz, J., & Hayes, N. 1988. Teaching business ethics. *Journal of Business Ethics* 7: 657–669.

Geary, W.T., & Sims, R.R. 1994. Can ethics be learned? *Accounting Education* 3(1): 3–18.

Gilbert, J.T. 1992. Teaching business ethics: what, why, who, where and when. *Journal of Education for Business* 68(1): 5–8.

The Hastings Center. 1980. *The teaching of ethics in higher education.* Hastings-on-Hudson, NY: The Institute of Society, Ethics and Life Sciences.

King, J.B. 1999. On seeking first to understand. *Teaching Business Ethics* 3: 113–136.

Kolb, D.A. 1982. *Experiential learning.* Englewood Cliffs, NJ: Prentice Hall.

Kracher, B. 1999. What does it mean when Mitchell gets an "A" in business ethics? Or the importance of service learning. *Teaching Business Ethics* 2: 291–303.

LeClair, D.T. 1999. The use of a behavioral simulation to teach business ethics. *Teaching Business Ethics* 3: 283–296.

Loeb, S.E. 1988. Teaching students accounting ethics: Some crucial issues. *Issues in Accounting Education* 3: 316–329.

McDonald, G.M., & Donleavy, G.D. 1995, Objections to the teaching of business ethics. *Journal of Business Ethics* 10: 829–835.

Mathison, D.L. 1988. Business ethics cases and decision models: A call for relevancy in the classroom. *Journal of Business Ethics* 7: 777–782.

Nielsen, R.P. 1984, Toward an action philosophy for managers based on Arendt and Tillich. *Journal of Business Ethics* 3: 53–161.

Pace, C.R. 1984. Historical perspectives on student outcomes: Assessment with implications for the future. *NASPA Journal* 22: 10–18.

Pincus, C. 1996. *Confidential business ethics pedagogy survey for the Times Mirror higher education group.* Burr Ridge, MA: McGraw-Hill.

Rest, J., & Narváez, D. (eds.). 1994. *Moral development in the professions.* Hillsdale, NJ: Lawrence Erlbaum Associates.

Sheppard, C.S. 1988. The ethical maze: Perspectives on business leadership and ethics. *William & Mary Business Review* (Spring): 26–31.

Sims, R.R., & Sims, S.J. 1991. Increasing applied business ethics courses in business school curricula. *Journal of Business Ethics* 10: 211–219.

Sloan, D. 1980. *Education and values.* New York: Teachers College Press.

Turnbull, W.W. 1985. Are they learning anything in college? *Change* 17: 6.

Ulrich, P. 1987. *Unternehmensethik—diesseits oder jenseits der betriebswirtschaftlichen Vernunft?* Dok. papier 42 der Wiss. Ges. f. Marketing u. Unternehmensführung, Münster, 67–86.

Chapter 3

The Environment for Teaching Business Ethics: Obstacles and Issues

INTRODUCTION

Agreement on the goals of teaching business ethics by the key stakeholders and good intentions do not work all by themselves. Good intentions can be controversial, too. A realistic understanding of the environment or working conditions for teaching business ethics is at least as important, in particular an understanding and handling of obstacles and conflicts. Brinkmann and Sims (2001) note that teaching business ethics faces three categories of obstacles and conflict potentials (see Figure 3.1), which need to be addressed and discussed:

- The existing business curriculum as a whole and the courses which it consists of.
- The students' working situation and mind-set.
- Faculty's working situation and mind-set.

This chapter discusses the environment for teaching business ethics. The chapter first focuses on obstacles to teaching business ethics. Next, issues that seem to cut across the three obstacles are then described. The chapter then highlights the importance of open communication and participation by all stakeholders involved, particularly faculty and students, to the success of achieving the goals of teaching business ethics. The chapter concludes with a summary presentation of a number of premises and recommendations important to teaching business ethics.

Figure 3.1
Curriculum-Related and Stakeholder-Related Obstacles to Business Ethics Teaching

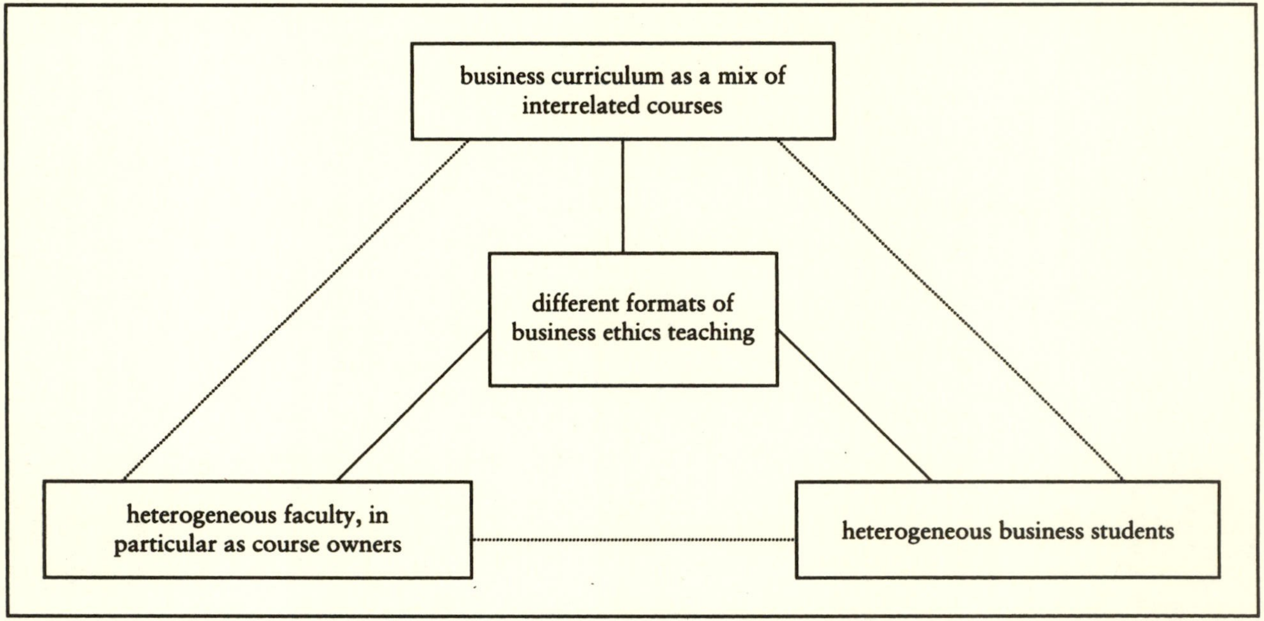

Table 3.1
Assumed Profile Differences between Core Business Courses and Business Ethics

Core Business Courses	Business Ethics
Money	Other values
Standard of living	Quality of life
Self-interest	Common interest, caring
Directly measurable	Indirectly measurable, if at all
Clear answers	Complex questions
Problem solving	Problem definition
Lecturing	Dialogue
Anti-academic	Academic
Typical testing by multiple choice	Typical testing by essay and/or case
Ahistoric, present and near future	Historic, past and distant future
Analytic	Holistic
Knowledge	Understanding
Modern	Premodern, postmodern
Objective	(Inter-)subjective
Pro-establishment bias	Anti-establishment bias
Positive functions of business	Negative side effects of business
Public	Private

Obstacle Type 1: The Existing Business Curriculum and Other Courses

Business ethics is not taught and perceived in a vacuum, but in relation to its business curriculum environment and to other courses. Without proper understanding and handling, such interdependencies easily become obstacles. There are differences between teaching business ethics and core business courses (such as accounting, marketing, finance) that should be taken into account. Such differences are usually experienced vaguely and not made explicit (see Table 3.1 as a suggested first example to list potentially relevant antonyms).

Unclear relationships between business ethics teaching and other courses can be even more problematic. If differences such as the ones mentioned in Table 3.1 are not explained and justified (e.g., as a broadening of perspective or as further elaboration of the other courses on the curriculum), business ethics can easily be perceived as irrelevant, disturbing, dissonant, and contradictory (see, e.g., Alam, 1999).

One can understand such problems in a systems perspective (i.e., look at business ethics in terms of its positive or negative functions for the business curriculum as a whole). Clear differences and contradictions (of the kind mentioned above) as such are not necessarily negative, as long as they are explained and justified vis-à-vis students and faculty, with reference to positive functions, internal or external ones, or both. Without such explanation and justification students and faculty tend to see only increased fragmentation, which is indeed only dysfunctional. Such differences between courses, contradictions, and possible system weaknesses should be addressed explicitly and offered for discussion.

While this first obstacle has to do with system weaknesses (i.e., business ethics as a system element and its frictions as well as potential catalyst functions in relation to a curriculum environment), the next two obstacles to business ethics as a teaching subject have mostly to do with lacking empathy (i.e., lacking understanding of target group mind-sets and lacking target group participation).

Obstacle Type 2: Students' Working Situation and Mind-Set

Business ethics is not the only subject students are taught. This means that business ethics competes with other subjects for short student working time and for short student attention. The subject is also perceived selectively with mind-sets that are acquired in previous courses. Before such conditions are discussed, two short preliminary remarks are necessary. First of all, students are not a homogeneous group (this point will be emphasized in the discussion on learning styles in Chapter 5). My experience suggests (and my course evaluation statistics, too) that there are not clear attitude differences toward business ethics and toward the issues raised by it among students. If my impression is right, business ethics is not popular or unpopular with business students, but rather controversial. Some students tend to like business ethics as a subject; others clearly don't. Popularity differences can be symptoms of differences in underlying moral maturity (in a Kohlberg perspective, see, e.g., Kohlberg, 1985) and differences in open-mindedness regarding the place of business and business professions in society. A second issue concerns responsibility. If many students feel frustrated and insecure about business ethics because of course profile differences and system frictions, one shouldn't blame the students. Rather, one should listen to them.

Students are not responsible for information overload and overscheduling of the curriculum either. When courses and terms are overloaded already, putting "more" on the agenda often means "less," taking attention away from what is defined as less relevant. A similar system-related obstacle involves the pressure of course level exams. Such pressure contributes to a short-sighted, course- and exam-focused mind-set and to "rational"[1] study behavior. More specifically, the relevance of what one is taught and reads in the books is defined narrowly, by immediate relevance of teaching and reading to the respective examination. Independent of the extent to which student mind-sets are symptoms of curriculum weaknesses and of who should be blamed, such mind-sets must be taken into consideration, both when communicating and when considering student participation.

The most obvious student-related obstacles, however, have to do with lack of receiver sensitivity, with mismatches of expectations, and with other communication barriers. While teachers, and in particular ethics teachers, tend to offer complex theory and abstractions, many students look for the opposite: for simple models, for checklists for "practice," for examples, and even entertainment. Even if students are wrong and the teachers are right, it is important to offer reasons why such types of expectations are frustrated. One should check communication effects, too, since students normally don't receive curriculum contents passively and completely, but selectively. Defence or "reactance" tendencies (i.e., boomerang effects) are possible, too, if students feel that personal, private values are addressed and fear that somebody is trying to manipulate something which is none of his or her business.

Business ethics teaching efforts should include a high degree of classroom discussion about ethical conflicts. Ethical discourse, however, is not the same as a courtroom-like competition about who is the best rhetorician. I share the impression of Fort and Zollers:

Being highly competitive, business students often try to "win" when they do engage in debate and problem solving. They seek to advance the stronger argument, the more convincing case, that is, the right answer. . . . Contentiousness (in the classroom) over issues that go to the heart of what students find valuable in life surely will produce lively debate, but that debate may neither be enlightening nor conducive to an atmosphere that hopes to encourage long-term discussion of difficult materials. Such an attitude also may teach students to avoid raising moral questions in business thereafter having had the experience of ethics being uncomfortably theoretical and conflictual. (1999, pp. 273–274)

Obstacle Type 3: Faculty's Working Situation and Mind-Set

Like students, business school faculty are more or less well-adjusted to a curriculum system with its strengths and weaknesses. One example of such adaptation is compartmentalization, with clear boundaries between courses and much less clear relationships between them. Faculty heterogeneity is even more obvious than student heterogeneity due to academic identification with research specialization rather than with teaching and due to traditional academic individualism. Of course, status and power differences also come into play. If Hosmer's observations (1999) are true, skepticism toward, and dislike of, business ethics is one of the few common denominators among faculty.

In a well-known report about how the Harvard Business School (HBS) has addressed business ethics teaching, faculty has received special attention (Piper et al., 1993). One chapter (written by M. Gentile) deals with "engaging the power and competence of the faculty" and lists 14 faculty-related "barriers," reconstructed from a survey among HBS business faculty (pp. 79–94). The "barrier report categories" are (somewhat abbreviated):

1. Assumptions about the definition of business ethics.
2. Assumptions about the school's goals with regard to business ethics.
3. Lack of rewards for attention to ethical issues in functional areas.
4. Lack of new research as a foundation teaching ethics in the functional areas.
5. Classroom norms that inhibit a necessary trusting climate for values-related discussion.
6. The fact that integration of ethics might require a reexamination of one's own value system.
7. Variation in willingness to integrate ethics.
8. Lack of a climate for planning ethics integration into course content.
9. The fact that efforts to increase attention to ethics could be perceived as reproach.
10. Mixed feelings about role model status.
11. Overcrowded courses that leave little space for ethics.
12. Compartmentalization of knowledge.
13. Unclear perceptions of what ethics is as a teaching subject.
14. Potential dangers related to ethical case discussion.

I will operate with fewer barrier categories, or maybe better barrier perception categories, and use them for structuring our observations:

- Information deficits
- Curriculum logistics
- Effort without appropriate reward
- Fears of personal dissonance and of losing control in the classroom

While the three first obstacle types are rational, the last one has to do with self-confidence in one's role as a teacher (i.e., it is more emotional). If one wants to, one could relate our categories roughly to the above-mentioned Harvard items:

- Information deficits (1, 2, 4, 9, 13)
- Curriculum logistics (7, 11, 12)

- Effort without appropriate reward (3, 8)
- Fears of personal dissonance and of losing control in the classroom (5, 6, 10, 14)

Information Deficits. Faculty disinterest in business ethics can be a natural way of handling information deficits. It is only fair not to have an opinion about something one knows nothing or very little about. As a point of departure, it seems wise not to overestimate how much faculty knows about how business ethics as a teaching and research field looks at itself. It is also wise to be prepared for misperceptions, simplifications, and perhaps even prejudice. Even if goal formulations of the type suggested above provide some information, it is not fair to invite a dialogue about ethical issues in business without first providing some easily accessible basic information about the field and its state of the art.

Curriculum Logistics. Business school faculty face a similar information overload and time pressures as their students. In such a situation a curriculum status quo tends to be perceived conservatively and in a constant sum fashion. Any newcomer or competitor for short space and time threatens the given course and topics establishment, in particular if most actors are content with the given status quo. Quite often business ethics and similar courses seem to enter when there are vacancies to be filled, when parts of the curriculum are redesigned, or when a prolongation of a curriculum is discussed and there is a need to fill it with something new. The curriculum logistics obstacle depends, of course, on which business ethics teaching format one considers—dedicated ethics courses or ethics as an integrated part of most other courses. Separate courses, in particular voluntary courses, are probably much less threatening than integration demands, since all new separate courses confirm rather than challenge compartmentalization. More will be said about the curriculum logistics category later in this chapter.

Effort without Appropriate Reward. University faculty, and in particular business school faculty, seem to have an economic attitude towards course development and course change. Developing a new course or changing an existing course is costly. At best it is an investment of energy and time, with expected return as a key variable.

Efforts to increase the number of business faculty who are willing to become experts in ethics (Prodhan, 1998) soon confront the issue of opportunity costs and of learning new tricks and new approaches. Increased research and publication pressure in recent years have furthered a tendency towards the publishable (and teachable), not necessarily issue-oriented and toward the empirical rather than the reflective (Power, 1991; Prodhan & AlNajjar, 1989). Such tendencies toward rational behavior for individual faculty and institutions are in the short run unlikely to foster an atmosphere of willingness to put one's "career" on the line in the long run. Those who are willing to put their careers on the line would do well to ensure that there is close coordination among their research, publication, and teaching, since spreading these activities is time consuming and risky. Both my own and other's experiences suggest that involvement in business ethics is often perceived as a distraction rather than as a chance to make research more problem oriented and interdisciplinary.

Fears of Personal Dissonance and of Losing Control in the Classroom. Teaching business ethics can be emotionally more challenging and more risky for instructors than teaching other subjects. Such challenges and risks relate to the instructor's self-image, to the communication climate in the classroom, and to the teacher's authority as a function of both. This seems to be particularly true for the discussion of provocative and controversial moral dilemmas in class (cf., e.g., Baetz & Carson, 1999, who discuss the use of adult-only video marketing in class). Faculty may be afraid that such a provocative and controversial approach could easily boomerang and instructors could be asked awkward Socratic questions about what they feel personally and what they would do themselves. The potential embarrassment of a given case may be hard to predict—adult-only videos, for example, can be particularly risky in one sociocultural setting, while questions about faith or racial prejudice can be at least as risky in others. I wonder if case discussions that raise fundamental questions regarding the moral legitimacy of capitalism, business, marketing, or the legitimacy of teaching professional sophistication in these fields are even more threatening, especially when instructors are asked to confess any contradictions between their private and their professional convictions. It has been my experience that nonrational faculty perceptions, in particular self-confidence problems, can represent obstacles that are harder to assess, and hence harder to work with, than "politically correct" rational ones, since this requires a greater climate of mutual trust and openness than usually found at a business school.

Handling curriculum logistics, exploiting interdisciplinarity, and assessing outcomes are issues that seem to cut across the three obstacles. The first issues will be discussed in the next section, while exploiting interdisciplinarity will be discussed in Chapter 4. Outcomes assessment will be discussed in Chapters 12 and 13.

HANDLING CURRICULUM LOGISTICS

As alluded to earlier, curriculum logistics is an important factor in how business ethics is perceived by students and faculty. Further, business ethics often enters the business school curriculum when there is a sudden opening and disappears equally suddenly whenever there is a shortage of curriculum space. Business ethics is often the posting used to balance the budget. Such a fate easily creates an add-on prejudice toward standard courses in business ethics and toward their content: the school offers and uses the business ethics course(s) when it is convenient, and skips them when convenient.

Like a number of my colleagues who teach business ethics, I have first-hand experience with this approach at my own business school (and business ethics conference hearsay indicates that such experiences are common). For example, at my own school an undergraduate course titled "Business and Society" is only offered: (1) when students complain about the lack of sufficient electives (2) when faculty recognize that while the course is listed in the course catalog, it has not been offered in two or three years, (3) when other stakeholders decry the school's failure to help develop "ethical" students in response to a recent questionable act by a student, and (4) when an important stakeholder (i.e., an alumnus with money to give) shows an interest in what the school is doing to help develop more "ethical" students and future employees. However, history continues to show that when these drivers are no longer present, the school just as easily decides to conveniently skip (not offer) the course, thus reinforcing the add-on prejudice towards the course and its content.

At a colleague's school, a business ethics course was developed and pre-tested as an elective. This course was made mandatory two years later after a merger with another business school, headed by a provost who was strongly in favor of ethics as a part of business education. Two years later the same course received increased credits and course hours in order to cover environmental ethics as well (and, as some might say, to increase the chances for program improvement by the Norwegian government). Then, claiming bad student evaluations were the primary reason (with a minority of students favoring and a majority disfavoring such a course), the school removed the course from the curriculum when the responsible faculty member was on sabbatical abroad—yet another example of less traditional courses giving way to more traditional business and marketing courses. And during the writing of this book, business ethics has been reintroduced, again because there was space available in the curriculum.

In such situations it might be wiser to offer smaller modules of business ethics than quarter- or semester-long courses. In other words, offering modules which fit the students' and future employers' needs might be better marketing for business ethics than offering full-format courses too early. This can be perceived as being too long and many students may feel they have learned enough after the first half of the course.

WHERE SHOULD BUSINESS ETHICS BE PLACED IN THE CURRICULUM? SEPARATE COURSE OR INTEGRATED ACROSS THE CURRICULUM?

Although the importance of incorporating ethics in business education is generally accepted in spite of the examples presented above, the method of teaching ethics (i.e., basic ways in which ethics can be taught such as a separate course, integrated with other courses, or both) remains an unsettled curriculum logistics issue. The fact that there are different views is another curriculum logistics issue that must be addressed by those responsible for teaching business ethics.

The debate over whether or not to integrate ethics across the curriculum or how best to integrate business ethics has been going on for the past four decades. Stakeholders at every level continue to be divided about whether business schools should attempt to incorporate business ethics into an existing curriculum or establish a new "values curriculum" (see, for example, Piper et al., 1993). There are studies that recommend that ethics to be taught as a discrete subject (Leung, 1991). Proponents of separate courses argue that this approach focuses more clearly on rational analysis in ambiguous situations and may provide a framework for decision making. In his comprehensive study of management education for the Carnegie Foundation in 1959, Pierson recommended that a full-year course on the "Places of Business and the Businessman in the Economic, Political, Legal, and Social Environment" be offered in the second year of an MBA program" (p. 92).

Gordon and Howell's report (1959) challenged the usefulness of a separate ethics course:

There is general agreement among business educators that the needed attitudes are not likely to be developed by formal courses in business ethics. . . . There is a widespread belief, based as much on hope as on fact, that students are exposed to ethical considerations in most business courses. We argue, however, that formal courses in business ethics accomplish little and are likely, if anything, to repel the students. (p. 111)

The latter position came under sharp attack in 1974. The Management Division of the Academy of Management's Committee on Curriculum and Standards of the Social Issues argued that unless the social environment were treated in a separate course, instead of receiving pro forma attention in courses devoted to the various functional segments of business, students would not develop an adequate understanding of the business-society relationship (Piper et al., 1993). "To permit this subject to be met by being frittered away as a matter of secondary concern in other courses, no matter how well taught, is to distort the perceived significance of the subject matter in the mind of the student (Powers and Vogel, 1980, pp. 27–28)," committee members wrote (Piper et al., 1993).

Clearly, the debate continues today, even though there are a number of studies that suggest that ethics be integrated into all courses rather than relegated to a separate course (Borowski & Ugras, 1998; Brinkmann & Sims, 2001; see also Gandz & Hayes, 1988). The opponents of the one-course approach to teaching business ethics maintain that it may not be as effective as the integrative approach, which helps enhance students' ability to identify and deal with ethical issues in a variety of situations. In addition, the one-course approach may create an impression that ethical considerations do not permeate all business decisions but are relevant only to issues covered in that one course (Bishop, 1992; Sims, 2000). Some other studies, on accounting education, also indicate that there should be a separate ethics course, and in addition to this course, ethical issues should be discussed in all accounting courses using "real world" situations (Langderfer & Rockness, 1989).

Instead of assigning the teaching of ethics to the philosophy department or confining it to specific business ethics or business and society courses, some schools incorporate the study of business ethics throughout many of the required courses within the various business majors (see, for example, the experiences of the College of Business at Northern Illinois [Bishop, 1992] and Nova Southeastern University [discussed in Sims, 2000]). The integrated, or across-the-curriculum, approach to teaching business ethics is in line with the views of Borowski and Ugras (1998), who suggest that "the earlier students learn that ethical behavior is valued by the business community, and the more it is [fully] integrated into applicable courses across the business curriculum, the sooner students may demonstrate more ethical behavior and attitudes" (p. 1124; see also Gandz & Hayes, 1988).

Integrated curricula that stress decision making, the formulation of values, and moral choice are nothing new in postsecondary education. Indeed, the efforts of others to integrate ethics throughout the curriculum have been well-documented (Bowman & Menzel, 1998). However, as suggested earlier, deliberations continue on whether ethics should be taught as a separate course or integrated into required foundations or core courses in the various functional areas of business.

Donald Warwick declared, "the teaching of ethics should be integrated into all forms of teaching rather than confined to a separate course" (1980, p. 49). Many business schools require a separate course in ethics, while others integrate ethical issues into courses. And still others do both. Oddo (1997) notes that when ethics is taught as a separate course, students often do not incorporate what they learn in the ethics course into other business courses. The ethics course, in a sense, is just "out there," and ethical principles are not applied to business problems in business courses. This view is similar to the point made earlier that there may be an add-on prejudice toward standard courses in business ethics and toward the course content. I believe, if ethics is to be taught at all, that the most effective business curriculum is interdisciplinary, with courses or units saturated with explicit coverage of business ethics, including references and questions on ethics (and values).

According to Bishop (1992), a main objective of an integrated approach to teaching business ethics is to encourage students to integrate their ethics into their problem-solving and decision-making approaches. And as suggested in Chapter 2, key stakeholders must come to agreement not only about the objectives but also about the methods of teaching business ethics. This means that decisions must be made about who is responsible for teaching ethics. Should general ethical theory be covered by the general education curriculum? Should the responsibility for teaching business ethics be delegated outside of the business curriculum? If the responsibility for teaching business ethics is not delegated outside of the business curriculum, then is there someone within the existing faculty who has the expertise to teach business ethics? If not, are the resources available to hire an expert in business ethics? What if the resources are not available? If a course is offered, where will it be placed in the curriculum? What if there is no room in the curriculum for a stand-alone course? Finding answers to these questions allows the key stakeholders to come to agreement on important points that impact business ethics teaching efforts, as was the case at the College of Business at Northern Illinois University.

The Principles of Management course at the College of Business at Northern Illinois University was selected as the vehicle to establish the ethics foundation in the curriculum. The course was one of the four courses on management principles (the others were marketing, finance, and production/operations) that students were required to take upon acceptance for major study in the college. It emphasized the following topics: planning, decision making (Bishop, 1992), and organizing and organizational control as carried out across business functions and levels. These factors supported the choice of the course as an appropriate medium through which to establish the ethics foundation. Ethics of business and management was the third of three learning units that made up the management principles course. The other two were the technical skills of management and the management of people and behavior. The ethics learning unit was organized into two conceptual levels: (1) societal-organizational ethics, which encompasses macro, intermediate, and organizational level analysis and (2) individual ethics, which emphasizes moral and ethical development, ethics specific to professions or occupations, and conflict over multiple role expectations.

Accepting the belief that ethics cannot be effectively integrated into the curriculum through a single course and thus there must be follow-up through additional coursework, each department in the College of Business was asked to identify several major specific courses through which discipline-related ethical issues might be addressed. Unlike the foundation course, it was not necessary for one-third of the curricula of these courses to be dedicated to ethics (Bishop, 1992). However, the objective for each department was the identification and application of the discipline's specific ethical issues throughout the normal teaching of the course. For further follow-up, all faculty were encouraged to integrate examples and applications of ethics into all of their courses where appropriate, which resulted in a comprehensive approach covering theoretical/conceptual foundations and discipline-related practical application. Recognizing the importance of the measurement or assessment of learning in the area of ethics, the college went beyond simply examining student learning through tests, which were clearly limited to measuring comprehension of factual material and conceptual models for analysis, and made use of written materials (essays, case reports) in an effort to further evaluate students' abilities to articulate ethical issues or to state positions on various issues.

Trying to find answers to the questions mentioned above can also result in a business school identifying ways that they may already be teaching business ethics and coming to agreement on policies for integrating ethics across the curriculum, which was exactly the case at Nova Southeastern University (NSU) (Sims, 2000).

At NSU primary faculty for courses in principles of management, organization behavior (OB), introduction to business, business research methods, personnel administration, marketing management, business policy and strategy, managerial accounting, and auditing volunteered to formally incorporate the study of business ethics within their course objectives (Sims, 2000). This began with formal statements in the course syllabi and led to the development of student assignments and/or classroom activities for each of these courses. In some instances, faculty elected to choose new textbooks that covered business ethics. The course assignments and/or activities selected by the faculty varied greatly from course to course. For example, the instructor teaching the principles of management course selected a case study with an ethical focus. In OB, miniature ethical dilemmas were selected from the text, and to ensure that ethical issues were raised in every class session, each student was assigned a dilemma to present to the class and required to lead a discussion. In the business strategy and policy course, where the students were already completing an extensive analysis of the financial and marketing aspects of a firm, students were now expected to analyze the ethical decision making and behavior of their assigned organization. Finally, in the accounting classes, classroom discussions focused on a mixture of textbook examples, current events, and problems students currently faced in their jobs, which meant that they needed to address issues of professional ethics and the expectations of the professional accounting associations.

Once agreement was reached about the courses to be included in the Ethics Across the Curriculum Policy, the key stakeholders at NSU agreed on the philosophical and applied statements, which were printed in their catalog, in brochures describing their majors, and in the course syllabus for each course designated as an Ethics Across the Curriculum course. Both of these statements are offered here, since I believe they provide excellent examples for those who may be interested in integrating ethics across the curriculum.

Policy statement for the college catalog: The Business & Administration Studies Division faculty believe that a socially responsible institution should not limit the study of ethical issues to a couple of courses, but that such study should be an ongoing endeavor embracing the experience of the student. To this end, the faculty is committed to making the study of ethical issues an integral part of our academic programs. We believe that by incorporating the study of ethics throughout the curriculum, the students will find an additional relevance and reality to their studies, and that it will help them become more responsible and productive citizens, as well as exemplary alumni of Nova Southeastern University.

Policy statement for the course syllabi: The Business & Administration Studies Division faculty is committed to ensuring that our students learn that ethical issues are relevant in every business field. We convey this message to our students by integrating the study of ethics throughout the undergraduate business curriculum. This course has been designated as one which highlights the relevance of business ethics.

As would be expected, there will be resistance to change within any organization, and as suggested by the obstacles to teaching business ethics discussed earlier in this chapter, the introduction of ethics into the business curriculum is such a change. This is why those responsible for introducing ethics into the business school curriculum must be sensitive to the obstacles discussed earlier in this chapter. For example, as Sims (2000) noted in the NSU experience, not all faculty feel comfortable covering ethical issues and thus there must be a commitment and action plan put in place to address those individuals' legitimate concerns. Meeting in small groups to discuss one another's concerns, sharing syllabi and handouts, and administrative support can go a long way to getting faculty to buy in to integrating ethics across the curriculum. Additionally, following the steps suggested by Sims in developing an Ethics Across the Curriculum Policy or program is a good way to start. The steps are (Sims, 2000):

1. Faculty agreement that business ethics is important.
2. Faculty agreement that universities should teach business ethics.
3. Faculty agreement that they should be the ones who teach business ethics.
4. Faculty discussions about how they currently handle business ethics within their courses.
5. A call for volunteers to formalize the teaching of business ethics within their courses.
6. Drafting of an Ethics Across the Curriculum Policy statement.
7. Provision of faculty support for faculty.

In concluding our discussion on separate course versus integrated approaches to teaching business ethics, I believe that it is important to understand that in the separate course approach the student is left to discern whether and to what extent discipline-based courses of study intersect or address similar ethical issues. On the other hand, an important attribute of the integrated approach is the explicit, continuous demonstration of intersections and ethical issues of joint concern within a business context. I also believe that as suggested by Brinkmann and Sims (2001), the separate versus integrated approach to teaching business ethics decision is perhaps less important than the mandatory versus elective choice.

MANDATORY VERSUS ELECTIVE COURSES

I believe that business schools (and their broader institutions) should make business ethics essentials mandatory (by integrating business ethics teaching with mandatory undergraduate business courses) and reserve a deepened state-of-the-art presentation for elective business ethics courses on the graduate level. This approach could also create a critical mass of motivated students for ensuring identity and continuity of this field as a necessary part of the curriculum.

Business ethics can be presented to students as mandatory (i.e., as a core business subject), or as a voluntary free space for second thoughts and reflection. For example, the Virginia Darden School offers a required first-year ethics class as well as several second-year electives. A recent study noted that many business schools offer an ethics course during the second year elective portion of their MBA programs. The result is that typically 24% of the students opt to take the ethics elective (Overell, 1999).

Mandatory status meta-communicates the indispensability of a given qualification. Elective status meta-communicates business ethics idealism (i.e., a hope that many students can be motivated to self-reflection and responsibility awareness). The main counter argument against mandatory teaching would be that such teaching would further rhetoric and reactance rather than reflection among unmotivated students. The main anti-elective argument would be that students who chose business ethics would need it much less than the ones who did not choose it. A quick review of what is happening in business ethics efforts at some business schools provides a picture of what is and is not occurring in regard to this issue.

A LIMITED LOOK AT CURRENT BUSINESS ETHICS CURRICULA

To explore the current ethics curricula situation at business schools, one must first turn to the Harvard Business School (HBS)—typically seen as a bellwether institution. Harvard produces multiple cases that address issues in ethics, and the *Harvard Business Review* is a prolific publisher of articles extolling the virtues of ethics in business. During the first phase of the MBA core program (the Foundations unit), students take a required ethics module as part of the Leadership, Values, and Decision Making class. HBS also offers many second-year elective courses that include ethics as a significant course component, including The Moral Leader, a course that uses novels to help students connect fictitious leaders and their actions with the students' own philosophies. The course also used philosophical works (Aristotle, Machiavelli) to help students develop an ethical decision-making framework.

As noted in the last section, the Darden School not only has a required first-year ethics class but also several second-year electives. One course, Business Ethics Through Literature, also uses novels and other literature to assist students in understanding the role of ethics in management. This approach seems to bring the characters and their ethical dilemmas to life for students.

Georgetown University's McDonough School of Business takes a holistic approach to ethics by weaving ethical decision making throughout its first-year core curriculum, along with a second-year elective course. Almost all of McDonough's core course descriptions mention ethics as a class component. The effort to implement an interdisciplinary approach appears to have a stronger foothold here than at many other schools.

Bentley College's McCallum Graduate School of Business and the MBA program at Loyola University in Chicago both offer students the opportunity to concentrate their MBAs in business ethics. These business ethics concentrations include courses that focus on both applied and theoretical ethics.

Some other well-known MBA programs only offer elective courses in ethics. At the Yale School of Management, the program website explains that ethics is incorporated into first-year course materials, but upon further inspection, this claim does not bear out. However, the school does offer an elective course that provides an in-depth look at the ethical responsibilities of managers to their companies, employees, customers, and communities. Cornell University's Johnson Graduate School of Management also offers an elective course on general business ethics. Dartmouth's Tuck School of Business offers a "mini-course" in ethics, and the syllabus explains that students address the classic arguments surrounding the morality of business—including many social responsibility topics.

All of these elective courses appear to be academically sound. They explore legitimate topics including sweatshops, exorbitant CEO pay scales, product safety, and discrimination. But they seem to lack an applied focus. In stark contrast to the fictionally or historically focused courses at other schools, the University of Maryland has a required and unique class, Business Ethics Experiential Learning Module, which incorporates into the course syllabus a field trip to meet current inmates at a prison. The prisoners who speak to the students are white-collar criminals, like lawyers and MBAs. One prisoner, who is an MBA, was convicted of money laundering and mail fraud. Current MBA students can immediately relate to this clean-shaven, young, former business student who talks about his post-MBA job and the series of bad decisions he made—and how easy it was to make those fateful decisions. This type of conversation prompts business students to realize that the "right" decision is not always clearly illustrated, nor does it typically lead to fast cash. Nevertheless, the correct decision can make an individual stand out over the course of his or her career as being principled and thoughtful. This applied tactic in teaching students the real-life results of being unethical brings alive the very confusing, but authentic, dilemmas that students will face in their corporate positions. Like the experience of others who teach business ethics, I have found that integrating ethics throughout the curriculum encourages students to recognize potentially uncomfortable situations and to learn how to address them appropriately.

As evidenced by the brief look at some of the current efforts to teach business ethics, there is no agreement about when in the curriculum business ethics should be taught or whether there should be prerequisites for this course. An important question is whether it is better to teach (or even require) the course early in the curriculum to inform the study of individual functional disciplines or to teach it at the end to make use of the knowledge gained in these courses. There is no doubt that there will always be a variety of ways business schools approach the teaching of business ethics, and some of them will have a module on ethics early in the functional courses to introduce considerations of ethical issues in their course material. Unfortunately, there is still little empirical evidence to let us know how widespread such practices are, or how effective they are.

Given the importance of business ethics, a case can be made for teaching it to all business majors and not just to those who take an elective course in this subject. However, it seems unlikely that all business schools will either add a required course, drop one of their presently required courses to make room for one, or integrate the teaching of business ethics across the curriculum. Addressing the issues concerning whether courses should be separate, integrated and mandatory, or elective will continue to offer challenges to those committed to teaching business ethics. These issues are, in my view, additionally challenging given the lack of empirical evidence to support any particular position. However, despite the lack of such evidence, I believe we must continue full steam ahead in our efforts to teach business ethics to our future leaders, and that, as Piper et al. (1993) suggest, the public debate on the separate versus integrated or mandatory versus elective approaches to teaching business ethics is flawed. Instead of the approaches being posed as alternatives, they should be viewed as mutually reinforcing complements. Like the experience Piper et al. refer to, it has also been my experience that the success of teaching business ethics results in part from a sustained discussion of the topic by the key stakeholders (i.e., students, faculty, administrators, alumni, potential employers, etc.). Thus, there is a need for conversations or dialogue on the assumptions and beliefs, various ideologies, goals and purposes, and obstacles and issues related to teaching business ethics.

I believe a good place to start the dialogue is to have the key stakeholders discuss the strengths, potential negatives, and neutralizers involved in offering required, elective or integrated courses. This has been suggested by Piper et al. (1993) (see Table 3.2) in their discussion of Harvard Business School's efforts to integrate leadership, ethics, and corporate responsibility (for our purposes simply referred to as ethics) into management education.

I have used Piper et al.'s suggestions in working with several groups that wrestled with the issues discussed in this section as a starting point for dialogue. I have also found success in encouraging groups to first develop and then compare and contrast their own lists of strengths, potential negatives, and neutralizers in an effort to increase community dialogue on these business ethics–related issues.

OUTCOMES ASSESSMENT: WHAT'S THE IMPACT OF BUSINESS ETHICS TEACHING EFFORTS?

Another working condition that is as important as deciding on where to start is whether or not business ethics teaching efforts actually achieve their intended goals—that is, how to assess the impact of teaching business ethics. As will be highlighted in Chapter 12, a variety of methods of assessment have been used in the research on the teaching of ethics (see for example, The Kohlberg Moral Development Interview and related tests built on the Kohlbergian model such as the Defining Issues Test [Rest, 1979; Thoma, 1994] and the Sociomoral Reflection Measure-Short Form [Snarey and Keljo, 1994]. Agreeing upon a common method of assessment for measuring student performance against shared standards or core competencies in business ethics also creates conflicts for those responsible for teaching ethics. Addressing and resolving such conflicts is especially important because agreement on an assessment instrument can ultimately lead to a common objective for business ethics and operationalization of the objective in terms of specific performance indicators.

STAKEHOLDERS, COMMUNICATION, AND PARTICIPATION

Thus far we have addressed the goals of teaching business ethics and some obstacles and issues to their realization. However, in order to address these obstacles and issues, it appears that the most important single condition for realizing goals and overcoming obstacles of the types mentioned is *open communication* and *active participation* of the stakeholders in-

Table 3.2
Required, Elective, and Distribution across Existing Courses

Strengths	Potential Negatives	Neutralization
Required Course		
Administratively easy	Seen as "the ethics course"	Encourage discussion of ethics in all first-year courses
Ensures focus	Failure to discuss issues as they arise across all courses feeds cynicism, takes an eraser to the work of others, and provides a flawed model of responsible leadership	
Careful teaching of reasoning process		
Strong signal from administration		
Energizes student interest		
Elective Courses		
Opportunity for advanced study	Many students do not take the electives	Include a required course on ethics at the outset of MBA (or BBA) program
Source of tested material for use in first-year required course	Because they are usually taken late in the program, electives have limited impact	Integrate discussion of ethics issues into all first-year courses
Opportunity for specialized teaching, research, and course development		
Distribution across Existing Courses		
Demonstrates that dilemmas and questions are not isolated problems but present throughout the organization	Fragmented teaching yields fragmented understanding of the issues and reasoning process	Include a required course on ethics at the outset of MBA (or BBA) program
Strong legitimization by faculty	Without strong student interest, treatment of these topics by many faculty tends to be intermittent	
Integrates a concern for ethics into the managerial decision-making process		

volved, in particular faculty and students as primary stakeholders. Such an assumption is consistent with modern business ethics positions. Open and fair communication can address conflicts, produce consensus, and prevent unneccessary conflict (see, e.g., French & Granrose 1995). And the parties affected by a decision or a change of a status quo have a moral right to be heard and to participate. As suggested by Sims and Sims (1991) and The Hastings Center (1980) report, pressure to teach business ethics has often come "from outside" or "from above" rather than from inside (i.e., from faculty and students as the key internal stakeholders). If faculty and students have not had the opportunity to discuss the goals of teaching business ethics or to participate in curriculum design decisions, then there should be no surprise if they exhibit superficial like or dislike for business ethics teaching, passive resistance to it, or repressive tolerance of it. As in any situation where those impacted most by a change are not included in the dialogue related to the change, resistance is inevitable.

In other words, to avoid such resistance and to ensure the active participation of all the key stakeholders, dialogue must start with the formulation of clear goals and agreement about them. They must be discussed openly and thoroughly by faculty and interested students alike. And schools must be prepared to revise them as a consequence of such discussion. My suggestion for such a catalogue of goals has been outlined already in this book. The design of such communication and participation co-determines their effect, and perhaps their success. In order to prevent domination by the most vocal or opinionated leaders, I have found that it is a good idea to start with an anonymous survey of goal acceptance and of views about various design alternatives (e.g., early versus late, mandatory versus voluntary, separate course versus integration into other courses, etc.). Well-monitored and power-free focus group discussion, with or without case references, should be the main focus, since this simulates real-life conflict handling and consensus building.

A curriculum discussion can benefit from a survey of concerns, questions, perceptions, and misunderstandings. With or without such a start-up survey, it is important to address openly as many of the obstacles mentioned above as possible (and other ones as well if raised by the respondents). The aim should be to reach at least a minimum consensus about all the issues. As a result of such "action research," I have found that it is much easier to identify best points of departure.

The HBS survey reference to misperceptions of business ethics teaching (Piper et al., 1993) suggests that business ethics and other key terms cannot be used unclarified and undefined. Additionally, one cannot underestimate the fact that if faculty feel they are asked to leave a secure professional platform, they must be provided with safety nets such as shared responsibility and team teaching (see Chapter 4 for a discussion of team teaching). Like Piper et al. (1993), my experience suggests that understanding and addressing faculty implications are the most crucial tasks in increasing business ethics teaching efforts. I'm sure we all have first-hand experience that confirms that there are interdepartmental rivalries and internal markets in business schools (especially in an atmosphere of resource constraints and "publish quick, or perish" reward structures), that faculty may lack self-confidence in being experts in ethics, and that there is an unwillingness to engage in broad dialogues about teaching business ethics. The traditional response would be that top-down organizational commitment is a necessary condition for overcoming such barriers. Heavy funding might be a sufficient condition. But, in reality, faculty support is essential to business ethics teaching efforts, and especially in any efforts to integrate ethics across the curriculum.

The story could end here and often does end here. In fact, not letting the story end here is similar to the very core of business ethics as an idealistic discipline. If there is a gap between realities and ideals, realities don't necessarily prove that better alternative realities are wrong or impossible. The challenge to teaching business ethics is to identify barriers to change and find realistic ways around such barriers. Like Brinkmann and Sims (2001), I wonder if one could and should modify the traditional argument about "there are no things that money can't buy," business ethics enthusiasm at a business school included. An alternative phrasing of the point could be "there are some things money shouldn't buy"—that is, if business ethics enthusiasm at a business school is bought by various material rewards, one never knows if there is any meaningful and trustworthy academic involvement behind it. In short, from my standpoint, there seems to be no other alternative than ongoing, open, and fair communication among faculty and students in the discourse-ethics tradition. I do hope, idealistically, that such dialogue and interaction build or at least further an open communication climate, which then might further more successful business ethics teaching effort in business school contexts. Additionally, as noted by Brinkmann and Sims (2001),

We hope that our idealism is not equivalent to naivete. Maybe it would be indeed naïve to expect that all colleagues and all students, or a majority of colleagues and students, can be convinced that teaching business ethics deserves a reserved place in a business school curriculum. To convince a critical mass of idealistic, non-conformist academics and students is probably sufficient but worth the ongoing effort. (p. 189)

SUMMARY AND RECOMMENDATIONS

As suggested in Chapter 3, business ethics is essentially about self-criticism of business practice, with a focus on moral dimensions. As a business school teaching subject, business ethics seems to be increasingly well-covered in the literature. To summarize the most important points about the goals and working conditions for teaching business ethics, the following premises and recommendations are offered.

Premises

1. Business school end-goal or mission statements regarding the development of moral responsibility are "empty rhetoric" that can create distancing rather than loyalty unless such statements have been discussed properly among faculty and students in an operational perspective.

2. Designing business ethics teaching efforts as an integrated part of business school curricula should start with a schoolwide dialogue about goals and working conditions.

3. The intention of business ethics teaching should not be to teach students certain attitudes or even morality, but to further awareness and critical examination of students' preexisting attitudes. As a result of such self-examination, students should acquire a more critically reflected, mature, and holistic understanding of their professional role, of business activity, and of the interdependence between business activity and the natural environment.

4. Knowledge of key terms and the most important schools of thought are important objectives. Such knowledge, however, should not be isolated from the function of key terms as useful critical tools. Learning the words and rhetoric is relatively easy and not very controversial. The correct words without critical enlightenment, however, can be worse than no words at all.

5. Furthering of critically reflected understanding should focus on six different but interdependent moral attitude components: self-conception, sensitivity, judgement, sharing, motivation, and courage.

6. Students should not wait to apply what they have learned until after completing school. Practice should start in other business school courses, with the asking of the critical questions that students have learned one can ask.

7. Essential questions concern how business ethics can function as a bridge-builder across disciplines, how it can serve as an integration mechanism for the business curriculum as a whole by promoting holistic understanding, and how, where necessary, it can take its legitimate place as an alternative way of thinking.

8. Business ethics is not the only subject students are taught. This means that business ethics competes with other subjects for limited student working time and attention. It also means that business ethics is perceived selectively with mind-sets that may be acquired in other courses.

9. Listening to students is important, since students quite often are better curriculum judges than most faculty, (e.g., of how well mixed and well integrated courses are as parts of a curriculum and how they compare).

10. Curriculum logistics is the obstacle that is most closely related to a business school's power and prestige structure. Interference with a colleague's course,

and in particular suggestions to shorten or even drop other courses, can easily challenge the faculty establishment.

11. Close coordination between one's research, publication, and teaching is attractive, while spreading one's activities is time consuming and risky. Business ethics involvement is often perceived as a distraction rather than as a chance to make one's research more problem oriented and interdisciplinary.

12. Nonrational faculty perceptions, in particular self-confidence problems, can represent obstacles that are harder to assess, harder to address, and hence harder to work with than "politically correct" rational ones because this requires more of a climate of mutual trust and openness than is usually found at a business school.

13. Superficial like or dislike of business ethics, passive resistance to it, or repressive tolerance of it is understandable when faculty and students have not had the opportunity to discuss goals or to participate in curriculum design decisions.

14. A curriculum discussion can benefit from a survey of concerns, questions, perceptions, and misunderstandings. With or without such a start-up survey, it is important to address openly as many of the obstacles mentioned above as possible (and other ones as well if raised by the respondents). The aim should be to reach a minimum consensus about each issue. As a result of such "action research," it is much easier to identify the best points of departure.

Recommendations

In concluding this chapter, the following recommendations are offered to help the reader think about how to design business ethics teaching efforts:

1. Fair and open communication, as well as stakeholder participation, is not only recommended *by* teaching business ethics but also *for* business ethics teaching, assuming that deeds convince more than words.[2]

2. Avoid the tendency to view the issues of separate versus integrated or mandatory versus elective as alternatives. Rather, view them as mutually reinforcing complements.

3. Business ethics recommends fair consensus building around common interests by power-free and open communication. It would be naive, however, to deny the existence of conflicting interests and power differences. Rather than preaching false consensus and uncritical acceptance of power, business ethics should look critically at illegitimate use of power in the business school world as well as in the real business world.

4. Developing communication and participation possibilities for stakeholders as early as possible through appropriate listening mechanisms is important (e.g., by inviting essay writing and group discussion about moral views and standpoints that individuals "bring with them").

5. Diversity of moral views and standpoints, documented by such data collection as mentioned or not, can be an important resource for simulation of real world moral and cultural diversity.

6. For the sake of developing the best possible communication climate in the sense of open and constructive pluralism, business ethics competence should be presented as open and interdisciplinary rather than as exclusive and dominated by one or by a few disciplines, such as mainstream business thinking and/or academic moral philosophy.

7. It is important to be sensitive towards various types of miscommunication risks (such as boomerang effects) and to unexploited communication possibilities (such as two-step communication in which students and/or faculty function as go-betweens in communication with students and faculty).

8. Course design should not come *before* an open discussion of goals and obstacles with faculty and students. It should come *after* to ensure a fair chance to suggest adjustments and revisions before it is too late in the process.

9. Business ethics teaching efforts should be evaluated continuously and thoroughly, going significantly beyond superficial customer satisfaction measures, and strive for institutionalization of continuous learning and revision by way of outcomes assessment.

10. Finally unnecessary conflicts should be avoided as much as possible. However, one must be prepared for conflicts regarding essential goal elements. Business ethics should be cooperative in the business world and business school world alike, but not at the expense of its integrity. If business ethics does not lead to an attitude of constructive self-criticism, it should perhaps be dropped rather than offered as moralistic rhetoric in which some parties are comforted by the words, while others are happy because they do not feel threatened. Negative examples and obvious lack of ethics can often have a better educational effect than preaching to the wrong target groups, at the wrong time, and in the wrong place.

NOTES

1. I am not sure about the relative importance of more irrational factors such as students' fears. Many students who have had few non-quantitative courses will be particularly uneasy. Such fears could be heightened by the fact that students view "values" as highly personal and therefore not subject to debate, examination, or preachment.

2. Cf. Fort and Zollers (1999) with detailed suggestions about how to demonstrate ethical theory in classroom practice. I would include consistent curriculum development practice, too, and use stakeholder participation and consensus building by communication as theory, from a position close to the one outlined by Reed (1999).

REFERENCES

Alam, K.F. 1999. Ethics and accounting education. *Teaching Business Ethics* 2(3): 261–272.

Baetz, M., & Carson, A. 1999. Ethical dilemmas in teaching about ethical dilemmas: Obstacle or opportunity? *Teaching Business Ethics* 3(1): 1–12.

Bishop, T.R. 1992. Integrating business ethics into an undergraduate curriculum. *Journal of Business Ethics* 11: 291–299.

Borowski, S.C., & Ugras, Y.J. 1998. Business students and ethics: A meta-analysis. *Journal of Business Ethics* 17(1): 1117–1127.

Bowman, J., & Menzel, D. (eds.). 1998. *Teaching ethics and values in public administration programs.* Albany, NY: State University of New York Press.

Brinkmann, J., & Sims, R.R. 2001. Stakeholder-sensitive business ethics teaching. *Teaching Business Ethics* 5: 171–193.

Fort, T.L., & Zollers, F. 1999. Teaching business ethics: Theory and practice. *Teaching Business Ethics* 3: 273–290.

French, W.A., & Granrose, J. 1995. *Practical business ethics.* Englewood Cliffs, NJ: Prentice Hall.

Gandz, J., & Hayes, N. 1988. Teaching business ethics. *Journal of Business Ethics* 7: 657–669.

Gordon, R.A., & Howell, J.A. 1959. *Higher education for business.* New York: Columbia University Press.

The Hastings Center. 1980. *The teaching of ethics in higher education.* Hastings-on-Hudson, NY: The Institute of Society, Ethics and Life Sciences.

Hosmer, T.L. 1999. Somebody out there doesn't like us: A study of the position and respect of business ethics at schools of business administration. *Journal of Business Ethics* 2: 91–106.

Kohlberg, L. 1985. A current statement on some theoretical issues. In S. Mogil & S. Mogil (eds.), *Lawrence Kohlberg, consensus and controversy.* Philadelphia: Falmer Press, pp. 485–546.

Langderfer, H.Q., & Rockness, J.R. 1989. Integrating ethics into the accounting curriculum: Issues, problems and solutions. *Issues in Accounting Education* 4: 58–69.

Leung, P. 1991. Ethics in accountancy—An innovative subjective in an accountancy degree program. Paper presented at the South East Asia Accounting Teachers Conference, January 21–23.

Oddo, A.R. 1997. A framework for teaching business ethics. *Journal of Business Ethics* 16: 293–297.

Overell, S. 1999. Business schools "ignore JR factor." *Supply Management* (June 10): 12.

Pierson, F.C. et al. 1959. *The education of American businessmen: A study of university-college programs in business administration.* New York: McGraw-Hill.

Piper, T.R., Gentile, M.S., & Parks, S.D. 1993. *Can ethics be taught?* Boston: Harvard Business School.

Porter, L.W., & McKibbin, L.E. 1988. *Management education and development: Drift or thrust into the 21st century?* New York: McGraw-Hill.

Power, M.K. 1991. Educating accountants: Toward a critical ethnography. *Accounting Organizations and Society* 16(4): 333–353.

Powers, C.W., & Vogel, D. 1980. *Ethics in the education of business managers.* Briarcliff Manor, NY: The Hastings Center.

Prodhan, B. 1998. Delivering ethics in business education. *Journal of Business Ethics* 1(3): 269–281.

Prodhan, B., & Al Najjar, F. 1989. *Accounting research database.* London: Routledge.

Reed, D. 1999. Stakeholder management theory: A critical theory perspective. *Business Ethics Quarterly* 9: 453–483.

Rest, J.R. 1979. *Development in judging moral issues.* Minneapolis: University of Minnesota Press.

Sims, R.L. 2000. Teaching business ethics: A case study of an ethics across the curriculum policy. *Teaching Business Ethics* 4: 437–443.

Sims, R.R., & Sims, S.J. 1991. Increasing applied business ethics courses in business school curricula. *Journal of Business Ethics* 10: 211–219.

Snarney, J., & Keljo, J. 1994. Revitalizing the meaning and measurement of moral development, essay review of "moral maturity: Measuring the development of sociomoral reflection" by J.C. Gibbs, K.S. Basinger & D. Fuller. *Human Development* 37(3): 181–186.

Thoma, S.J. 1994. Trends and issues in moral judgment research using the defining issues test. *Moral Education Forum* 19(1): 1–7.

Warrick, D. 1980. *The teaching of ethics in the social sciences.* Hastings-on-Hudson, NY: The Hastings Center.

Chapter 4

Who Should Teach Business Ethics?

INTRODUCTION

As the interest in teaching business ethics grows among faculty, the debate about who should teach this topic begins. Because many business faculty have not had formal training in ethics, the argument is made that faculty trained specifically in ethics should assume this responsibility (see Frederick, 1998; Klein, 1998). One of the consistent arguments against ethics faculty, many of whom are trained from within the philosophy field, is that philosophers do not always have the requisite experience or background in business to be convincing to students (see Oddo, 1997; Sims, 2000).

As noted in the previous chapters, business schools may choose to develop separate courses or integrate ethics throughout the curriculum. Additionally, business schools may decide to take an interdisciplinary, or team, versus single disciplinary approach to teaching business ethics. Regardless of which approach is taken, the question of *who* will teach business ethics must be answered. Providing an answer to the "*who*" question is the focus of this chapter. More specifically, the chapter will first briefly discuss the issue of exploiting interdisciplinarity. Next, the chapter addresses the question of who should teach business ethics. Then, the focus turns to a discussion of an interdisciplinary team approach to teaching business ethics that includes specific examples of such an approach.

EXPLOITING INTERDISCIPLINARITY

Business students today live in a world where ethical issues, problems, dilemmas or challenges appear to pile up faster than solutions. They will

likely continue to live in such a world in the future. Furthermore, many of
the challenges or problems will increasingly be "world" problems, that is,
they are of a global nature. One need only think of environmental pollution, an increase in the gap between the "haves" and "have-nots," ethnic
warfare, and an increasingly global and competitive business environment
as just a few on a long list of growing ethical dilemmas or challenges that
seem to defy simple solutions. Unfortunately, none of these ethical issues
come in the tidy packages of disciplines. Although the fundamental views
of ethics created by disciplines may be indispensable in addressing certain
ethical issues or problems, ultimate solutions require people who are skilled
in using many kinds of knowledge or perspectives when confronted with
ethical dilemmas. Interdisciplinary, or team taught, business ethics courses
are well-suited to developing the skills most needed to deal with the often
complex ethical issues students will encounter in today's society.

I, along with a number of others, believe that higher education should
be a liberating process that helps students become independent and critical
learners. The essence of "higher" education is criticism; all students should
think critically about the knowledge they already possess. Reflecting on
knowledge in a wider context demands a curriculum that is genuinely interdisciplinary and enables students to reflect on knowledge that transcends
any one particular discipline (Barnett, 1990; Macfarlane, 1998). Critical
interdisciplinarity, as Barnett terms it, encourages students to take a critical
attitude to knowledge and transform the way they look at the world.

Business ethics is genuinely interdisciplinary and beyond the narrow confines of the business curriculum. One writer notes that philosophy, economics, politics, sociology, literature, history, and management are among
the disciplines that contribute strongly to business ethics (Macfarlane,
1998). While subjects like corporate strategy, often taught in the final year
of business programs, help students synthesize and make sense of a broad
range of business disciplines, business ethics gives students an opportunity
to critically evaluate business knowledge.

Unfortunately, it seems that students often experience business school
curricula as a fragmented mix of single courses. Business ethics should build
bridges across existing courses rather than further intercourse fragmentation (i.e., business ethics teaching should be interdisciplinary rather than
single disciplinary). This means that an interdisciplinary approach to business ethics teaching builds bridges across different courses by demonstrating the relationship between the subject areas studied (i.e., accounting,
marketing, economics, organizational theory, etc.), opening both faculty
and students to new points of view, new questions, and new discoveries.
Such multifaceted teaching connects learning about ethics and ethical issues
with real business life—which is messy and complex—and presents many
viewpoints and alternative solutions to ethical dilemmas and issues. Students' values and prior learning and experiences are applied to business

situations, questioned, and reinforced. Critical thinking and analytical skills develop just like other skills important for success in business (i.e., financial analysis, operational analysis, market analysis, etc.). Analyzing and making decisions when ethical issues are involved, for example, calls for understanding and viewing issues from the perspective of each subject area and holistically within the context of each ethical decision (financing, human resource management, plant location, etc.). In the end, an interdisciplinary approach to teaching business ethics leads to increased student understanding of the congruence between business decisions and ethical behavior.

There are many arguments in favor of interdisciplinary teaching and learning. An interdisciplinary teaching and learning approach by its very nature does something that can't be done in a single disciplinary approach. It increases faculty cooperation and enhances student learning by exposing them to a variety of perspectives on a given comment" (Davis, 1995).

An interdisciplinary approach to teaching business ethics will undoubtedly require change and integration of faculty as well as students. Faculty themselves are often required to integrate knowledge, attack the teaching of business ethics from multiple perspectives, communicate effectively with others having different disciplinary language, listen to students and other stakeholders, negotiate and compromise in order to achieve a common purpose, learn from one another, and build something new by learning and utilizing the strengths of other faculty (team members). In effect, the steps required to build an interdisciplinary approach to teaching business ethics parallels the skills and mind-set to be taught and learned by students in ethics courses or modules.

BUSINESS ETHICS DOES NOT HAVE A SINGLE DISCIPLINARY HOME, SO *WHO* SHOULD TEACH BUSINESS ETHICS?

There do not appear to be any firm data on the background of those currently teaching courses in business ethics. It is still true that "those publishing in the field come from a variety of academic backgrounds, as evidenced by autobiographical information in journals. This also seems to be the case for those teaching the subject" (Gilbert, 1992, p. 6).

In teaching business ethics a single disciplinary viewpoint typically fails to discover and integrate inputs from other disciplines (i.e., sociology, psychology, philosophy, and other specialized fields that make up the business school curriculum). It has been my experience that these inputs can help broaden the perspectives of faculty teaching business ethics, strengthen their conceptual understanding, provide needed and valuable external input to reviews of an ethics course or module quality, and enhance student learning and enjoyment of the whole business ethics teaching effort. Further, single disciplinarity tends to ignore the complexity of many moral problems in business activity in general and business ethics in particular. The requirement to match such complexity to an interdisciplinary approach to teaching business ethics has been suggested by many authors (see, e.g., Brinkmann & Sims, 2001; McDonald, 1992). For our purposes, complexity, reflection (i.e., moral reflection as offered as a goal of teaching business ethics introduced in Chapter 3), and interdisciplinarity are closely related. Complexity is neither easily discovered (without reflection) nor easily handled (without interdisciplinarity). Interdisciplinarity furthers insight into single-dicipline limitations and, one hopes, academic humbleness and openmindedness towards what other disciplines have to say.

The fact that business ethics does not have a single disciplinary home is an important factor that has implications for teaching of business ethics and in deciding *who* should teach business ethics. Even as many urge that business should be a required component of business curricula, questions about who should teach it remain a matter of debate—one which often divides along disciplinary lines (Gilbert, 1992; Holt et al., 1998).

Traditionally, ethics is a branch of philosophy, but the study of business belongs to disciplines such as marketing, management, accounting, business law, economics, and finance. Studies over the years have found that the academic background of instructors in business and society courses (which were either business ethics courses or included significant ethics components) varied widely from management, marketing, and law, on the one hand, to political science, sociology, and philosophy, on the other hand (Holt et al., 1998). The mix has changed over years. For example, from 1978 to 1990, the percent of schools using instructors in philosophy increased from 4 percent to 28 percent while the percent using instructors with degrees in management decreased from 61% to 58 percent. But the variation in academic background continues to be significant (Collins & Warrick, 1995). Frederick (1998) has recently noted that there are far more philosophers-in-residence at business schools now than 20 years ago, and several of them occupy handsomely endowed professorships (p. 576).

The issue of who should teach ethics not only arises between disciplines, such as philosophy and business, but also among business faculty. This is especially the case when some business faculty, like their philosophy counterparts, have had formal training in the fundamentals of philosophical thought and take a more theoretically based approach to teaching ethics. Such an approach often creates additional tension between faculty, since those business faculty who often are not formally trained in the fundamentals of philosophical thought are more inclined to focus on clear-cut issues of right and wrong than they are to focus on the gray areas found in the reality of business (see White & Dooley, 1993 for a more detailed discussion of this point).

Perhaps nowhere is the division between disciplines so apparent as between philosophy and business faculty. Oriented towards career preparation and rooted in the social sciences, the business stresses the application of empirical methods to "real world" problems. In contrast, philosophy is a humanistic discipline that applies nonempirical methods such as conceptual analysis and textual interpretation to the clarification of our basic beliefs and values (Holt et al., 1998). While acknowledging that ethical theory is a traditional area of inquiry in philosophy, business professors may feel that "philosophers [do not] give business students what they need"—practical know-how for real life decision making (Parmenthal, 1991). Philosophers for their part, may be heard complaining that precisely what business students need is a solid grounding in ethical theory and the humanizing effect of a liberal education, which they are not getting from business professors. As White and Dooley suggest,

traditionally, the realm of ethical studies has been located in the philosophy departments of universities. Instruction has been theoretically based, and has lacked the pragmatism necessary to bridge the gap with the business environment. Professors . . . in business schools, on the other hand, are often not formally trained in the fundamentals of philosophical thought . . . and are more inclined to focus on clear-cut issues of right and wrong than they are to focus on the gray area found in the reality of business. (White & Dooley, 1993, p. 644)

So, *who* should do the teaching? One neutral and clear answer is people with advanced degrees in ethics (i.e., philosophers and perhaps people in religious studies). The curricular inference is that we need more courses in ethics and more ethicists in schools of business. However, this approach is insufficient for two reasons, one methodological and the other institutional. The latter reason is less controversial. If all the ethics teaching in business schools is to be done by ethicists, only a limited amount will be done. There aren't enough ethicists and, in particular, there aren't enough with the credibility to work in business schools.

It is also not clear that approaches to ethics honed in departments of philosophy are sufficient, even on the level of normative theory. Philosophers must be partners in the conversation, to be sure, but it is less likely that they will be solvers of problems. It appears that in trying to decide who should teach business ethics one has to necessarily grapple with the multiple conceptions and reasoning of ethics offered by faculty within philosophy (and even theology) and the wide range of business practices within the disciplines of business school faculty, who often have no formal training in ethics. It seems that the key question remains the identification of faculty who can bring a proper balance between philosophy and business practice, particularly with regard to moral principles and material practices, into business ethics teaching efforts. The frustration of deciding who should teach business ethics is often compounded by the fact that when one turns to philosophers to teach business ethics, one encounters a form of moral relativism. And when one turns to business faculty with no training in ethics, one discerns that they tend to focus too heavily on the impact of ethical decisions on business profits. Given the diversity between the disciplines and the different perspectives of philosophy and business faculty, it is important to recognize that the decision on *who* should teach business ethics is not a choice between philosophy or business professors but rather it involves an appreciation of what each can contribute to the teaching of business ethics. Thus, the best choice is an interdisciplinary approach to teaching business ethics that relies on faculty *who* can effectively contribute to the teaching and learning of business ethics, regardless of their discipline.

AN INTERDISCIPLINARY TEAM APPROACH TO TEACHING BUSINESS ETHICS

An interdisciplinary approach to teaching can be defined as the work undertaken by two or more teachers in planning, implementing, and assessing the curriculum. This partnership may take one of several forms but generally allows a group of teachers to share their knowledge and skills in an integrated curriculum that provides positive, connected learning experiences for students. A key characteristic of an interdisciplinary team approach to teaching business ethics is "integration"—faculty working together to pool their interests, insights, and methods, usually with the hope of gaining and presenting new understandings that could not be derived from working alone.

Team teaching has been used to teach ethics for a number of years (see Callahan, 1980, pp. 79–80; The Hastings Center, 1980; Loeb, 1988, pp. 325–326) and the advantages and disadvantages of team teaching have been considered in some of these sources (e.g., The Hastings Center, 1980, pp. 65–66). More recently team teaching used in teaching business ethics has also been highlighted (see Loeb & Ostas, 2000). For our purposes, interdisciplinary team teaching refers to teaching done in interdisciplinary business ethics efforts (i.e., either in separate or integrated courses across the curriculum, modules, or exercises) by several faculty members who have joined together to produce that course, module, or exercise. The arrangements vary considerably among teams, however, and it is not always easy to agree on what constitutes the "team" part of team teaching.

Team teaching in business ethics can range along a continuum. At one end of the continuum, courses may be planned by a group of faculty and then carried out in segments by individual members of the group. For example, two faculty members might plan a business ethics course to be delivered over the two semesters of an academic year, with the first faculty member taking responsibility for the first semester and the second for the second semester. They plan the general content of the two semesters together to avoid overlapping and to ensure continuity, but once this general planning is done they teach their "own" sections serially, one after the other. They do not attend each other's classes, they devise their own teaching strategies, and they employ their own evaluation procedures. Some would ask whether or not this is team teaching? And many would say "no." The degree of collaboration is low, and the amount and kind of interdisciplinary interaction is limited. The enrichment that comes from the interrelationship of multiple perspectives is minimal.

On the other end of the continuum are business ethics teaching efforts that are both planned and delivered by a group of faculty working together closely as a team. They develop a common syllabus, they struggle to integrate their various perspectives, they come to agreement about the ordering of topics, and they intermingle their teaching activity throughout the business ethics course. They take primary responsibility for individual class sessions, but sometimes two or more faculty members are involved in planning and teaching a particular class. They attend one another's classes and actively participate and provide feedback and support for one another in their teaching. They agonize together over facilitating experiential learning exercises and other pedagogical issues like grading and evaluation procedures. When the course is evaluated, they are attentive to the results. The degree of collaboration in this team approach to teaching business ethics is high, and the amount and kind of interdiciplinary integration is extensive. The learning and enrichment that comes from the synthesis of their multiple perspectives is what gives the business ethics teaching effort its distinctive character.

Wherever the course may fall on the continuum, it is important to recognize that team teaching in business ethics involves two or more faculty involved in some level of collaboration in the planning and delivery of the course. However, for our purposes, it is important to understand that optimal arrangements for interdisciplinary integration and for team teaching involve higher levels of collaboration. The reason for this, of course, is linked to the goal of providing integrative interdisciplinary perspectives to the teaching of business ethics. If the reason for team teaching in business ethics—its justification—is to create and deliver ethics from an interdisciplinary perspective, the achievement of that goal, in ways that are significant and not superficial, will require collaboration. In fact, one might generate the following principle: *The greater the level of integration of ethics desired, the higher the level of collaboration.*

I have found that there are two important questions to ask about interdisciplinary team teaching of business ethics: "Why decide to team teach business ethics?" and "If this is team teaching, what is the type and level of collaboration among team members?"

WHY DECIDE TO TEAM TEACH BUSINESS ETHICS?

Why do faculty decide to work in interdisciplinary teams in teaching business ethics? What and whose needs are being addressed? Several reasons can be found. First, faculty who choose to work collaboratively in interdisciplinary planning and teaching of business ethics have accepted the idea that ethics should not necessarily be taught by a single discipline. Rather, the various disciplinary perspectives should be woven together so that students see the connections *between* and *within* the disciplines. Team collaboration draws upon the expertise and experience of faculty with strengths in different subject areas who share a common belief about the ways in which to best teach business ethics. Working from this perspective, faculty look for teaching and learning strategies that best allow them to deliver or facilitate the understanding and learning of business ethics.

Secondly, in planning business ethics courses, modules, exercises, and assessments, interdisciplinary teaching teams combine their knowledge and skills in designing thoughtful, integrated, and stimulating experiences for students. I have found that collaboration in teaching business ethics seems to foster increased creativity and insight in ways that working in isolation does not. In approaching a three-session (one and a half hours for each session) unit on the social responsibility of U.S.-based global organizations in the oil industry, for example, organizational behavior (OB), marketing, accounting, philosophy, and sociology faculty bring to the table their unique understandings of that topic. As they work together, the faculty develop a unified presentation of the topic, tying together OB/management, marketing, philosophical, and sociological issues and events. This interdisciplinary approach to teaching this business ethics unit benefits students because they see the social responsibility of the organizations not just through the narrow lens of one discipline but as an ethically or socially complex case or situation that must be viewed from political, social, cultural, economic, and other lenses.

Finally, I have found that faculty have long expressed the need for increased opportunities to share professionally their successful (and not so successful) business ethics teaching strategies and lessons. While professional communication is often limited to coffee and lunch conversations in the faculty lounge (if you are lucky enough to have one), interdisciplinary team teaching in business ethics not only allows but necessitates regular planning, comparing, and sharing. Teaming relationships in teaching business ethics encourage reflective thought and discussion, as faculty review goals, plans, teaching strategies, and assessment approaches. In the process of reflecting together on teaching and learning in business ethics situations, teams of faculty can analyze, clarify, and rethink classroom situations and experiences, leading to confirmation or change of previously held ideas or practices. Vygotsky (1978) pointed out the relationship between learning and social interactions. Engaging in reflective dialogue with team members allows faculty to develop and refine their ideas about teaching and learning business ethics, which in turn may lead to improvement in the planning and implementation of interdisciplinary team teaching.

What Is the Type and Level of Collaboration of Team Teaching?

What is the type and level of collaboration among team members in interdisciplinary teaching of business ethics? There are several criteria that can be applied to any team-taught business ethics effort, whatever the mix of disciplines. These can serve as useful guidelines both for analyzing existing courses and for making decisions in the planning stage about the level of intended collaboration for interdisciplinary efforts. The criteria for judging the degree of collaboration are as follows:

Planning. What is the involvement of the faculty and other key stakeholders in planning this business ethics teaching effort (hereafter referred to as course)? Are all members of the team involved in planning, or do some members of the team play a more important role in planning the course than others? If so, why? Does the leader of the course (its coordinator) have more responsibility and more authority for planning the course (assuming it is only one course) than other team members? To what extent does the team use collaborative decision-making (democratic) processes in planning the course? How much time and effort have gone into planning the course? How well have the goals of the course been elaborated, and to what extent do the goals of the course reflect the views of all the participants? Remember the importance of coming to agreement on the purposes or goals of teaching business ethics as discussed in Chapter 2.

Content Integration. In what ways, and to what extent, have the multiple disciplinary perspectives of the faculty been represented? Are the differing perspectives seen as contradictory or complementary? Do the various disciplines provide different lenses for viewing the same phenomena (ethical principle, case, situation, dilemma, etc.), or do the disciplines examine different phenomena? Are the perspectives distinct and related in some logical way, such as serial or chronological order, or have the perspectives been integrated to produce some new way of thinking about the substance of the business ethics course, module, topic, or exercise? Is some unifying ethical principle, theory, or set of questions used to provide unity and coherence to the course? Content integration focuses on issues of scope and sequence and breadth and depth, as will be highlighted in Chapter 7.

Teaching. Who will teach and how will it be done? Do all team members participate more or less equally in the delivery of the business ethics course or management of student learning? Is there a core of key faculty who teach regularly but are supplemented by less frequent guests (i.e., business school faculty may teach regularly and be supplemented by faculty from the philosophy department or members of the business community)? Are teaching responsibilities divided into identifiable time segments, such as a term or unit of instruction, or do faculty intermingle their instruction day by day? Do faculty sometimes work together during a single class session? How are decisions made about what teaching strategies (i.e., experiential learning exercises, etc.) to employ and what readings and other materials to use? Pedagogical approaches used in teaching business ethics are discussed in Chapters 7 and 8.

Testing and Evaluation (Outcomes Assessment). How is agreement reached about what kind of learning outcomes are to be measured and how they are to be measured? What kinds of tests, papers, and other devices are used to assess or measure student learning or achievement? How are the various components of the testing and evaluation process weighted? How do the faculty involve themselves in this process? Who is included, and who is left out? Who takes charge of this process, and where is the highest court of authority when students challenge the process, including their grade? In addition, who decides what mechanisms will be used to get faculty feedback about the course, not only on what students appear to be learning but also on their satisfaction and concerns about the course? Chapters 12 and 13 discuss outcomes assessment, including student satisfaction with a business ethics teaching effort.

I suggest that faculty who teach business ethics use these criteria in examining the extent of collaboration in team teaching in their interdisciplinary efforts before, during, and after each course. It is possible to locate any business ethics teaching effort on a continuum of collaboration. When a course is examined to determine the degree of collaboration in specific areas—planning, content integration, teaching, and evaluation or assessment—faculty are able to look for opportunities to improve their collaboration in all four areas. In the end, there are many ways for business school faculty and others to work together to achieve their goals in teaching business ethics from an interdisciplinary team teaching approach.

Opportunities and Benefits of the Interdisciplinary Team Approach to Teaching Business Ethics

All key stakeholders, and especially faculty in business schools, must recognize that an opportunity exists to integrate their various perspectives and resolve their differences. In an interdisciplinary team teaching approach to business ethics, faculty have an opportunity to successfully meet the challenges of "connecting learning," while students have a chance to see relationships they don't get to see in other courses or faculty teaching initiatives. This is one of the great payoffs when business faculty work collaboratively in integrating their various perspectives in teaching business ethics. Faculty also have the opportunity to think about and give attention to those outcomes important to collaboration and the interdisciplinary process itself. These outcomes are as follows: an appreciation for perspectives other than one's own; openness to dialogue; an ability to evaluate the opinions of experts; tolerance for ambiguity; increased sensitivity to ethical issues; an ability to synthesize or integrate; enlarged perspectives or horizons; more creative, original, or unconventional thinking; increased humility or listening skills, and sensitivity to disciplinary, political, or religious bias.

In the ideal integrated effort, learning outcomes for the students have been discussed by the faculty team. Learning outcomes (i.e., goals) become specific and are based on some rational scheme agreed upon by the business school faculty, the administration, and all the important stakeholders. Because learning outcomes in business ethics teaching efforts can get complicated and ask a lot of faculty (and students), decisions need to be made about which outcomes are most important, given the underlying idea of the course and the focus on business ethics.

More specific opportunities and benefits to an interdisciplinary team approach to teaching business ethics include the following:

- An interdisciplinary/collaborative or team approach to teaching business ethics provides more opportunities for students to learn about ethics holistically, as they would in real work situations.
- Faculty has the opportunity to get experience in working on interdisciplinary teams; that is, to have an enriching and broadening experience instead of engaging in a power struggle brought on by disagreements.
- There is the opportunity to increase dialogue among faculty and for further integration of course material and pedagogical approaches.
- All concerned take the time to wrestle with, and to some extent resolve, the differences in pedagogical, theoretical, and disciplinary perspectives. This is hard work, but it should result in more integrated and connected approaches to teaching business ethics and improve student learning.
- There is also the opportunity to create a better learning climate/community, which is responsive to, or takes into consideration, students' fears.
- In addition, there is the opportunity to discuss learning outcomes in sufficient detail to make clear to the faculty, administrators, and ultimately to the students the kinds of learning intended by the teaching of business ethics.
- Learning outcomes are specific and based on some rational scheme. Faculty are better able to make decisions about which outcomes are most important.
- Faculty have the opportunity to divide up the teaching tasks and bring different talents into play from different functions.
- They also have the opportunity to watch other faculty members and their unique styles and pedagogical approaches, which stimulates growth and development in teachers as well as students.

- Some faculty can specialize or develop strengths in various pedagogical approaches (i.e., lecturing, facilitating case discussions, and work with students to identify and address ethical situations). Students ultimately gain the advantage of dealing with experts in these various roles.

- Faculty have an opportunity not only to play roles in which they have expertise but also to get additional training in those roles within the context of teaching business ethics.

- All faculty involved get the opportunity to see how their work contributes to the whole business ethics teaching effort. They also see that achieving this perspective requires training and learning in those specialized pedagogical roles in which they lack expertise.

- Opportunities are provided through such things as group projects (i.e., requiring students to engage in research into the current state of issues) that engage students in integration of theory and practice, appreciation of the shifting and evolving nature of business issues, and development of skills that can be transferred to other emerging issues.

- Finally, an opportunity exists for faculty and institutional administrators to more fully explore the possibility for those faculty who are already experts in business subjects to take on ethics. Giving special attention to the conflicts that often exist between individual faculty members' interests and those of the organization should provide for a better climate in which business schools can develop and deliver a more consensus-based approach to offering ethics in the curriculum.

Limitations of the Interdisciplinary Team Approach to Teaching Business Ethics

One of the great ironies of life in business schools is that we expect students to put the various curricular pieces together into something called a liberal or general education when teachers themselves make no claim to having done so. We expect students to emerge from our schools with a sense of citizenship when the faculty seldom works together, which is the beginning of citizenship. A useful principle to keep in mind is that the logical consequence of the separation of faculty from one another is a fragmented sense of knowledge and of self among learners. When faculty, and especially those responsible for teaching business ethics, work in isolation, when subjects like ethics are taught in isolation, why should we not expect students to view the learning of ethics as fragmented. And why should they themselves not feel isolated?

The primary purpose of this chapter has been to extol the virtues of the interdisciplinary team approach to teaching business ethics. But like anything else, no matter how beneficial, it can be both overdrawn and misapplied. The two most potentially damaging applications of interdisciplinary team teaching of business ethics are (1) its siren call of superficiality and (2) the temptation to use it when a separate subject approach would better serve both teachers and students. Let us look at each of these problems in turn.

Among traditionalists and subject-matter specialists there is great reluctance to abandon the separate approach to teaching of important subjects like business ethics. This is so because they fear that ethics will be watered down and treated superficially in an attempt to meet the compromising demands of teaching from an interdisciplinary perspective (see Klein, 1998). There is the accompanying concern that the orderly progression of knowledge and skills taught when a subject like ethics is treated as a curriculum in and of itself will be lost in a random, patchwork attempt to relate it to the particular theme. Finally, what one is left with, the critics note, is a shallow, disorganized treatment of ethics, or whatever, lacking both depth and continuity. Thus, the integrity of a typical ethical concept, such as ethical reasoning, is sacrificed in order to meet the demands of a theme, such as "social responsibility." Because of the focus on the organizing theme in a typical interdisciplinary business ethics unit, a subject like business ethics that could be treated in depth as an end in itself becomes merely a means to another end. When this is the case, business ethics itself is susceptible to superficial, random treatment.

The other related problem—an interdisciplinary approach to teaching business ethics when a separate discipline approach might well be superior—can be just as vexing. This is an issue that those responsible for teaching business ethics must address carefully. The question should be tied to the curricular goal structure. What are the important things that students must study (and is business ethics one of them), and how should they study them? Of course, there is no predictable answer to such a question because local circumstances must always be taken into account. The important thing is not to assume the inherent superiority of one approach over another but to think through the implications for student learning. The answer to this question is to consider carefully the implications of teaching business ethics from an interdisciplinary team approach as opposed to a single disciplinary approach. We should search for meaningful ways in which to integrate business ethics into a seamless whole, but we should never assume that integration is the only answer. For many, the burden of proof should be on integration and not the other way around (see Klein, 1998).

EXAMPLES OF TEAM TEACHING

The University of Denver's experience trying to reinvent its Masters in Business Administration (MBA) curriculum provides a first-hand look at the use of interdisciplinarity and team teaching in business ethics (see Wittmer et al., 1998). More specifically, in order to make a new two quarter "values" course (which replaced three required, self-standing courses in the old curriculum) more integrative, team teaching was viewed as an essential part of the larger curriculum change. Two types of teams were formed for the design and implementation of the values course. A collegewide review team representing each of the traditional disciplines and programs was created in order to make the course truly interdisciplinary. In addition to those who traditionally taught in law, public policy, and ethics, stakeholders realized the importance of including the perspectives of scholars in accounting, finance, statistics, and other traditional core business disciplines.

The second team was the core teaching team, and individual faculty members were selected for this team from among those who had taught two of the three required courses, thus maximizing community, integration, and overlap. Two cores were created and these pairs functioned as "true teaching teams" (as opposed to "tag teams," or sequential teaching), with both instructors being present for virtually all classes (Wittmer et al., 1998). Members of the larger design and review team provided spot lectures and participated in topics appropriate to their areas of interest and expertise.

As suggested earlier in this chapter and in our discussion of obstacles and issues to teaching business ethics in Chapter 3, change and integration were required of faculty and students at the University of Denver MBA program. For example, faculty themselves were required to integrate knowledge, attack problems from a multiple perspectives, communicate effectively with others having different disciplinary languages, listen to students and stakeholders, negotiate and compromise in order to achieve a common purpose, learn from one another, and build something new by learning and utilizing the strengths of other faculty (team members). In effect, the steps and skills required for building the values course paralleled the skills to be taught in the new, integrated program.

In designing their team-taught business ethics course, two authors recently noted that they approached the task from different backgrounds, different disciplines, and different preferred teaching strategies in an MBA program at the University of Maryland's Robert H. Smith School of Business (Loeb & Ostas, 2000). The authors noted that despite differences in background (for example, one instructor's doctoral training and discipline is accounting, while the other instructor's educational background is in law and business economics) and differences in preferred teaching strategies (the accounting instructor preferred an "interactive" and "experiential" approach, while the other instructor preferred lectures and Socratic-style case analysis), they were able to complement one another and facilitate successful team teaching.

The authors attribute much of their success in team teaching to the fact that their backgrounds and disciplines had something in common. For example, at the time of the course, they were both faculty in the same school of business. Additionally, both learned much of what they knew about business ethics and the teaching of business ethics through self-instruction, attendance at relevant professional conferences, teaching ethics-related courses, and conducting ethics-related research. The authors offer the following further insights into successful team teaching of business ethics:

- Instructor teams should consist of individuals who are familiar with business ethics and who come from business or business-related backgounds and/or disciplines that minimize the need for new learning.
- Members of the team should have a strong interest in business ethics and be willing to learn from the other faculty member(s) as well as on their own.
- Faculty with business-related backgrounds and/or disciplines should be used on business ethics teams to reduce the possibility that students get different messages from different instructors.
- Team teachers must jointly and effectively participate in all aspects of the course. For example, similarities between the two authors enabled them to plan the course, design the syllabus, participate in all classroom activities, and grade student performance together (i.e., students were evaluated for the quality and the quantity of their participation following each class period, both instructors wrote examination questions for the final exam, etc.).

The authors note in concluding their discussion that team teaching likely involves increased cost to the educational institution as suggested by other researchers (see, for example, Callahan, 1980, p. 79; Caplan 1980, p. 23; The Hastings Center, 1980, p. 65). However, they believe that the benefits to the students and to the instructors may be worth the possible increased costs.

LeMoyne College's MBA program also offers a team-taught required course "Business Ethics—BUS 601" (Schonsheck, 1998). The course is taught by a philosopher (Johnathan Schonsheck of the Department of Philosophy), and business professor (Daniel L. Orne of the Department of Business Administration). Increased sensitivity to moral issues is one of the goals of the course. Increased proficiency in resolving moral issues is also one of the central goals. To achieve the very broad personal goal for each student to develop a moral position that is consistent, coherent, and adequate to the subtleties and complexities of modern moral life (beginning with what one has internalized of "common morality"), students study three of the great traditions in moral philosophy: those of Aristotle, Immanuel Kant, and J.S. Mill. In addition, a critique of capitalism from the Marxian perspective is offered (Schonsheck, p. 402). The authors use a casebook (*The Corporate Social Challenge: Cases and Commentaries* by James E. Stacey and Frederick D. Sturdivant), aided by a secondary source (*Business Ethics: Concepts and Cases*, 3rd edition by Manuel G. Velasquez), and also require students to read significant portions of primary texts: Aristotle's *Nicomachean Ethics*, Kant's *Grounding for the Metaphysics*, and Mill's *Utilitarianism*.

The guiding metaphor for the course is "navigating the stream of life": a journey that requires both "white water skills," and "still water wisdom." One portion of each class is taught by the business professor and is devoted to case analysis through which students are expected to acquire white water skills as they answer rapid-fire questions, respond to misdirection, and role-play to enhance sensitivity to the ethical issues raised in business and to help them work on their resolution and be mindful of the continuing viability of the company. The other part of each class is led by the philosophy instructor, who focuses on acquiring the "still water wisdom" of philosophy, including sensitivity to the occasional need to get out of the "white water" of business and to be able to pause and reflect. The two instructors actively discourage the attitude that in the first part of class they will get a "tool" and in the second part of the class they will "use" that tool.

An important goal of this team-taught course is to help students develop a step-by-step way (Moral Decision Procedure) to apply abstract philosophy to ethical issues in business (Schonsheck, 1998). Written case analysis assignments are incorporated into the course, leading to the "capstone assignment" (The Grand Synthesis), which is designed to integrate the philosophical material of the course with the practice of business. The format of the final paper is a standard business case analysis of the *SCA Corporation* case and includes the following sections: executive summary, introduction, problem statement/analysis of problem (symptoms and causes), options/analysis of options, recommendations, implementation plan, and conclusion. Each student submits two copies of "The Grand Synthesis," one to each of the instructors who grade them independently.

While Schonsheck provides no specific information about the team teaching process, I believe he provides additional opportunities for us to learn about team teaching in business ethics. In particular, the situation described by Schonsheck demonstrates the viability of successful team-taught business ethics efforts in which team members are not from the same department/school (i.e., school of business or philosophy department). It appears that the real key to successful team-taught business ethics efforts is the interest and commitment on the part of the team members to simply make the effort "work."

In the end, I believe that deciding *who* should teach business ethics can be best determined by answering a simple question: What is best for students? In other words, decisions made not with reference to an abstract policy that favors business or philosophy professors, or separation or integration of business ethics, or an interdisciplinary or single disciplinary approach but with reference to contextual matters such as the development of morality, knowledge, skills, and self-realization will be the best decisions. One can only conclude that sometimes the best answer is "it all depends."

RECOMMENDATIONS

As suggested several times already in this book, business ethics teaching efforts must begin with making decisions about goals or objectives. This means that each faculty member (and other key stakeholders), regardless of their discipline, must think about how ethics applies to the overall mission of student learning, growth, and development. The following recommendations are offered for deciding the *who* and (at least partially) *how* of teaching business ethics:

- Avoid power struggles that usually result when faculty members from different disciplinary perspectives recognize that they have differing points of view on ethics and on teaching goals and objectives. These disagreements, initially quite rational, often lead to serious power struggles because each faculty member believes his or her views are superior. Faculty must not only avoid attacking one another's ideas but also one another.
- Faculty (and others) must work to resolve differences in perspectives. This means that they must do something to confront the assumptions and limitations of their disciplinary paradigm. Resolving differences involves a great deal of "homework" on the part of faculty, but the end result is a more integrated or team approach to teaching ethics. This also means that faculty must develop enough comfort with their differences to make them explicit.
- Faculty (and others) should pay significant attention to both content and process levels of the business ethics teaching initiatives and settle on desired outcomes. The content level focuses on the subject of ethics, and the process level has to do with the kind of learning taking place and the way that learning is occurring.
- Faculty members must recognize and be open to the value of the various pedagogical approaches offered by other faculty.
- They must also be prepared to address the heightened need for coordination in all aspects of the interdisciplinary team approach to teaching business ethics. Otherwise, both individual faculty time and business school time will likely be used inefficiently.
- In the end, those responsible for teaching business ethics must recognize contrasting perspectives; learn how to synthesize, think critically and reexamine the world they take for granted; and develop learning outcomes that are not vague, unarticulated, or fail to spell out the purpose of teaching ethics.

In my view, teaching business ethics is enhanced by an interdisciplinary team approach, using resources from various disciplines (i.e., philosophy, religion, business, literature, etc.). Additionally, an interdisciplinary approach to teaching business ethics infuses business education with moral theory and reasoning that helps students develop important tools for addressing diverse business situations, situations that best represent the world in which our students live. This is a world that is permeated with ethical and value questions that don't fall clearly within one subject area or discipline. Business schools can scarcely claim to have educated their students to cope with that world if they have not encouraged them and helped them to refine a holistic view of their moral sensibility. But there is a more fundamental reason for concern with an interdisciplinary or team approach to teaching business ethics. It pertains to the relationship between helping students acquire useful business knowledge and exposing them to ethical issues, the link between ways of knowing and ways of being that don't fall within the purview of a single discipline.

In my experience, when a business school faculty helps students understand a business situation and the ethical implications from a multifaceted or holistic viewpoint, they are "doing" their job. An interdisciplinary approach to teaching business ethics builds bridges across different courses by demonstrating the relationships among subject areas (i.e., accounting, marketing, economics, organizational theory, etc.), opening both faculty and students to new points of view, new questions, and new discoveries. Such multifaceted teaching connects learning about ethics and ethical issues with real business life—which is messy and complex, with many viewpoints and alternative solutions to ethical dilemmas and issues. Students' values, prior learning, and experiences are applied to business situations, questioned, and reinforced. Critical thinking and analytical skills develop just like other skills important for success in business (i.e., financial analysis, operational analysis, market analysis, etc.). Analyzing and making decisions when ethical issues are involved, for example, calls for understanding and viewing issues from each subject area's perspective as well as holistically within the context in which ethical decisions are set (financing, human resource management, plant location, etc.). In the end, an interdisciplinary team approach to business ethics teaching leads to increased student understanding of the congruence between business decisions and ethical behavior.

CONCLUSION

Team teaching is one strategy that can be effectively used in planning, teaching, and assessing an interdisciplinary approach to teaching business ethics. Working collaboratively to teach business ethics results in a more connected, holistic learning experience for students. This is especially the case when those engaged in team teaching work towards a real integration of their perspectives.

I do not assume that effective collaboration requires that the faculty engaged in team teaching come from different or similar backgrounds. What is important is that there is a true willingness to commit to the planning necessary to integrate different perspectives, or any other differences, so that insurmountable difficulties will not result. There is always the likelihood that integrating the content of various fields, the costs of team teaching, faculty from different disciplines, and the possible problems due to the department organization of many schools of business may be potential barriers to teaching business ethics. However, successful team teaching overcomes such barriers. Especially, when members of the teaching team have a strong interest in business ethics and are willing to learn from one another. In the end, each participating faculty member and all students are likely to learn and have a positive experience in an integrated, interdisciplinary approach to teaching business ethics, since they get the best of "all" worlds. Additionally, perhaps business schools can meet the challenge posed by Trevino and McCabe (1994) to "integrate ethics education into functional area courses and expand ethics education to the program's 'hidden curriculum' by developing and building just communities and 'honorable business school communities.' " I hope the discussion to this point has provided some guideposts for those who are interested in undertaking this challenge.

REFERENCES

Barnett, R.A. 1990. *The idea of higher education.* Buckingham: Society for Research into Higher Education/Open University Press.

Brinkmann, J., & Sims, R.R. 2001. Stakeholder-sensitive business ethics teaching. *Teaching Business Ethics* 5: 171–193.

Callahan, D. 1980. Goals in the teaching of ethics. In D. Callahan & S. Bok (eds.), *Ethics teaching in higher education.* New York: Plenum Press, pp. 61–80.

Caplan, A. 1980. Ethical engineers need not apply: The state of applied ethics today. *Science, Technology and Human Values* 6 (Fall): 24–32.

Collins, D., & Warwick, S.L. 1995. Business and society/business ethics courses: Twenty years at the crossroads. *Business and Society* 34(1): 51–89.

Davis, J.R. 1995. *Interdisciplinary courses and team teaching.* Phoenix, AZ: American Council on Education and the Oryx Press.

Frederick, W.C. 1998. One voice? Or many? *Business Ethics Quarterly* 8(3): 575–579.

Gilbert, J.T. 1992. Teaching business ethics: What, why, who, where, and when. *Journal of Education for Business* 68(1): 5–8.

The Hastings Center. 1980. *The teaching of ethics in higher education: A report by the Hastings Center.* The Teaching of Ethics I. Hastings-on-Hudson, NY: The Hastings Center, Institute of Society, Ethics and the Life Sciences.

Holt, D., Heischmidt, K., Hill, H.H., Robinson, B., & Wiles, J. 1998. When philosophy and business professors talk: Assessment of ethical reasoning in a cross disciplinary business ethics course. *Teaching Business Ethics* 1: 253–268.

Klein, E.R. 1998. The one necessary condition for a successful business ethics course: The teacher must be a philosopher. *Business Ethics Quarterly* 8(3): 561–574.

Lampe, M. 1997. Increasing effectiveness in teaching business ethics to undergraduate students. *Teaching Business Ethics* 1: 3–19.

Loeb, S.E. 1988. A separate course in accounting ethics: An example. In B.N. Schwartz & D.E. Stout (eds.), *Advances in accounting education: Teaching and curriculum innovations.* Vol. 1. Stamford, CT: JAI Press, pp. 235–250.

Loeb, S.E., & Ostas, D.T. 2000. The team teaching of business ethics in a weekly semester long format. *Teaching Business Ethics* 4: 225–238.

Macfarlane, B. 1998. Business ethics and the idea of a higher education. *Teaching Business Ethics* 2: 35–47.

McDonald, M. 1992. The Canadian research strategy for applied ethics: A new opportunity for research in business & professional ethics. *Journal of Business Ethics* 11: 569–583.

Masden, P. 1995. A theoretical ground for the practice of business ethics: A commentary. *Teaching Business Ethics* 5: 451–462.

Oddo, A.R. 1997. A framework for teaching business ethics. *Journal of Business Ethics* 16(3): 293–297.

Parmenthal, G.L. 1991. The course in business ethics: Why don't philosophers give business students what they need? *Business Ethics Quarterly* 1: 385–394.

Rosen, B., & Caplan, A.L. 1980. *Ethics in the undergraduate curriculum.* The Teaching of Ethics IX. Hastings-on-Hudson, NY: The Hastings Center, Institute of Society, Ethics and the Life Sciences.

Schonsheck, J. 1998. A team-taught course in business ethics and its synthesizing capstone assignment. *Teaching Business Ethics* 1: 399–429.

Sims, R.L. 2000. Teaching business ethics: A case study of an ethics across the curriculum policy. *Teaching Business Ethics* 4: 437–443.

Trevino, L.K., & McCabe, D. 1994. Meta-learning about business ethics building honorable business school communities. *Journal of Business Ethics* 13: 405–416.

Vygotsky, L.S. 1978. *Mind and society: The development of higher mental processes.* Cambridge, MA: Harvard University Press.

White, C.S., & Dooley, R.S. 1993. Ethical or practical: An empirical study of students' choices in simulated business scenarios. *Journal of Business Ethics* 12: 643–651.

Wittmer, D., Holcomb, J., Hutton, B., & Nelson, D.R. 1998. Reinventing the master of business administration curriculum: Integrating ethics, law, and public policy. In J.S. Bowman & D.C. Menzel (eds.), *Teaching business ethics and values in public administration programs: Innovations, strategies, and issues.* Albany: State University of New York Press, pp. 63–84.

Chapter 5

Teaching Business Ethics for Effective Learning: Experiential Learning

INTRODUCTION

As a business professor, I am dedicated to the proposition that students can learn from experience. Most people adhere to the notion of "trial and error" learning. Many, like myself, who are committed to experiential learning, have used the following quote, attributed to Confucius, to express their conviction that experiential learning is effective:

> I hear and I forget
> I see and I remember
> I do and I understand.

The AACSB Memorandum (Carter et al., 1986) used a slightly different version: Tell me and I'll forget. Show me and I'll remember. Involve me and I'll understand. Others have cited Sophocles' quote from 400 B.C., "One must learn by doing the thing, for though you think you know it—you have no certainty, until you try." Or one could quote George Santayanna, "The great difficulty of education is to get experience out of ideas" (Gentry, 1990). It is hard to argue that experience will not lead to learning under the right conditions. However, it will be argued that the resultant learning can be in error unless care is taken by the business ethics teacher to ensure that those conditions occur. The purpose of this chapter is to present a model of curriculum design and business ethics teaching based on how different people think and learn. The model is organized around a theory that describes both experiential learning and learning styles. This chapter will delineate the components of "experiential learning" so that the necessary conditions for learning business ethics can be specified.

TEACHING BUSINESS ETHICS: LESSONS TO BE LEARNED FROM *THE WIZARD OF OZ*

The movie *The Wizard of Oz* (LeRoy & Fleming, 1939) offers three lessons that have direct application to teaching business ethics experientially. In one of the final scenes, Dorothy and her three friends return to the Wizard after defeating the Wicked Witch of the West and ask that their wishes be granted as he had promised. Dorothy wants to go home to Kansas; the Scarecrow wants a brain; the Tin Woodsman wants a heart; and the Cowardly Lion wants courage. Therein lies our first lesson: *Although they may all participate in a shared activity, individuals are likely to have different needs.* Students in business ethics education efforts have different learning styles.

Dorothy and her friends soon discover that the Wizard, rather than being all-powerful, is a mere mortal with a great multimedia projection system. Luckily, he's also a great improviser. Reaching into his carpetbag, he presents each of the characters with symbols of their learning that represent the fulfillment of their wishes. The Tin Woodsman is given a pocket watch in the shape of a heart to honor his compassion. The Scarecrow receives a diploma to recognize his intelligence. The Wizard awards the Cowardly Lion with a medal for courage. He even offers to take Dorothy back to Kansas in a balloon. Now here is the second lesson: *If you are not an all-powerful wizard, it helps to have a bag of useful items to help you out in a bind.* When applied to a business ethics teaching plan, this lesson suggests that it is important to offer individually designed rewards to meet the needs of different individuals. In a business ethics teaching environment, these rewards come in the form of appropriate learning experiences that stimulate different types of students (i.e., learners).

Interestingly, the Wizard did not actually grant the wishes of Dorothy and her friends, yet all were able to gain what they needed. How did they attain their aspirations? Through experience! The Tin Woodsman found his heart by being in a situation that required compassion. By responding with quick thinking, the Scarecrow recognized his brain. Protecting his friends from danger allowed the Cowardly Lion to find his courage. Dorothy eventually realized that she had the power to go home all along. The third lesson from *The Wizard of Oz* is this: *Individuals learn best through experience.* If we can create an active and experiential learning environment when teaching business ethics, then it is possible to encourage students to recognize their own compassion, intelligence, and courage, and to take this learning home with them to parallel work and other life situations.

Teaching Business Ethics for Effective Learning

Teaching business ethics for effective learning means that there is an emphasis on the development of competence or skill building, interactive or collaborative learning among students, and application of new learning. Other emphases include increased knowledge and personal awareness or self-improvement. These different emphases are briefly discussed below.

Competency or Skill Building. Business ethics teaching that emphasizes skill building is aimed at equipping students with specific skills that they can use in their personal or work lives. For example, building skills in ethical decision making or handling ethical dilemmas or problems.

Problem Solving. Business ethics teaching that focuses on problem solving creates opportunities for students to work together to find solutions to ethical or other related problems. For example, students could work to find new organizational strategies for preventing unethical behavior.

Increased Knowledge. Increasing knowledge can also be the emphasis of teaching business ethics. However, if knowledge is only transmitted in a didactic fashion, it is considered a lecture and does not fit our definition of teaching business ethics for effective learning. Although I believe that most business ethics teaching efforts do result in increased knowledge, they also provide opportunities for students to use and apply their newfound knowledge. For example, business ethics education can be used to inform students of the results of research about being socially responsible to an organization's bottom line. For this educational experience to be experiential, the students would need to be provided with the opportunity to practice using their new knowledge in real-world work situations.

Systemic Change. Systemic change is another possible emphasis for teaching business ethics that can fall into the context of consultation or organizational development. For example, developing skills in conducting an ethics audit intended to diagnose an organization's culture might be offered within a real or simulated company after there have been reports of unethical behavior that has tarnished the company's reputation. The aim of the business ethics teaching effort would be to change attitudes and behaviors within the workplace in order to create a more positive ethical environment for all of the company's employees (perhaps by developing a code of ethics or other means of institutionalizing a more ethically oriented culture).

Personal Ethical Awareness/Self-Improvement. Personal awareness, self-improvement, or both are the goals for other business ethics teaching efforts. These may focus on issues like ethical self-awareness, self-esteem, or positive thinking and promote change by helping students become aware of their own values, attitudes, ethics, or behavior and by helping people make changes in their lives.

Interaction among Emphases. It should be pointed out that these emphases may overlap substantially. Rarely is it possible to isolate a process like awareness from related emphases like skill building or problem solving. For example, a business ethics teaching effort that promotes personal ethical awareness in an area such as self-reflection frequently will be tied to skill building in areas such as moral judgement.

Teaching Business Ethics Experientially: A Definition

In addition to the characteristics mentioned above, the business ethics teaching model described in this chapter emphasizes three interrelated elements: experiential learning, sensitivity to different learning styles, and the use of a variety of learning activities. The following definition of teaching business ethics for effective learning will be used:

> Teaching business ethics is a series of learning experiences that encourages active, experiential learning and uses a variety of learning activities to meet the needs of diverse students.

I see an experientially oriented approach to teaching business ethics, which uses a variety of teaching and learning approaches, as an ideal way to address the needs of students with different learning preferences. Throughout the next few chapters, I will offer further information about learning styles, learning activities, and facilitation skills important to creating an effective learning environment that is sensitive and responsive to diverse student learners.

When Is Teaching Business Ethics Not Teaching Business Ethics for Effective Learning?

Have you ever attended a business ethics class or taken a course that relied on lectures? While preparing this book, I attended several classes on ethics taught at my own and other institutions. Several were exclusively lectures with no attempt to provide active learning. A couple of others included videotaped or live demonstrations. One had students respond in writing to material presented by the faculty member. And only one had students break down into dyads and small groups for interactive or collaborative learning. Although I do not question the value of lectures and demonstrations, these elements alone do not fit my definition of teaching business ethics for effective learning. The class that involved students in responding to material in writing took an important step toward active learning. (It might be noted that the instructor had close to 80 students in her class, and it was impressive that she found a way to include an active exercise at all.) However, the class that included student interaction met the definition of teaching business ethics for effective learning.

THE BUSINESS ETHICS TEACHER AS A FACILITATOR

In order to enact this vision of teaching business ethics, it is important for faculty who teach business ethics to act as facilitators of experiential learning rather than merely as teachers or instructors. In my experience, more than any other aspect of business ethics teaching efforts, students will be impacted by the business ethics teacher. When creating an interactive, experientially oriented learning environment, the business ethics teacher as the facilitator can often be more important than the content. The business ethics teacher is the most important tool!

When the word facilitator is used rather than teacher, instructor, or leader, it implies a different approach to teaching and learning business ethics. These implications are critical to understanding the environment for teaching business ethics and the experiential learning that occurs within a business ethics teaching effort. Many traditional business ethics teaching formats depend upon the teacher primarily as an expert source of information.

The teacher who takes on the role of a facilitator can stretch beyond the expert role by encouraging learning through participatory experience and among the students. This expanded role can be more effective because it promotes learning on many different levels. Creating powerful learning experiences and guiding and encouraging individual and group learning can generate change that complements and encourages greater and deeper learning than merely providing information on business ethics to students.

The initial reaction of many of my colleagues to the idea of experiential learning and the facilitator role may include resistance. They may wish to defend traditional, didactic, content-oriented business ethics instruction. For example, after one colleague first tried to use the model suggested here, she earnestly suggested that "When you are dealing with a topic as complex as business ethics and there is so much material to be covered, we don't have time to create an engaging environment or to facilitate active involvement." People who do not see the value of experientially oriented business ethics education may be depending upon a traditional educational paradigm. Embracing experiential learning as a valuable endeavor may require a paradigm shift (Kuhn, 1970).

A traditional, unidirectional, content-based learning paradigm has dominated Western ideas of education for centuries. This paradigm is so pervasive that it can be difficult to see beyond it. Experientially oriented business ethics education and the accompanying facilitator role represent a paradigm shift that can revolutionize the way people learn about business ethics. Although the idea of experiential ethics education has been discussed for the past decade or so, there is still considerable resistance based on adherence to a traditional ethics educational paradigm. An important paradigm shift for faculty responsible for teaching business ethics is the shift in the perception of their own role as educators. A facilitator in teaching business ethics is likely to value experience and growth as much as knowledge and attend as much to process as content. In my own experience, the facilitation of learning in teaching business ethics is often more informal and multidirectional than traditional instruction. For example, in response to a question, a traditional business ethics instructor might choose to offer his or her expertise, whereas a facilitator might choose to "bounce" the question back to the class and ask other students what they think.

When educating students about business ethics as a traditional instructor, the individual might start by collecting as much information on business ethics as possible and plan on spending most of the time lecturing from this material. In contrast, in my experience, experiential facilitators are more likely to identify key ethical theories or frameworks, or a set of ethical rules or guidelines but not limit themselves to focusing on the content alone. A facilitator might also identify ways to encourage students to reflect on their own experience in order to increase motivation, design ways for people to experiment and practice using their newfound knowledge, and ensure that students are prepared to apply what they have learned. As a facilitator, the instructor provides opportunities for interaction, feedback, and making choices so that learning is active and individualized. This expanded role of the teacher as facilitator in business ethics is a key ingredient of experiential learning.

USING EXPERIENTIAL LEARNING THEORY IN BUSINESS ETHICS EDUCATION

Ethics education is an increasingly important priority for business schools, the workplace, and the community. Its purposes can range from raising awareness and understanding of ethics in one's personal life, work, or in the broader society to a number of other purposes.

Learning about or teaching business ethics poses difficult educational challenges:

1. Business ethics education requires not only acquisition of knowledge but also a change of attitude as well as personal change. It must address emotional, perceptual, cognitive, and behavioral issues.

2. Resources for business ethics education must be organized to be maximally responsive to what each student wants to (and should) learn and the manner in which that learning is to be achieved. One student may enter a business ethics course or module seeking to understand ethical principles, a goal that may require her to read related concepts and theories. Another student, who wants to learn what it means to strive to always act ethically, might engage in self-reflection and dialogue with his classroom peers. Such individualized learning sometimes comes into conflict with a particular instructor's view that learning

involves a one-size-fits-all ethical or moral view of the world and a learning environment of sameness.

3. Perhaps, because business ethics education addresses core feelings and values, it requires a climate of psychological safety and trust. Students must feel empowered and in control of their own learning. When students feel threatened, they adopt defensive and conformist postures. Teaching, then, is experienced as coercive and manipulative, and learning becomes secondary.

Business ethics education summons to the classroom social and personal issues and the act of learning in unique combination. Teaching about ethics compels a framework that is considerably broader than traditional classroom methodology—one that recognizes the relevancy of education to the student's life situations. Theories of experiential learning provide educational strategies for responding to the challenge of ethics education in business schools. Other important points on experiential learning theories are:

1. Experiential learning theory describes learning as the holistic engagement of affective perceptual, cognitive, and behavioral processes (Kolb, 1984). Learning results from the interplay of these processes, which are positioned along two primary dimensions of knowledge. Prehension, knowing by taking in data, involves the affect of concrete experience and cognition of abstract conceptualization. Transformation, knowing through modification of data, requires perception in reflective observation and behavior in active experimentation. Experiential learning theory is an inclusive paradigm that allows for a range of responses to the learning requirements of ethics education in business schools.

2. Experiential learning theory offers a perspective for addressing individualized learning in ethics education. Each student is unique in the way he or she learns and equal in his or her contribution to a larger holistic learning cycle that values, acknowledges, and includes all ways of knowing. There is no one best way to learn. The assumption is equal worth in all ways of knowing. Experiential learning theory also provides guidelines for creating learning environments that address the special learning needs of each learning style.

3. Experiential learning theory proposes that the foundation of learning resides not in business schools, books, or even faculty. Rather, it rests in the experiences of students. This approach to education emphasizes self-directed learning and the role that sharing, dialogue, and discussion play in the creation of a psychologically safe climate of learning.

Holistic Learning

I believe that experience is a crucial aspect of teaching business ethics for effective learning. Therefore, Kolb's model of experiential learning will be used to inform and direct our considerations because it has a crucial advantage over other models. For example, Curry (1987) identified more than 18 models that describe stages of learning organized as a cycle. Likewise, there are different theories that describe individual differences related to human learning.

Curry also observed that at least four variations of Kolb's model are in use. Two derivatives have been developed for business applications: McKenney and Keen (1974) and Honey and Mumford (1982). A third variation of Kolb's model is by Marshall and Merritt (1985) and is applied in educational settings. A fourth inventory, by Gregorc and Ward (1977), is a Kolb-like bipolar scale (abstract/concrete and sequential/random). The Kolb Learning Style Inventory is the only one of the 18 identified by Curry to have stimulated the development of four other learning style inventories.

Kolb's model is most useful in our consideration of business ethics education because it describes both individual learning styles that can be used to understand students in ethics courses or modules and a cycle of learning that can be used to organize teaching activities and facilitation skills for the business ethics teacher. In addition, Kolb's (1999) *Learning Style Inventory III* (LSI III) provides instrumentation to operationalize these concepts. For these reasons, I will use Kolb's model as the primary theoretical base for the business ethics teaching approach described in the next few chapters.

KOLB'S EXPERIENTIAL LEARNING MODEL

Experiential learning theory is distinct from traditional approaches to learning. Unlike the epistemology of behavioral theory or cognitive and other rationalist theories, experiential learning theory is based on the epistemology of radical empiricism—a knowledge theory that affords equal status to multiple ways of knowing. Its intellectual roots are traceable to the pragmatism of John Dewey, the Gestalt and action research perspectives of Kurt Lewin, and Jean Piaget's structural dimensions of cognitive development.

David Kolb (1984) proposed a model of experiential learning in his book *Experiential Learning: Experience as the Source of Learning and Development*. Kolb drew upon the foundational work of Kurt Lewin and Piaget to develop his experiential learning model. According to experiential learning theory, learning proceeds as a cycle and results from the integration of four learning modes: concrete experience, reflective observation, abstract conceptualization, and active experimentation (Kolb, 1984). Students must be able to fully and openly engage in new experiences; reflect on, observe, and consider these experiences from various perspectives; create concepts that assimilate these experiences into sound theories; and appropriately apply these theories to their life situations. This cycle of learning is at the heart of Kolb's experiential learning model. Thus, the underlying premise of Kolb's cycle or learning sequence is that learners learn best when they are active, take responsibility for their own learning, and can relate and apply it to their own context.

Kolb's cycle of learning proposes four learning modes: concrete experience, reflective observation, abstract conceptualization, and active experimentation. Learning occurs most effectively when all four modes in the cycle of learning are completed. This cycle of learning is depicted in Figure 5.1.

In addition to describing learning as a cycle, Kolb (1984) also used four learning modes to suggest that there are two primary dimensions to the learning process. The first dimension, prehension, represents concrete experience and abstract conceptualization. Knowledge acquired through concrete experience—affective, immediate, and intuitive—is called apprehension. Knowledge gained through abstract conceptualization—cognitive, rational, and symbolic—is referred to as comprehension. The second dimension of knowing, transformation, represents reflective observation and active experimentation. Knowing through reflective observation—perceptual, appreciative, and diffuse—is intentional. Knowing through active experimentation—behavioral, focused, and goal directed—is extensional. McCarthy (1980, 1990) labeled these continua perception (anchored by concrete experience and abstract conceptualization) and processing (anchored by active experimentation and reflective observation). The synthesis of these four forms of knowing results in higher levels of learning.

The transformation dimension of knowing is well illustrated in the two primary psychological dimensions of introversion (intention) and extraversion (extension) in dialectic relationship (Jung, 1971). The radical pedagogical concept of praxis—"reflection and action upon the world in order to transform it"—depicts the interplay between intentional knowing and extensional knowing (Freire, 1974, p. 36).

By considering the ways that different people perceive and process, individual learning styles can be identified. These two dimensions can visually serve as horizontal and vertical axes to create four quadrants that represent four individual learning styles. The concept of learning styles is another important aspect of Kolb's model that can be used to direct this consideration of teaching business ethics.

The first learning style describes *divergers* (Kolb, 1984, 1985), who perceive primarily through concrete experience and process primarily through reflective observation. The second learning style describes *assimilators* (Kolb, 1984, 1985), who perceive primarily through abstract conceptualization and process through reflective observation. Third, *convergers* (Kolb, 1984, 1985) have the opposite strengths of divergers and perceive primarily through abstract conceptualization and processes primarily through active experimentation. Fourth, *accommodators* (Kolb, 1984, 1985) (I prefer *implementers*, Sims, 1990) have the opposite strengths of assimilators and perceive primarily through concrete experience and process primarily

Figure 5.1
Learning Modes, Learning Styles, and Learning Environments

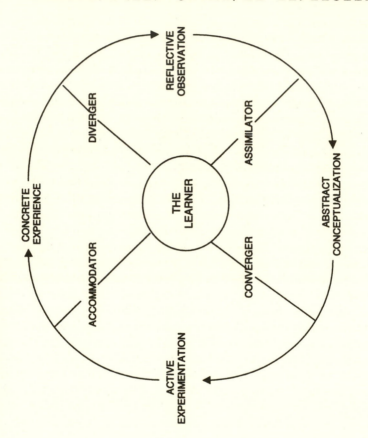

AFFECTIVELY ORIENTED ENVIRONMENT

PERCEPTUALLY ORIENTED ENVIRONMENT

BEHAVIORALLY ORIENTED ENVIRONMENT

COGNITIVELY ORIENTED ENVIRONMENT

CONCRETE EXPERIENCE

REFLECTIVE OBSERVATION

DIVERGER

ASSIMILATOR

THE LEARNER

ACCOMMODATOR

CONVERGER

ABSTRACT CONCEPTUALIZATION

ACTIVE EXPERIMENTATION

through active experimentation. Both of Kolb's (1984) views of learning—as four parts of a continuous cycle and as two complementary dimensions or continua that can be used to identify learning styles—are useful to this consideration of business ethics teaching.

APPLYING KOLB'S MODEL TO TEACHING BUSINESS ETHICS

Now that Kolb's (1984) model of experiential learning has been introduced, it can be applied to the domain of developing business ethics teaching efforts. A major premise of the model is that there are three major tasks involved in successful business ethics teaching efforts. The first task is coming to a better understanding of the students involved in the business ethics teaching effort. The second task is developing a business ethics teaching design that addresses a particular group of students within a particular context or learning environment. The third task is facilitating the teaching effort in a way that promotes active learning.

Experiential learning theory can inform us about all three of these tasks. First, when experiential learning is applied to the task of understanding an audience and its individual students, the concept of individual learning styles can be used to identify four clusters of learning needs and preferences. Second, in addressing the design of teaching efforts, the four learning processes can be used to promote different types of learning environments. Third, four sets of facilitation skills for the business ethics teacher can be identified that correspond to the four basic learning processes. In developing a particular business ethics teaching effort, an instructor might use Kolb's LSI III (1999) to measure the needs of students and use this information to choose which activities to plan and to anticipate the types of skills they are most likely to use.

Using Learning Styles to Understand Students and Guide Curriculum Design

One key to being a successful gardener is knowing that different plants need different conditions to thrive. Some plants need lots of water, others need little. Some need direct sunlight, others need shade. Some plants need fertilizer, others don't. The same is true of learners. Each has different needs and preferences. To be a successful business ethics teacher, I have found that one needs to recognize individual variations in learning styles and respond to these differences with conducive learning environments and activities. In this way, the learners in your garden will grow and flourish.

To design and facilitate business ethics teaching efforts that appeal to learners and address their diverse needs, it is important to consider the impact of individual learning styles. Most of us have ideas and impressions about how we, ourselves, learn best and what we prefer in new learning situations. A business ethics teacher or facilitator, however, often has 30 or more students with strongly held learning preferences that differ from the facilitator's and from one another's. The challenge is to use knowledge of learning styles to design a business ethics teaching effort that is responsive to all of these needs.

As noted above, I have organized the approach to designing and facilitating teaching business ethics around Kolb's (1984) model of experiential learning and his learning styles. Kolb's four learning styles can be used as a guide or strategy to develop or design teaching efforts that will meet the needs of different learners. Both of these strategies will be discussed in more detail below. Of course, Kolb's model is only one of many that could be used to direct our thinking. Two other models will be described briefly in Chapter 6.

Understanding Students: Two Design Strategies

Exploring different ways to respond to individual differences in students has led me to identifying two strategies for designing business ethics teaching efforts: "flexibility and diversity" in putting together content and "customization." These two strategies will be described along with a further elaboration of Kolb's learning styles, and then the two will be combined to demonstrate their applicability to teaching business ethics.

Flexibility–Diversity. The flexibility–diversity strategy begins with the assumption that business ethics teachers will face a variety of learners and that teachers should select learning activities that correspond to all of their students' needs. This strategy does not require measuring the needs of students ahead of time but does involve using a specific theory or model to guide design. The model that the business ethics teacher can use as a guide can be a general description of learning or a theory that is more closely related to the content of the business ethics teaching effort. For example, to apply the flexibility–diversity strategy to a business ethics teaching effort for managers, one could use a model that describes different management or learning styles and select activities that correspond to the needs of each style. In this way, the design attends to the preferences of all students. The advantage of the flexibility–diversity strategy is that it is easy to use and does not require formal needs assessment. The disadvantage is that it does not allow teachers to customize the business ethics effort to the specific needs of a particular group of students.

Customization. In contrast, the customization strategy identifies students before a business ethics effort begins and uses needs assessment methods to collect information that will guide the instructor's design. This allows the business ethics teacher to tailor the business ethics teaching effort to the needs of particular students by selecting learning activities that correspond to their preferences or to a more specific measure related to the business ethics teaching effort. Applying the customization strategy to a business ethics teaching effort for managers, one could assess the management or learning styles of students and tailor the design to meet the needs of the predominant styles in the group. The advantage to the customization strategy is the ability to use accurate knowledge of individual students' needs to design a unique learning environment. Sometimes, however, the results of a needs assessment reveal a diversity of learning styles. In this case, the teacher can offer activities for all styles, just as would have been done when using the flexibility–diversity strategy. The obvious disadvantage is that the customization strategy can be used only in situations in which one can identify students and have them complete an instrument or survey like Kolb's LSI III.

Either of these two strategies can be used with almost any theory or model related to teaching business ethics. Teachers can decide which theory or model works best for them. As noted thus far, Kolb's model works best for me, and I will review Kolb's model of learning styles in more detail and then identify ways to apply flexibility and diversity or customization to his model.

Kolb's Model of Learning Styles

Kolb (1984) applied his ideas about experiential learning to the concept of individuality in learning to identify four different learning styles. He identified these based on individuals' preferences for each of four modes of the learning process: concrete experience, reflective observation, abstract conceptualization, and active experimentation. Using these modes, Kolb (1984, 1985) described the four groups of learners that he referred to as divergers, assimilators, convergers, and accommodators. The four learning styles are described in more detail next.

Divergers are oriented toward concrete experience and reflective observation (Kolb, 1984). The greatest strength of this orientation lies in imaginative ability and awareness of meaning and values. The emphasis in this orientation is on adaptation by observation rather than by action. Kolb notes that this style is called "diverger" because a person of this type performs better in situations that call for generation of alternative ideas and implications, such as a "brainstorming" idea session. These individuals want to construct personal meaning from learning. Learning environments that allow personal involvement and interpersonal interaction are a good match for divergers. Divergers may particularly enjoy business ethics teaching activities that allow them to share what they already know, that allow them to learn from one another, and that address personal values.

Assimilators are oriented toward abstract conceptualization and reflective observation. The greatest strength of this orientation lies in inductive reasoning, in the ability to create theoretical models, and in the ability to assimilate disparate observations into an integrated explanation. They learn by thinking through ideas. As with convergers, this orientation is less focused on people and more concerned with ideas and abstract concepts. Ideas, however, are judged less in this orientation by their practical value. Here, it is more important that the theory be logically sound and precise. Assimilators value expert knowledge and data. Traditional educational settings often allow assimilators to excel because they focus on information and analysis. Business ethics teaching efforts that are particularly helpful for assimilators are those that present factual information derived from research or expert opinion and that involve data and statistics.

Convergers are oriented toward abstract conceptualization and active experimentation. The greatest strength of this approach lies in problem solving, decision making, and the practical application of ideas. Kolb calls this learning style the "converger" because a person with this style seems to do best in such situations as conventional intelligence tests where there is a single correct answer or solution to a question or problem. In this learning style, knowledge is organized in such a way that, through hypothetical-deductive reasoning, it can be focused on specific problems. Convergers want to put new information to immediate practical use. They want to be involved in a process of hands-on learning that involves experimenting with new knowledge. They prefer dealing with technical tasks and problems rather than with social and interpersonal issues. A learning environment that promotes direct involvement, practice, and active experimentation is beneficial for convergers. Business ethics teaching efforts or activities like role-plays, simulations, and in-basket exercises encourage the hands-on experimentation that convergers desire.

Accommodators are oriented toward concrete experience and active experimentation. Their greatest strength lies in doing things, in carrying out plans and tasks, and in getting involved in new experiences. The adaptive emphasis of this orientation is on opportunity seeking, risk taking, and action. Kolb calls this style "accommodator" because it is best suited for those situations in which one must adapt oneself to changing circumstances. In situations where the theory or plans do not fit the facts, those with an accommodative style will most likely discard the plan or theory. (With the opposite learning style, assimilation, one would be more likely to disregard or reexamine the facts.) People with an accommodative orientation tend to solve problems in an intuitive trial-and-error manner, relying on other people for information rather than on their own analytic ability. Individuals with accommodative learning styles are at ease with people but are sometimes seen as impatient and "pushy." A learning environment that builds a bridge from learning to application and points toward actively using new learning is valuable for accommodators. Brainstorming solutions, homework, action plans, and other business ethics teaching activities that anticipate the future are particularly helpful for accommodators.

In the introduction to this chapter, I used *The Wizard of Oz* (LeRoy & Fleming, 1939) as a metaphor to teach three lessons about business ethics teaching efforts. The analogy can be extended to learning preferences, and the characters from the story can be used to represent the four learning styles. Divergers share something in common with the Tin Man because they want learning that appeals to their hearts. The Scarecrow is a symbol for assimilators, who need to use their brains. Convergers are similar to the Cowardly Lion because it takes courage to try new things. Dorothy represents the accommodators, who want to take their learning home with them.

Applications to Teaching Business Ethics Efforts

Kolb's model of learning styles can be used to apply either flexibility–diversity or customization to business ethics teaching efforts.

Flexibility–Diversity. When the flexibility–diversity strategy is combined with Kolb's model and applied to the design of business ethics teaching efforts, the outcome includes a balance of activities that correspond to each of Kolb's four learning styles. Learning activities that allow students to recall their own past and integrate personal values into a business ethics teaching effort are especially appealing to divergers. The opportunity to learn new facts and theories and apply these ideas to new areas will stimulate the thinking of assimilators. Convergers enjoy practicing new skills and experimenting in a supportive environment. A business ethics teaching effort that includes making concrete plans for the future is responsive to the needs of accommodators.

In my experience, the combination of the flexibility–diversity strategy and Kolb's model of learning styles forms an important approach to designing effective business ethics teaching efforts. Designing and selecting activities that meet the needs of learners with these learning styles is important to effective learning.

Customization. To combine the customization strategy with Kolb's model, business ethics teachers can use Kolb's LSI III as part of needs assessment. The LSI is a brief questionnaire that requires respondents to rank order a series of responses. Advantages of the LSI include its brevity (it takes about 10 minutes to complete) and the fact that it has been empirically validated (Veres et al., 1987). By assessing the student learning styles in a business ethics class, the teacher can design activities that appeal to the needs of the predominant learning styles represented or to others' learning styles, depending on the teacher's philosophy about teaching to students' learning styles. If one were teaching business ethics to a group of accountants, one might use the LSI during the needs assessment and find that most of the students are assimilators. To match the needs of this group it might be necessary to provide a lot of didactic material about business ethics to build a conceptual foundation before experimenting with new skills that might require these students to stretch beyond their own comfort zone.

CONCLUSION

This chapter introduced experiential learning theory and specifically Kolb's experiential learning model, which forms the theoretical basis for the approach to teaching business ethics discussed in this book. The chapter also discussed the use of learning styles as a means of better understanding students and designing business ethics teaching efforts for effective learning. Flexibility–diversity and customization are two strategies that can be combined with Kolb's model to design business ethics teaching efforts.

The next chapter builds on the experiential learning and learning styles discussion in this chapter by highlighting the importance of creating learning environments and learning processes that enhance effective learning in business ethics teaching efforts.

REFERENCES

Carter, P., Hickman, J., McDonald, P., Patton, R., & Powell, D.C. 1986. *Memorandum on applied and experiential learning curriculum development.* AACSB Task Force Report, March.

Curry, L. 1987. *Integrating concepts of cognitive or learning style: A review with attention to psychometric standards.* Ottawa: Canadian College of Health Service Executives.

Friere, P. 1974. *Pedagogy of the oppressed.* New York: Continuum.

Gentry, J. 1990. What is experiential learning? In J. Gentry (ed.), *Guide to business gaming and experiential learning.* East Brunswick, NJ: Nichols/GP Publishing, pp. 9–21.

Gregorc, A.R., & Ward, H.B. 1977. Implications for teaching and learning: A new definition for individual. *National Association of Secondary School Principals Bulletin* 61: 20–26.

Honey, P., & Mumford, A. 1982. *The manual of learning styles.* Maidenhead, UK: Peter Honey.

Jung, C. 1971. Psychological types. In J. Campbell (ed.), *The portable Jung.* New York: Viking Press. (Original work published 1921; original translation 1923.)

Knowles, M. 1984. *The adult learner: A neglected species* (3rd ed.). Houston, TX: Gulf Publishing Company.

Kolb, D.A. 1984. *Experiential learning: Experience as the source of learning and development.* Englewood Cliffs, NJ: Prentice Hall.

Kolb, D.A. 1985. *Learning styles inventory* (rev.). Boston: McBer & Company.

Kolb, D.A. 1999. *Learning styles inventory III.* Boston: McBer & Company.

Kuhn, T.S. 1970. *The structure of scientific revolutions.* Chicago: University of Chicago Press.

LeRoy, M. (Producer), & Fleming, V. (Director). 1939. *The Wizard of Oz.* [Film]. Washington, DC: MGM/UA Home Video.

McCarthy, B. 1980. *The 4MAT system: Teaching to learning styles with right/left mode technique.* Arlington Heights, IL: EXCEL.

McCarthy, B. 1990. Using the 4MAT system to bring learning styles to school. *Educational Leadership* (October): 31–37.

McKenney, J.L., & Keen, P.G.W. 1974. How managers' minds work. *Harvard Business Review* 52: 79–90.

Marshall, J.C., & Merritt, S.L. 1985. Reliability and construct validity of alternate forms of the learning style inventory. *Educational and Psychological Measurement* 45: 931–937.

Sims, R.R. 1990. *An experiential learning approach to employee training systems.* Westport, CT: Quorum Books.

Veres, J.G., Sims, R.R., & Shake, L. 1987. The reliability and classification stability of the learning styles inventory in corporate settings. *Educational and Psychological Measurement* 47(4): 1127–1133.

Chapter 6

Learning Environments and Experiential Learning Processes

INTRODUCTION

A crucial component of teaching business ethics for effective learning is considering the necessary learning environments. The learning environment may be more about how a classroom or other environment feels than what it looks like. Content, context, conduct, and character are key dimensions of designing a business ethics education effort, each dimension having its own pedagogical consideration. What is the appropriate context or learning environment to foster? What is the process or conduct to use? What is the character or role of the business ethics teacher?

This chapter builds on the discussion of experiential learning theory introduced in Chapter 5 as a guiding framework for effectively teaching business ethics. First the chapter describes four learning environments conducive to enhancing the teaching and learning of business ethics. Next, the chapter describes four experiential learning processes that correspond to the four learning styles that can be used to guide the development of business ethics teaching efforts. Four types of facilitation skills teachers can use are also identified. The chapter then describes two alternatives to Kolb's learning styles model developed by Grasha and Reichmann. The theory of psychological types is also discussed. These types collectively comprise a powerful and readily available approach that business ethics teachers can use to understand and respond to individual differences in learning. The next section of the chapter discusses the importance of managing the learning process in business ethics teaching efforts by adapting teaching methods to students' learning styles. The chapter concludes with a look at the implications of a greater understanding of teaching and learning styles and learning environments.

LEARNING ENVIRONMENTS

Particular learning styles seem better suited for particular learning environments (Fry & Kolb, 1979). Students perform better in environments and with approaches that complement their learning styles than in environments or approaches that are inconsistent with their learning styles (Dunn et al., 1989). In addition to conceptualizing individual learning styles, experiential learning theory provides a structure for the learning environment that is consistent with the learning cycle (Fry & Kolb, 1979) and appropriate for teaching business ethics.

Any business ethics teaching effort can be viewed as having degrees of orientation toward each of the four learning modes in Kolb's experiential learning model, labeled as affective, perceptual, symbolic, and behavioral to connote the overall climate they create and the particular learning skill or mode they require (see Figure 6.1). Thus, an *affective environment* emphasizes the experiencing of concrete events. A *symbolic or cognitively oriented environment* emphasizes abstract conceptualization. A *perceptual environment* stresses observation and appreciation. And a *behavioral environment* stresses taking action in situations that have real consequences. Any particular learning experience can have some or all of these orientations, to differing degrees, at the same time. According to Fry (1978), each learning environment can be measured by observing key variables in the context of a course: the purpose of the major activities, the primary source or use of information, the rules guiding learner behavior, the nature of feedback, and the faculty role. These are useful dimensions to guide faculty in planning classroom interactions, provided that provision is made for individual differences among both faculty and students. These variables create four distinct components of a learning ecosystem. Table 6.1 structures each learning environment against the five variables with examples of activities for each.

A typical lecture on, say, an ethical theory obviously has perceptual and symbolic orientations because it requires students to listen to and interpret the presentation (reflective observation skills) and to reason and induce conceptual relationships from what they hear (abstract conceptualization skills). But there may be an affective orientation as well. Some students may be experiencing the business ethics teacher who is lecturing as a role model. Or if the teacher directs questions or poses dilemmas to the class, he or she increases the behavioral orientation by urging students to take action by speaking up and testing out their ideas in public.

Each type of environmental orientation can be measured by observing the following variables in the context of an ethics course: the purpose of

Table 6.1
Learning Environments and Their Distinct Variables

	Learning Environment			
	Affectively Oriented	*Perceptually Oriented*	*Cognitively Oriented*	*Behaviorally Oriented*
Purpose	Develop personal ethical or self-awareness and insight	Appreciate and understand how and why things relate	Acquire and master knowledge and skills	Actively apply learning to real-life situations
Information source	"Here and now" concrete experience	Multiple data sources viewed in different ways	"There and then" abstract concepts and facts	Activities directed toward requirements of task completion
Rules of behavior	Free expression of feelings, values, and opinions	Emphasis on process and inquiry	Adherence to prescribed objective criteria	Minimal rules in support of learner autonomy
Nature of feedback	Personalized and immediate from business ethics teachers and peers	Non-evaluative suggestions rather than critiques	Evaluation of correct or incorrect learner output	Learner judges own performance based on established standards
Faculty role	Role model and colleague	Process facilitator	Interpreter of a field of knowledge (i.e., business ethics)	Coach and advisor
Activities	Check-in, guided imagery to create experience, or debate	Casual mapping, maintaining a diary/journal or brainstorming	Presenting concepts, developing personal theories, or traditional testing	Developing action plans, a simulation, or group ethical norms

the major activities, the primary source or use of information, the rules guiding student behavior, the faculty member's role, and the provision for feedback. These are useful cues because to a great extent they are controlled by the business ethics teacher and are independent of the student as a learner. Most decisions affecting these aspects of learning environments are made before learner-classroom interactions take place. Using these variables, different views of learning environments and faculty responsible for teaching business ethics result.

Affectively Oriented Environments

This learning setting focuses on attitudes, feelings, values, and opinions generated from "here and now" experiences. Tasks and activities often change from prior design and are more emergent as a result of students' immediate needs. Procedures and guidelines are geared toward free expression of personal feelings, values, and opinions. Feedback is personalized with regard to the personal needs and goals of the student rather than comparative and comes from both faculty and peers. Faculty members serve as role models and colleagues. Typical activities are exploring feelings with students at a particular time or asking the class what might be useful to do given the dynamics of the moment. In the affectively oriented environment the emphasis is on experiencing what it is actually like to be a professional in the field of study (i.e., in a real-world business situation where one is confronted by ethical dilemmas, etc.). Students are engaged in activities that simulate or mirror what they would do as graduates, or they are encouraged to reflect upon an experience to generate these insights and feelings about themselves. The information discussed and generated is more often current/immediate and often comes from expressions of feelings, values, and opinions by students in discussions with peers or faculty. Such expressions of feelings are encouraged and seen as productive inputs to the learning process. There is accepted discussion and critique, for example, of how a business ethics course is proceeding, and thus, specific events within a single-class session are often more emergent than prescribed.

Perceptually Oriented Environments

This learning setting emphasizes appreciation and understanding of relationships between events and concepts. Students are encouraged to view business ethics or ethical theories and models from multiple perspectives to clarify their position (their own experience, expert opinion, literature) and in different ways (listen, observe, write, discuss, act out, think). If a task is being done or a problem is being solved, the emphasis is more on how it gets done—the process—than on solutions. Students are evaluated on methodology of inquiry rather than on getting a particular answer. Faculty members serve as process facilitators, inviting students to step back and attempt to appreciate opposing viewpoints or engaging the class in a casual mapping of the concept of ethics or ethical theories and models.

In this learning environment, the faculty member does not measure success or performance against rigid criteria. Instead, students are left to conclude, answer, or define criteria of success for themselves. Individual differences in this process are allowed and used as a basis for further understanding. Students are thus free to explore others' ideas, opinions, and reactions in order to determine their own perspective. In this process, the faculty member serves as a "mirror" or "process facilitator." He or she is nonevaluative, answers questions with questions, suggests instead of critiquing, and relates current issues to larger ones. The faculty member creates a reward system that emphasizes methodology of inquiry versus getting a particular answer. In class sessions, time is planned to look back at previous steps, events, or decisions in order to guide students in future activities.

Cognitively Oriented Environments

This environment is one characterized by skill mastery. Activities are directed toward problem solving based on "there and then" objective criteria. Business ethics teachers function as interpreters of a field of knowledge. Lecturing on ethical models or asking students to create their own personal ethical theories are typical activities. In this environment students are involved in trying to solve a problem for which there is usually a right answer or a best solution. The source of information, topic, or problem being dealt with is abstract. It is removed from the present and presented via reading, data, pictures, lecture inputs, and so on. In handling such information, students are both guided and constrained by externally imposed rules of ethical performance, jargon, theorems, or protocols. There is often a demand on students to recall these rules, concepts, or relationships (i.e., these are usually in the form of ethical guidelines, etc.).

In this learning environment, the teacher is the accepted representative of the body of knowledge—judging and evaluating student output, interpreting information that cannot be dealt with by the rules of inference, enforcing methodology and the rigor of the use of particular guidelines, and so forth. The teacher is also a timekeeper, a taskmaster, and an enforcer of schedules of events so that students can become immersed in the analytical exercise necessary to reach a solution and not have to worry about having to set goals and manage their own time. Student success is measured against the right or best solution, expert opinion, or other rigid criteria imposed by the teacher or accepted by experts or others. Decisions concerning flow and nature of activities in the class sessions are essentially made by the faculty member and mostly prior to the course.

Behaviorally Oriented Environments

This setting is geared toward application of knowledge and skills to deal with real-life situations. Activities are directed toward the planning necessary to complete a task. Students are left to judge their own performance based on criteria they establish. Business school faculty serve as coaches. They provide friendly advice and leave responsibility for outcome to the student. Assigning students the task of developing strategies for using what they have learned about ethics in their everyday lives or developing role-plays that demonstrate effective ethical behavior in the workplace are illustrations of activities.

The emphasis in this setting is upon actively applying knowledge or skills to a practical business problem or situation. The problem or situation need not have a right or best answer, but it does have to be something the student can relate to, value, and feel some intrinsic satisfaction from having solved. This would normally be a real-life business problem/situation with ethical implications, or a simulation of a situation that students could expect to face as professionals. In attacking the problem, the focus is on doing.

Completing the task is essential. Although there may be an externally imposed deadline or periodic checkpoints for which reports or other information are required, most of the students' time is theirs to manage. They are concerned with the effect their present behavior will have vis-à-vis the overall task. The next task students engage in will not occur independently of the one they are currently in.

In this learning environment, the business ethics teacher ensures that students are left to make decisions or choices about what to do next or how to proceed. The faculty member can coach or advise, but primarily at the request or initiative of students. Student success is measured against criteria associated with the task: how well they handled the particular situation or dilemma, feasibility, salability, client acceptance, cost, and so on.

When those responsible for teaching business ethics view students and the instructional environment in terms of learning styles and learning environments, useful relationships can emerge concerning the design of learning activities or situations in courses, in a particular class, and in the business school as a whole. As a result, managing the learning process allows learning to become a skill that can be managed, improved, and coached. Managing the learning process by working with learning styles and learning environments allows faculty members to design opportunities to learn about business ethics that match students' learning strengths and weaknesses. Empathy and communication become central to the business ethics teaching process. Teachers then become concerned with how learning styles can be addressed when students are in courses that deal with complex topics like business ethics, topics that may be foreign to their preferred learning style.

USING EXPERIENTIAL LEARNING PROCESSES TO DESIGN BUSINESS ETHICS TEACHING EFFORTS

To guide the development of business ethics teaching efforts, I suggest using four experiential learning processes that correspond to the four learning styles. These four learning processes are: reflecting on experience, assimilating and conceptualizing, experimenting and practicing, and planning for application.

Reflecting on experience occurs when students are encouraged to recall important ethical aspects of their past experiences. This process increases motivation and prepares students for learning by reminding them of what they already know (Kolb, 1984). A business ethics teaching effort might start by having students share with one another times they were confronted by an ethical dilemma.

Assimilating and conceptualizing moves students from reflection and observation to abstract conceptualization. Assimilating and conceptualizing may include more didactic teaching but also encourages students to compare the didactic material to their own experience. A business ethics class or activity focusing on ethical leadership could include a role-play to demonstrate common mistakes leaders make that contribute to the development of an unethical organizational culture. This encourages the students to identify the leaders' errors or misjudgments and suggest alternative behaviors.

Experimenting and practicing encourages students to move from abstract conceptualization to active experimentation. In this process, students are asked to use new ethical knowledge and practice skills in an experimental way. For example, in a business ethics class students are given scenarios printed on index cards and asked to sort each of the index cards into one of three piles based on whether they think unethical behavior did not occur, whether the scenario constituted unethical behavior, or whether it was not clear whether unethical behavior did or did not occur.

Planning for application prepares students to move from active experimentation back to concrete experience. Since much of the process of application occurs, by necessity, outside an ethics course, class, or activity in one's work or personal life, this process emphasizes planning and preparation. At the end of a business ethics class or activity, students might be given time to do some writing in a journal or to complete a personal application assignment (PAA) concerning how they will apply what they have learned to parallel or other related situations.

In designing a business ethics teaching effort, learning activities can be used that encourage each of these four types of learning. Using these four processes accomplishes two important goals. First, different learning experiences are provided to meet the primary needs of students with different learning styles. Second, a learning experience is created that provides a complete cycle of learning which deepens learning for all students.

Examples of *reflecting activities* are:

- Dyadic or small-group sharing: a simple but effective way to encourage reflection by asking students to pair off and share past experiences (i.e., dealing with ethical dilemmas, etc.).

- Role-plays: planned role-plays structured by the business ethics teacher and presented to the students.

- Games: engaging activities used to activate students' thoughts about ethical, moral, or related topics. Games tend to be enjoyed by extroverted students.

- Storytelling: a way to provide a common experience on which the group can reflect together and that can provide insights related to the focus of the business ethics effort.

Examples of *assimilating activities*:

- Lectures/lecturettes: used to provide factual content information about an ethical theory, for example. (A short lecture is called a "lecturette.")

- Values clarification: allow students to explore their own values and experiences and how they differ from those of other students in an involving and nonthreatening way.

- Questionnaires/instruments: allow students to gain new knowledge about themselves. Questionnaires to access information about students in a way that does not require verbal participation.

- Modeling role-plays: used to demonstrate effective behavior related to the focus of the business ethics teaching effort. These can be presented by the business ethics teacher or a guest lecturer.

- Case studies: accounts of actual events that are used to prompt exploration and discussion.

- Fishbowl discussions: structured exercises in which a group of students sits in a circle while another group silently observes from outside the circle. These activities are used to help students gain knowledge about the group itself. Fishbowl discussions allow students in the observer role to gain "inside information" from another group that might not be expressed in an open discussion between groups. An open discussion can follow the fishbowl discussion, focusing on why different groups have different perceptions or experiences.

Examples of *experimenting activities*:

- Practice role-plays: used to practice new behaviors or skills.

- Simulations: used to present realistic or metaphorical situations so that students can practice using knowledge related to the focus of the business ethics teaching effort.

- Open discussions: allow students to share their ideas with one another, with little interference from the business ethics teacher.
- Structured discussions: require the business ethics teacher to provide more guidance or control questions, time limits, or other structures. Structured discussions are an organized way for students to share their ideas in an interactive manner.
- Scenarios: exemplary situations that provide specific examples with stimulus questions and that are used to activate learning in structured discussions.

Examples of *planning activities*:

- Personal practice of skills learned in role-plays: provides an opportunity for students to incorporate knowledge from the business ethics teaching effort into their own personal behaviors.
- Action plans: offer students the opportunity to contract with one another and the business ethics teacher the opportunity to take knowledge gained in the teaching effort and apply it to students' outside lives.
- Goal setting: involves stating specific, measurable goals and dates when those goals are expected to be accomplished. This specificity increases the likelihood that application will occur.
- Brainstorming solutions: can be used as a way for the group to cooperate in identifying possible solutions to an individual or collective difficulty.
- Quizzes: allow business ethics teachers to measure how much has been learned by students and to help consolidate material into students' behavior and memory.

Adaptation of Activities

The categorization of learning activities into different learning quadrants is based on my experiences and is not absolute. The classification is based on the type of learning I think is most often promoted rather than the structure of the activity. Therefore, it is possible for many of the previously listed activities to be modified to facilitate different types of learning. Obviously, the activities can be adapted to address a wide variety of focuses in business ethics teaching efforts.

For example, role-plays can be used to promote all four types of learning. Stimulus role-plays are considered reflecting activities. Modeling role-plays tend to promote assimilation. Practice role-plays are a useful way to encourage experimentation. Personal practice of skills can be used as a planning activity. Similarly, a carefully planned activity may meet more than one type of learning need. For instance, an ethical self-awareness survey about ethical dilemmas faced by managers can interest students in the topic (reflecting) as well as provide information about different types of management styles (assimilating).

USING FACILITATION SKILLS TO ENCOURAGE EXPERIENTIAL LEARNING

In the same way that learning styles are used to identify learning processes, learning style quadrants can be used to identify four types of facilitation skills teachers can use in their business ethics teaching efforts. As noted earlier, instructors must take on the role of facilitator as opposed to the traditional role of teacher. The facilitation skills related to reflecting on experience and the diverger learning style are referred to as *engaging facilitation skills* because an important role of the business ethics teacher is to help the students engage in experiential learning. The skills that correspond to assimilating and conceptualizing and the assimilator or analytic learning style are called *informing facilitation skills* and highlight the role of the business ethics teacher as facilitator or provider of information. Skills that are related to experimenting and practicing and the converger learning style are called *involving facilitation skills* because of the importance of actively involving students in the process of experimentation. The last set of skills, which corresponds to planning for application and the accommodator learning style, are called *applying facilitation skills*.

The four facilitation skills relate to Kolb's four learning styles. I recommend using all four types of facilitation skills for the same reason that I advocate including all four learning activities: you can meet the primary learning needs of each student as well as encourage all students to complete the experiential learning cycle. These four types of facilitation skills for business ethics teaching efforts will be described next.

Engaging Facilitation Skills. Engaging skills are used to invite students to be fully engaged and actively involved in the learning environment. Engaging skills help students reflect on their own experience and prepare them for interactive learning. These skills are used to activate knowledge that students already possess and to get them motivated and interested in business ethics. Engaging skills are employed to create curiosity and energy for learning. They help create personal meaning and encourage interpersonal connections. Engaging skills build bridges between students' past experience and the current learning experience. Engaging facilitation skills most closely correspond to the needs of divergers and are often used in reflecting activities.

Informing Facilitation Skills. Informing facilitation skills help students learn new information and conceptualize their own observations. Informing includes teaching factual information and allowing students to gain new knowledge. Informing skills involve both content information from outside the group of students and process information about the group itself. Content information is frequently presented in a lecture format and includes facts and theories. In contrast, process information can be collected in the form of surveys, scoring exercises, and internal group activities. Once information is assimilated, facilitation skills can be used by the business ethics teacher to encourage students to use the concepts to understand their own experiences. Informing facilitation skills best meet the needs of assimilators and correspond most closely to assimilating activities.

Involving Facilitation Skills. Involving facilitation skills create an opportunity for active experimentation with new knowledge and skills, encourage learning by practice, and allow students to use the knowledge that has been gained in the business ethics teaching effort. Involving skills often are used to increase interpersonal interaction among students. Because this type of learning occurs when the students themselves practice new skills and gain hands-on experience, these facilitation skills require a shift in focus away from the business ethics teacher and toward the students. Involving facilitation skills correspond most closely with the needs of convergers and are most often used in experimenting activities.

Applying Facilitation Skills. Applying facilitation skills allow students to personalize their new learning by planning to apply the knowledge to their own personal or professional lives. Applying skills are used to build bridges between the learning environment and real life outside the course, module, or exercise. These skills meet the needs of accommodators and correspond most closely to planning activities.

ALTERNATIVE APPROACHES FOR TAKING INDIVIDUALIZED DIFFERENCES INTO CONSIDERATION

As suggested thus far, an understanding of individual differences is indispensable to the effective design and delivery of business ethics education. With a better understanding of individual differences, learning opportunities can be designed that match students' strengths and weaknesses with learning objectives. The challenge is to identify those factors that are most valuable and employable to permit faculty to make distinctions that lead to meaningful differences. In addition to Kolb's experiential learning described earlier, the learning styles model developed by Grasha and Reichmann and the theory of psychological types collectively comprise a powerful and readily available approach to help business ethics teachers understand and respond to individual differences in learning. While these theories are not mutually exclusive, each perspective makes an important contribution to understanding and responding to individual differences.

In my view, a person has learned something when either or both the following descriptions apply:

- They know something they did not know earlier (e.g., an ethical theory) and can show it.
- They are able to do something they were not able to do before (e.g., apply ethical guidelines to a particular situation).

The descriptions require combining the characteristics of learning and problem solving. Kolb's (1984) experiential learning theory is based on his understanding of how people exrapolate from their experiences to generate the concepts, rules, and principles that guide their behavior in new situations and how they modify these concepts, rules, and principles to improve their effectiveness. Remember that Kolb approaches learning as a circular process in which concrete experience is followed by reflection and observation. This in turn leads to the formulation of abstract concepts and generalizations, the implications of which are tested in new situations through active experiments. The LSI III describes the way people learn and how they deal with ideas and situations in their day-to-day lives.

As noted earlier, any business ethics teaching effort can be described using Kolb's four styles. The *Grasha-Reichmann Learning Styles Questionnaire* (GRLSQ) (Reichmann, 1974) and the *Myers-Briggs Type Indicator* (MBTI) (Briggs & Myers, 1988) can also help business ethics teachers understand individual differences and in turn enhance the effectiveness of their teaching efforts.

GRLSQ

The GRLSQ can be used to further differentiate approaches to learning. It provides the basis for classifying three distinct approaches to learning: dependent, collaborative, and independent. A student who scores high as a dependent learner generally prefers a teacher-directed, highly structured course with explicit reading assignments, explicit class assignments, and a predetermined number of tests. A student who scores high as a collaborative learner prefers a discussion class with as much interaction as possible. A student who scores high as an independent learner likes to have significant influence over the content and structure of the course.

The implications of these three approaches for business ethics are straightforward. A student who is a dependent learner would most likely prefer a lecture course without term papers. If a term paper were to be assigned, the dependent learner would want the topic to be assigned by the teacher, with fairly detailed instructions. A student who is predominantly a collaborative learner would prefer group projects and collective assignments, such as case studies, that require interaction and collaboration. The independent learner prefers to have a voice in determining the material covered, the number of tests or other assignments given, and so forth. Independent learners also prefer the faculty member to serve as resource person rather than as a formal lecturer. If a paper is to be assigned, independent learners would prefer to choose their own topics instead of having the faculty member assign specific topics.

MBTI

A third and complementary perspective on the learning process is drawn from the theory of psychological type, originally developed by Carl Jung and popularized by Myers and Briggs (Briggs & Myers, 1988) through the *Myers-Briggs Type Indicator* (MBTI). The MBTI assesses four bipolar dimensions: extraversion-introversion (orientation towards the outer and inner words), sensing-intuition (ways of perceiving), thinking-feeling (ways of making choices), and judging-perceiving (ways of responding to the outer world).

In business ethics teaching efforts, students and faculty with a preference for extraversion will generally prefer learning approaches that emphasize participation and interaction (for example, an opportunity to ask and answer questions). Students and faculty with a preference for introversion will generally prefer individual work that emphasizes the importance of reflection.

Sensation and intuition refer to cognitive approaches for acquiring knowledge. Sensate learning emphasizes facts, patterns, rules, procedures, and a mastery style of learning. Intuitive learning focuses on new possibilities, unstructured problems, and an understanding style of learning.

Thinking and feeling refer to the process of making choices. An ethical decision, for example, based on feeling emphasizes subjective factors such as personal values and inclinations, group values, and concern for particular issues and people. An ethical decision based on thinking stresses the importance of justice and objectivity. Effective use of the feeling mode can greatly enhance communications and contribute to success in teamwork and developing new business. Correspondingly, effective use of the thinking mode will promote logical reasoning and the pursuit of fair, correct solutions to problems.

Judging and perceiving describe how individuals process information. A student with a preference for judging will seek closure, structure, and resolution. A student with a preference for perception is inclined to gather more information and postpone making decisions.

A brief look at the accounting profession should further highlight the applicability of psychological types to the learning process. Historically, the accounting profession has been closely identified with sensate and thinking-based teaching methods, with the result that accounting education has overemphasized both sensate and thinking-based approaches. The complex forces reshaping the profession in recent years demand the application of intuitive and feeling-based approaches. Students, for example, are expected to use creative problem-solving skills in a consultative process, to solve diverse and unstructured problems in unfamiliar settings, and to comprehend an unfocused set of facts. They are expected to identify and, if possible, anticipate problems and find acceptable solutions. All of these examples are consistent with the ambiguity that accountants often encounter in actual practice and should be incorporated into business ethics teaching efforts.

Like their students, business ethics teachers have different styles that are reflected in how they approach their teaching responsibilities. For example, business professors vary in terms of how explicitly they give instructions, how much they expect students to learn on their own, and how actively they encourage group work. The GRLSQ can be used to help faculty examine how they use dependent, collaborative, and independent teaching styles. Similarly, the LSI and the MBTI can be used to help faculty assess how they plan their classes and how they use their own strengths and preferences in the classroom.

ADAPTING TEACHER AND STUDENT LEARNING STYLES IN BUSINESS ETHICS EDUCATION

Teaching business ethics in a manner that fosters student learning, growth, and development requires identification and management of those aspects of the educational system that influence the learning process. This section discusses the importance of managing the learning process by adapting teaching methods to students' learning styles. In my experience, such an approach creates learning activities and learning environments that improve the effectiveness of business ethics teaching efforts.

In the planning and development of most business school curricula very little attention is given to the interaction of teacher and student learning styles. One limitation of this oversight is the failure of faculty to take into account different learning styles (i.e., how students prefer to learn—for example, lecture, group discussion, or independent projects) or preferred teaching styles (i.e., highly structured lectures, group discussion, experiential learning, case studies, and so forth). For instance, if in an introductory business ethics survey class taught by the lecture method, the instructor decided to experiment with the case-study approach, the results, if measured by student achievement and attitude scores, may be inconclusive. If student preferences are randomly distributed with regard to learning styles, the gains to some students from a change in method may be offset by the losses to other students unless one can control for the differences in student learning styles.

To increase the potential for success, learning objectives (for example, master the use of ethical guidelines, think analytically, communicate effectively) must be clarified and made explicit. These objectives must be coordinated with the ways students learn. This is especially true in the process in business ethics because it is important to avoid the one-size-fits-all philosophy utilized by many faculty members. Students learn in different ways, and different learning objectives are more or less compatible with various approaches to the learning process. Failure to provide for differences in student learning styles may mean that a gain to some students from a change in method will be offset by losses to other students. Also, failure to provide experience through a variety of learning approaches may severely limit a student's effectiveness when confronted with ethical dilemmas because of an inability to address a wide range of problems that require different approaches.

Learning is an interactive process that involves both faculty and students. It is important to acknowledge that the reality of the classroom is more complex than the simple pursuit of knowledge. Students may want to be entertained in the class, engage in dialogue with other students, simply achieve a particular grade, send a message to a parent, or attain some other goal not directly connected to the learning process. Faculty responsible for teaching business ethics may also be interested in diverse goals, such as obtaining good student evaluations, being well liked, getting students to enroll in more advanced courses, obtaining more business majors (especially in a time of stable or declining overall enrollments), and so forth. While motives such as these are commonplace, the planning process should continue to focus on the learning objectives as the central concern.

The exchange between faculty and students is more effective if there is a "fit" between teaching styles of faculty members and cognitive or learning styles of students (Goldstein and Blackman, 1978; Kolb, 1985). A greater understanding of "successful" teaching may emerge from answers to the following questions:

1. Are there certain teacher styles that work best with specific learning styles? If so, what are they?
2. Do effective faculty members adapt their teaching style to match both the learning style of specific students and the learning objectives?
3. How can faculty learn to adapt teaching styles to student learning styles?
4. Can learning environment profiles be identified? If so, can the learning process be managed in business schools generally and in business ethics teaching efforts specifically?

The answers to these questions will provide a starting point for the planning process needed to help faculty responsible for teaching business ethics.

Teaching styles are personal and develop over time. If a business ethics teacher's teaching style (for example, highly structured lectures, group discussion, experiential learning, and case studies) is highly incompatible with either students' learning styles or the learning objectives, the teacher will need to make a more successful accommodation. For this to occur, business ethics teachers must be aware of alternative pedagogies, learning activities, and useful insights that will allow them to differentiate the ways in which students learn.

As suggested earlier in this chapter, an important step in developing and maintaining an effective teaching method is to determine the needs of the students and identify learning opportunities or environments for satisfying these needs. Broadening student learning and developing skills they can use when confronted with such things as ethical dilemmas can be enhanced by assessing students' individual orientation toward learning or problem solving and identifying their particular learning style. Then the teaching method that is most likely to suit students' learning styles can be adapted.

HOW CAN BUSINESS ETHICS EDUCATION BE ENHANCED FOR MORE EFFECTIVE LEARNING?

To improve the potential success of business ethics teaching efforts and to assist in the development (broadening) of a particular skill or learning style, faculty members must remember that no single learning style has any overwhelming advantage over any other. They all have their strengths and weaknesses (though it is important to be cautious about labeling strengths and weaknesses since, to some extent, which is which depends on the context in which they are viewed). The effectiveness of business ethics education can be enhanced by being clear about the relative strengths and weaknesses of each style because selecting appropriate learning opportunities essentially involves finding activities where strengths will be used and where weaknesses will not prove too much of a handicap.

Students can also be screened before they attend a business ethics course or program to provide advance warning about the predominant learning styles of the students in a given course or program. This information is very useful to teachers. It helps them prepare for the course or program and, possibly, slant parts of their teaching efforts to better accommodate the learning style preferences of the group. If there are a number of interchangeable faculty members available to teach business ethics, then their teaching styles can be taken into account to get the most compatible match between students and faculty.

A rather more ambitious possibility is to use the learning style information to assign certain students to specific courses, classes, or ethics activities. For example, if it was felt desirable to have an equal number of accommodators, divergers, assimilators, and convergers together in one course, class, or ethics activity, this could be engineered by administering some sort of quota system. This would ensure that the group, as a whole, would be well balanced, with all the different learning skills equally represented. If, on the other hand, it is considered more practical to have as homogeneous a group as possible, then it is possible to invite, say, accommodators, divergers, assimilators, and convergers to attend separate ethics courses, classes, or activities. While attempting to achieve the same objectives, business ethics efforts are easier to plan and run with the likes and dislikes and strengths and weaknesses of more homogeneous student populations clearly in mind. The syllabus, therefore, remains the same, but the methods differ, catering to learning style preferences. Thus, there could, for example, be many service learning or related projects for accommodators, reading time built in for divergers, question-and-answer dialogue sessions for assimilators, and practical demonstrations for convergers.

If it is considered impractical to offer different versions of the same course, module, class, or ethics activities, then it might be considered more feasible to design different options or branches within the same program. The course would contain some core ethical activities standard for all, irrespective of differences in learning style preferences. At intervals, however, the course or class would split into branching business ethics activities tailor-made to meet the needs of students with specific learning styles.

IMPLICATIONS FOR TEACHING BUSINESS ETHICS

A greater understanding of teaching styles or preferences, learning styles, and learning environments has several implications for business ethics education:

1. Matching students and faculty who possess similar learning and teaching styles should improve student learning, growth, and development as well as student attitudes towards business ethics. If maximizing these outputs is the main goal, then this type of matching would increase teaching efficiency.

2. Faculty and administrators should take teaching and learning styles into consideration when reviewing student evaluations. These evaluations may reflect students' responses to differences in teaching styles rather than being evaluations of teaching or of the faculty.

3. Business education researchers who evaluate different methods of teaching business ethics may need to control for teaching and learning styles.

4. Faculty members who use only the dependent teaching style can improve understanding and attitudes toward business ethics by using other teaching methods, such as case studies, experiential exercises, independent projects, and so forth.

5. The inconclusive results reported in surveys of the literature on student evaluations of business ethics teaching efforts may occur, not because a new teaching method is "bad," but because students with different learning styles react differently to various methods. Thus, some students may gain and others may lose from using a new teaching method. Taking these different learning styles into account may provide more conclusive results in evaluations of different methods used to teach business ethics. Researchers may be able to discover which types of students gain (or lose) from different methods used to teach business ethics.

6. Many educational research designs are costly to implement and to replicate because the need for research data requires "artificial" changes in teaching methods. For example, switching to a case-study approach or a self-paced method requires that a number of faculty members deliberately and explicitly alter their method of teaching. Obtaining the necessary number of faculty members to do that (especially more than once) may be difficult. On the other hand, researchers could use existing teaching and learning styles as factors to help study differences in business ethics teaching outcomes, without imposing undue costs on the faculty.

CONCLUSION

Just as some students are heavily dominated by one learning style, or are particularly weak in one style, so some business ethics learning activities are dominated by explicit or implicit assumptions about learning styles. The activity may be so geared to a particular style of learning that it causes a mismatch with any student whose major preferences are different. For example, marketing students have generally been identified as having an accommodator learning style and learn primarily from "hands-on" experience. They also have a tendency to act on "gut" feelings rather than on logical analysis. Most business schools, however, tend to emphasize rationality, logic, and system values, which are best suited to the assimilator learning style when teaching those interested in marketing. In addition, courses most often reflect the learning styles of faculty members, not the learners.

Of course, just as there is wide variation in students' learning styles, there are business ethics teaching and learning activities that contain opportunities to learn in different styles. An example of this would be an ethics course that involves role-plays. A strongly accommodation-oriented learner will enjoy actually playing roles, even if the person may feel uncomfortable and ineffective when asked to provide a logical analysis of ethical issues involved in the role-play. Our concern then becomes establishing how students' learning styles can be addressed when we are designing business ethics teaching efforts to develop ethical knowledge, understanding, or practice aspects that may be foreign to students' preferred learning style.

Learning styles can be used to advantage during the development and implementation of efforts to teach business ethics. First, learning styles can be used to predict learning difficulties—for example, to anticipate who will talk most and talk least, who will find the course too fast or too slow, who will be keen to observe or be keen to take part. Predictions like these are useful because they open up the possibility that faculty members can handle the design of a particular learning environment more appropriately from the start, rather than feeling their way for a period as students' behavioral tendencies gradually reveal themselves. Second, learning styles can assist in discussing the learning process. Discussion helps students understand what is involved in the learning process and can assist them in learning from the various opportunities built into an ethics course, class, or activity.

Third, knowledge of learning styles can help students plan and expand their own learning styles. This suggestion is an extension of the previous one because it presupposes which students in a particular ethics class, course, or program have completed an LSI or GRLSQ and scored/interpreted it. Instead of leaving it at that, however, the idea is now to invite students to analyze their responses to the questionnaire in more depth, with the goal of producing some personal action plans.

Fourth, learning styles can be used to assign roles in experiential exercises or while working on service learning projects. Often, within the framework of an ethics-oriented exercise in a class or course, faculty members are able to decide which roles to distribute to which students. Role-play exercises are an obvious opportunity to do this, but other exercises may also lend themselves to this approach.

Finally, using learning style can help in constituting groups or learning teams. Much has been written about methodologies for bringing together individuals who can blend their different strengths to form a coherent team. Learning style information offers another basis for mixing groups in efforts to teach business ethics. Perhaps the most obvious way to use learning styles is as a basis for putting groups, classes, or courses together to ensure that all groups are matched and that the full range of learning styles is available to each group.

REFERENCES

Briggs, K.C., & Myers, I.B. 1988. *Myers-Briggs type indicator: Form G.* Palo Alto, CA: Consulting Psychologists Press.

Dunn, R., Beaudry, J., & Klavas, A. 1989. Survey of research on learning styles. *Educational Leadership* 46: 7.

Fry, R.E. 1978. *Diagnosing professional learning environments: An observational framework for assessing situational complexity.* Unpublished Ph.D. thesis, Massachusetts Institute of Technology.

Fry, R.E., & Kolb, D. 1979. Experiential learning theory and learning experiences in liberal arts education. *New Directions for Experiential Learning* 6: 79–92.

Goldstein, K., & Blackman, S. 1978. *Cognitive style: Five approaches and relevant research.* New York: John Wiley & Sons.

Kolb, D.A. 1984. *Experiential learning: Experience as the source of learning and development.* Englewood Cliffs, NJ: Prentice Hall.

Kolb, D.A. 1985. *Learning styles inventory* (rev.). Boston: McBer & Company.

Reichmann, S. 1974. *The refinement and construct validation of the Grasha-Reichmann student learning styles scales.* Master's thesis, University of Cincinnati.

Chapter 7

Structuring and Delivering Business Ethics Teaching Efforts

INTRODUCTION

As the goals and objectives of teaching business ethics are discussed by faculty and others, they must also address issues related to curriculum planning. And they must find answers to important questions like: Where does teaching business ethics begin and end? How should business ethics content be ordered? How deeply should the topic of business ethics be explored? And, of course, what pedagogy should be used? Finding answers to questions like these are particularly important when faculty from different disciplines are involved because more individuals or team members involved in curriculum planning generate more potential answers to their questions, and therefore more choices are required.

This chapter first takes a brief look at the issues of scope, sequence, breadth, and depth in business ethics curriculum planning. Next, the discussion turns to a categorization of course content based on a review of the goals, objectives, and purposes identified in a number of syllabi used in teaching business ethics or in Business and Society courses. The chapter concludes with a look at some of the philosophical or ethical theories often used to develop students' theoretical knowledge base in business ethics education.

ESTABLISHING SCOPE, SEQUENCE, BREADTH, AND DEPTH

As decisions are made about teaching business ethics and learning outcomes are developed, important additional questions need to be addressed:

Where does this course begin and end? How should its content be ordered? How many topics should be included? How deeply should one topic be explored? In my experience, these issues are addressed by careful planning. That involves clarification of the concepts of scope, sequence, breadth, and depth in teaching business ethics.

Scope

When those responsible for curriculum planning speak of "scope," they are referring to the boundaries that have been set for the inclusion of material. When faculty from different disciplines are involved in teaching business ethics, the boundaries are not obvious; they have to be defined through dialogue about scope. What is meant by business ethics? For example, when a team of faculty sets about to integrate ethics across the curriculum or create a course, module, exercise on business ethics, it is not clear, exactly where that course should begin and end. (For purposes of discussion in this section we will use the term course when discussing business ethics teaching efforts.) Faculty must come to a consensus about scope. This means they must understand that there is no a priori logic about how to set up the course. The boundaries of the course must be agreed on by the faculty. They must make decisions, often difficult and painful ones, about what they want to do. The decisions should not be arbitrary, but reasoned and justifiable. Without clear agreement about scope, the course can wander and lose focus, both for the faculty and, of greater importance, for the students.

Sequence

Once questions about scope have been settled, more detailed business ethics topics must be ordered in a reasonable sequence. Unlike a disciplinary approach to teaching business ethics, there is no inner logic curriculum planners can rely on to determine the sequence of topics or materials to be taught when multiple disciplines are involved in the curriculum development. There is no involved process for ordering skills, as in accounting, which requires students to master the prerequisite skills needed to perform advanced skills. There is no chronological logic, as with marketing, or a "structural or conceptual logic," as with a course in finance. In an interdisciplinary team approach to teaching business ethics, the rules for determining the sequence of topics or material must be created by curriculum planners (i.e., faculty, administrators, etc.). Without some sense of the logic for sequencing the topics or materials or courses on business ethics, students as well as faculty will feel lost.

Breadth and Depth

Curriculum planners also need to make decisions about the breadth of topics or material to be included and the depth of treatment given to each ethics topic. In teaching business ethics from a disciplinary context, the distinction is most likely to be made in describing the difference between, say, an introductory survey course and an advanced topic seminar. The survey course touches on general topics lightly, introducing students to many aspects of the subject of ethics or business ethics. The seminar format, on the other hand, focuses on one or two specific ethical topics, going into significant depth. Because an interdisciplinary team approach to teaching business ethics consists of a team of faculty who possess a broad range of expertise, there may be a tendency to emphasize breadth, including a broad range of material, because the faculty know about many things.

The breadth is one of the advantages of an interdisciplinary approach to teaching business ethics, since the topic can be examined in depth from several disciplinary perspectives. Teaching business ethics requires faculty and administrators to make conscious choices about the breadth and depth of the topic for modules, courses, and the whole curriculum. As with other questions that must be answered in developing an interdisciplinary team approach to teaching business ethics, the appropriate balance of breadth and depth needs to be struck through an informed decision reached by all concerned parties after adequate discussion, as emphasized in Chapter 2.

In planning the teaching of business ethics, curriculum planners need to make conscious and justifiable decisions about the scope, sequence, and the appropriate balance of breadth and depth. Increasing the relevance of business ethics education by choosing appropriate materials and pedagogies, with an emphasis on active rather than passive learning, is also an important issue that the teacher and others involved with teaching business ethics must address. More will be said about the relevance issue in Chapter 14.

PEDAGOGICAL APPROACHES TO TEACHING BUSINESS ETHICS

One difficulty confronting those responsible for teaching business ethics lies in the fact that there is little agreement regarding the scope, nature, and guiding perspectives for ethics courses or classes. Thus, faculty members teaching in this area must select the content they will cover, recognizing that embedded in their decisions to include certain materials and omit others are a host of contentious ideological and practical positions that impact their choice of pedagogical approaches.

According to one writer, there are traditionally two alternative approaches to teaching business ethics (Hosmer, 2000). The first method stresses background knowledge and analytical procedures clearly needed for rigorous moral evaluation. This theory/policy method of instruction is often referred to as the *philosophical approach*. There is extensive exposure to alternative ethical systems, with readings—generally in excerpt or summary form—from authors ranging from Socrates and Aristotle to Rawls and Nozick, interspersed with discussions of corporate policy issues such as advertising deception, environmental damage, sexual harassment, and so forth. The philosophical approach is advocated by individuals like Donaldson and Werhane (2002), who stress the importance of the philosophic content in teaching business ethics.

The second approach focuses much more on the strategic and functional problems of business organizations. Cases are used extensively to convey those problems to students, often with considerable operational and financial detail. The intent is that students recognize the need for alternative choice mechanisms and gradually develop those different ways of looking at moral issues.

Is there support for this categorization of pedagogical approaches to teaching business ethics? In an effort to determine whether or not there was any validity to this categorization, I reviewed the goals and objectives listed in 24 different business ethics teaching efforts (i.e., 16 syllabi from business ethics courses and objectives from eight business ethics workshops) forwarded to me by professors as part of a survey. An analysis of these proved to be extremely useful in that they reinforced, clarified, and amplified the fact that there is support for the two pedagogical approaches to teaching business ethics as well as a combination of the two, as suggested by Hosmer and others. For our purposes we will refer to these three categories as: (1) those that focus on developing students' theoretical knowledge base, (2) those that focus on analyzing issues facing people in business situations, and (3) those that focus equally on theory and practice. The first category is cognitive in its orientation, with the goal of developing and nurturing ethical knowledge in students. The second category focuses on issues—usually problems—arising in everyday business situations and encourages students to consider the ethical commitments and reasoning processes that might assist in addressing troubling business situations. The last category usually finds one half of business ethics teaching time focused on ethical theories and the other half on using concepts to address ethical dilemmas.

Developing Students' Theoretical Knowledge Base

Business ethics teachers with strong cognitive underpinnings focus on covering various schools of philosophical ethics. In this theory/policy method of instruction there is extensive exposure to alternative ethical systems through readings. For example, one might see the business ethics teaching effort taking a distinctly historical approach in a course intended to serve as an introduction to the study of the place of values in business. Students taking this course could trace the development of beliefs about morality in business, in particular professions in general (i.e., accounting), and in society from ancient times to the present. Further, business ethics teachers using this approach might encourage students, through various readings and written assignments, to consider the ways Judeo-Christian or other traditions continue to shape prevailing ethics or contemporary thinking.

Another approach to developing students' theoretical knowledge base might cover various approaches to moral thought and reasoning. Yet another might take an even more philosophical approach by exploring various schools of thought in a dialectic fashion (i.e., contrasting utilitarianism and Kantian ethics and alternative approaches to utilitarian theory, including John Rawls's theory of justice). Either of these two approaches could also be used in early classes focused on describing and analyzing the various perspectives. Later meetings could then be devoted to considering the "moral imperatives of business leadership."

An important point about what Hosmer (2000) refers to as this "philosophical" approach to teaching business ethics is that it stresses the background knowledge and analytical procedures clearly needed for rigorous moral evaluation. By exposing students to alternative ethical systems through readings generally in excerpt form interspersed with discussions of corporate policy issues such as affirmative action, sexual harassment, business bluffing, environmental damage, and advertising deception students can increase their ability to argue from ethical principles. The philosophical approach is best represented by Donaldson and Werhane (2002) who have succinctly summarized their views on the importance of the philosophic content in both the title—*Ethical Issues in Business: A Philosophical Approach*—and the prefix of their best-selling text: "Some theoretical perspectives maintain importance as foundational materials for the study of business ethics. The insights of Adam Smith and John Locke and the challenges of Karl Marx are no less relevant today than in the eighteenth and nineteenth centuries" (2002, p. ix). More will be said about various philosophical or theoretical frameworks later in this chapter.

Practical Issues Facing Business People

The objectives of this pedagogical approach to teaching business ethics include the analysis of issues or situations students might encounter throughout their business careers. Ethical theories, principles, and reasoning strategies are usually studied in order to assist students in developing wise approaches to problems, challenges, and dilemmas. Hosmer (2000) notes that this approach focuses more on the strategic and functional problems of business firms. This approach to teaching business ethics can take on a number of forms. For example, business ethics teachers might structure their classes around very specific ethical dilemmas and ask students to consider principles that might prove useful in solving (or at least coping) with these problems. Business ethics teachers might also organize their classes around more general concerns (e.g., increasing globalization or competitiveness, collection and use of information in the new economy, downsizing and reengineering, and organizational and employee commitment or loyalty) that are likely to affect most people in business. In these situations, business ethics teachers might organize these topics as the starting point of discussions and ask students to contemplate the ways ethical commitments might inform or confound efforts to deal with them. In contrast, other business ethics teachers might spotlight examples of good ethical behavior or practice (i.e., auditing) rather than problems. In these situations, business ethics teachers might ask students to reflect upon the organizational contexts and personal and professional moral perspectives that would likely support appropriate performance in a business situation.

Business ethics teaching efforts that focus on specific cases or dilemmas tend to use case-oriented texts. The cases in the books serve as springboards to encourage students to consider principles and decision-making strategies. It is not unusual, however, for business ethics teachers to ask students to analyze cases in slightly different ways. For example, as a guideline for addressing textbook scenarios, one might focus exclusively on the professional responsibilities of an individual or a leader and look at codes of ethics governing an accountant or an information technology manager. In another example, a business ethics teacher might show a particular interest in making students aware of their own beliefs and values. An early assignment in this situation might invite students to clarify their own values/ethics so that they will have a clear basis for their decision making and behavior by writing a paper that describes who they are and where they see themselves going in the next three, five, and 10 years. A later assignment might involve the investigation of cases in light of students' personal ethical commitments. A final example might find the business ethics teacher emphasizing personal, professional, and organizational morality, asking students to compare and contrast their own code of ethics with that of a professional or organizational code and to confront the tensions inherent in this process. Hosmer (2000) appropriately notes that the classic case example of the practical or problem/choice method of teaching business ethics is "H.B. Fuller in Honduras" (Bowie & Lenway, 1992). Few students can read the account of the hallucinogenic addiction of homeless street children to a useful industrial adhesive manufactured by a North American chemical company for sale in a third world economy without thinking that there must be other gauges of corporate value than return on sales. Like Hosmer, I have found that there is no equivalent text here. Most instructors who purse this methodology assemble their class materials from the various case clearing houses.

In a final example of focusing on business situations or issues in teaching business ethics, faculty might eschew a discussion of problems or dilemmas and, instead, underscore the relationship between excellent leadership and the commitments of today's business leaders. Business ethics teachers might expose students to many manifestations of skillful leadership in business and encourage them to think about the ways good leaders are shaped by carefully considered personal philosophies. Or faculty might place the major focus of their business ethics teaching efforts on teams of five or six students responsible for designing an ethical business organization (e.g., Internet start-up company, financial brokerage firm, manufacturing firm, etc.). Business ethics teachers using this approach would emphasize the importance of building a comprehensive ethical environment in the organization while broadening and deepening students' understanding of an ethical worldview by working toward organizational transformation.

The intent of the practical issues approach to teaching business ethics is that students recognize the need for alternative choice mechanisms and gradually develop those different ways of looking at moral issues. More will be said about practical or problem/choice methods in the business ethics teaching efforts in Chapter 8.

Equal Focus on Both Theory and Everyday Practice or Reality

The two categories of pedagogical approaches discussed thus far certainly blend, to some degree, ethical theories and issues of everyday business situations or practice. They tend, however, to focus heavily on one dimension or the other, and the two methods obviously conflict. Iyer (1998, p. 315), in a recent and relevant article, spoke of the tension between ethical theory and disciplinary applications, and between abstract reasoning and practical actions, and then confirmed the bifurcated structure of our discipline in the following terms:

Business ethics are often taught through two dominant approaches. The first is the descriptive enterprise of outlining various ethical systems and perspectives (such as Utilitarianism, . . . etc.) and providing accounts of how actions may differ within such systems. Such methods involve the a priori identification of ethical principles that could be applied to particular circumstances. The second is the argumentative approach of providing case instances and identifying the ethical decisions and guidelines as they emerge from the particulars of the case. Such methods use the case context as the ground for moral reasoning and provide the background for the emergence of particular rules and principles. (p. 327)

In my experience, most business ethics teachers fall somewhere between the philosophical and practical extremes. Like other texts, the Donaldson and Werhane (1999) text contains a number of case applications, and the case clearing house catalogs offer a number of theoretical summaries, even though we may not be satisfied with the compromise. The business ethics teaching efforts briefly discussed in this section are portrayed in terms of a conscious effort on the part of faculty to devote approximately equal amounts of time to developing students' knowledge of ethical theories, principles, and reasoning strategies and to investigating ways these might be of use to students in solving (or addressing) day-to-day business problems.

One example of an equal focus on ethical theory and everyday practice would find the business ethics teacher spending the early sessions of a course following a fairly traditional academic format with lectures and discussions on various philosophical perspectives and theories of moral development. Beginning with a consideration of "historical perspectives on ethics as a field of study," students would be exposed to the writings of a number of scholars in order to acquaint them with the literature on ethics and values. Later classes would be centered on moral dilemmas, with writing assignments aimed at setting students to examine the meaning of philosophical constructs in their lives and work.

Another way to think of this dual-emphasis approach to teaching business ethics is to clearly articulate in both the course catalog description and the syllabus that there are two major objectives in the course: to examine the central features of ethical theory and to consider problems in business involving ethical considerations. The first part examines philosophical views of ethics, morality, and business. The second part focuses on fundamental ethical issues and dilemmas. Topics covered might include: breaches of confidentiality, enticements to practice beyond one's professional competence, price fixing, lying, cheating, sexual harassment, the unfair distribution of scare resources, whistleblowing, authority, favoritism, justice, leadership, conflicting professional/personal obligations and loyalties, and so forth. In order to achieve these purposes, faculty would spend part of each class meeting discussing ethical theories or principles (e.g., relativity and diversity in morals, ethical relativism, justification and truth) and part inviting analyses of cases.

As with other pedagogical issues, business ethics teachers and other stakeholders must reconcile theory and practice as they come to agreement on the purposes or goals of their business ethics education efforts. Some insight in addressing the theory and practice challenge can be garnered from a look at several authors who, while not concerned centrally with pedagogical problems, offer useful suggestions in their early efforts to reconcile theory and practice in the classroom (Nash, 1996). Edward Stevens (1974) argued that the teaching of ethics should never freeze at the level of particular do's and don'ts because this can lead to a "specious moralism" that degenerates into oversimplistic moral formulas, rules, and codes. Stevens contended that ethics instruction should take a broader view: It should help students become less the "uncritical captive" to unstated moral assumptions they may already hold. Arthur Dyck (1977) went one step further. He said that effective ethics teaching should encourage "systematic reflection" upon the specific acts of individuals and groups, what they ought to do, and how they ought to behave. And Tom L. Beauchamp and James F. Childress (1979) argued that only when teachers undertake a systematic examination of moral principles in order to determine how they apply to specific cases would they be able to bring "some order and coherence" to a discussion of ethics. For Beauchamp and Childress, two bioethicists, applied ethics is "the application of general ethical theories, principles, and rules to problems of therapeutic practice, health care delivery, and medical and biological research" (p. 9).

For our purposes, these authors provide a basic understanding that the study of ethics represents a modest yet effective way for business ethics teachers and their students to discover, before and after they act, how they would best like to act—and then imaginatively test in advance some of the difficult choices that lie ahead. By trying to get students to look ahead and back, on the basis of a critical examination of their already present, deepest moral presuppositions, there is an increased likelihood of success in clarifying the goals for teaching business ethics and in heading off a certain amount of unnecessary goal bewilderment (and resistance to philosophical or ethical concepts) on the part of students. By helping students get a firm and articulable grasp on the moral principles they already hold, via pertinent business ethics texts, case studies, and experiential learning exercises, students learn to see where their moral perspectives might be flawed, in need of enrichment, or inconsistent with their everyday behavior.

The last section of this chapter offers a more detailed discussion of some of the philosophical or ethical theories included in the theory/policy method of teaching business ethics. The next chapter will describe the more traditional and practical pedagogical approaches used in the analysis of issues or situations that students might encounter throughout their business careers.

PHILOSOPHICAL OR ETHICAL THEORIES: DEVELOPING STUDENTS' THEORETICAL KNOWLEDGE BASE

First, I offer no independent argument that the philosophers or philosophical/ethical theories discussed in the remainder of this chapter are all encompassing or that any one is any better than the others. However, they do seem to be the major ones focused on in business ethics teaching efforts. The mix of philosophers or philosophical/ethical theories covered and the way they are taught is up to each business ethics teacher. I do not presume to offer any significant original scholarship on these philosophers or philosophical/ethical theories. Rather, since this is a book about teaching business ethics, my goal is to offer a summary or brief description of philosophers' views and philosophical/ethical theory so that you, the reader, can decide if you want to investigate these in more detail or incorporate the information in your assigned readings and business ethics teaching efforts.

Ethical actions and feelings result from beliefs about what is "right" or "wrong" or "good" and "bad" in society and the world. In simple terms it can be said that ethics determines how a person reacts to the question "What should I do?" when faced with a moral dilemma. None of us can provide a single method or formula to help our students arrive at ethically correct decisions, either as learners in business ethics education efforts or in life or work situations. Indeed, the very nature of ethics limits the possibility that a universally accepted approach may be found or taught by an institution of higher learning or a business school. Nevertheless, there is a great deal that can be learned about ethics and ways to understand and analyze the issues involved when ethical concerns arise in business situations.

MORAL REASONING

Throughout the years, several approaches to moral reasoning have prevailed and are most often incorporated in the teaching of business ethics. These are teleology/consequentialism, deontology, and virtue ethics. Each of these is discussed in turn below.

Teleology/Consequentialism

This approach focuses on consequences. That is, it considers the amount of good that is produced in the end. This approach to ethical reasoning is called a teleological approach (the most prominent version of which is consequentialism). Teleology is derived from the Greek word *telos*, which means "outcome" or "result." Some of the most influential philosophers in the Western tradition—including Jeremy Bentham and J.S. Mill—have determined that moral worth of personal conduct can be determined solely by the consequences of that behavior (i.e., the rightness or wrongness of an action is to be decided in terms of its consequences). Perhaps one of the best ways to understand this approach is through its committment to the principle of benefit maximization. This principle holds that whenever an individual is faced with a choice, the best and most just decision is the one that results in the most good or the greatest benefit for the most people. Thus the principle of benefit maximization judges the morality of an act or decision by its consequences. An act or decision is "right" if it results in benefits for people and it is "wrong" if it leads to damages or harm.

It is important for students to understand that according to the teleological or consequentialist theories, the concepts of right, wrong, and duty are subordinated to the concept of the end or purpose of an action. As one scholar notes, "The overall objective is to create the greatest degree of benefit for the largest number of people while incurring the least amount of damages or harm" (Hosmer, 1996). Therefore, the best action is the one with the best overall results. We are not told, however, what is to count as a benefit or a good. That requires additional reflection. The theory merely says that once an individual knows what is good, the best decision is the one that maximizes good outcomes. Thus, if an individual wishes to decide the merits of blowing the whistle on her boss by using consequentialist reasoning, she would have to balance the benefits and harms of blowing the whistle against the benefits and harms of not blowing the whistle. She would seek to maximize the good. But what is to count as good?

To talk about the good is to talk about those kinds of things that are intrinsically valuable (i.e., something worthwhile for its own sake). A good consequentialist is not simply interested in producing any results that are intrinsically good. Consequentialists are interested in maximizing the good—that is, producing the most good. After all, it is relatively easy to produce some good results. Every gray cloud has a silver lining. In fact, it is difficult to do something that produces no good. But the point is to choose that action which has the best set of consequences. One must not only show that they produce some desirable consequences, but that the consequences produced are better than those consequences that would result from whatever else might be done. The good must be maximized.

There are at least two types of consequential theory. The first—advocated only by a few consequentialists, such as Thomas Hobbes and Frederick Nietzsche—is a version of what philosophers call ethical egoism. It places the main concern on what brings an individual the most pleasure. In this instance a person makes a decision in order to maximize her/his best interests, with less regard for the consequences to others. It construes right action as action whose consequences, considered among all alternatives, maximize *my* good—that is, action that benefits me the most or harms me the least.

The second type—advocated by most consequentialists, including Jeremy Bentham and John Stuart Mill—is termed utilitarianism. Utilitarianism focuses on net consequences, not individual intentions. The name of the philosophy is derived from the word utility, whose eighteenth-century meaning referred to the degree of usefulness of a household object or a domestic animal. That is, a horse could be said to have a utility for plowing beyond the cost of its upkeep (Hosmer, 1996). Utilitarianism is in stark contrast to ethical egoism, which has as its objectives the maximization of utility for the individual actor. Utilitarians, however, may not always agree on what values to promote. Utility may be understood as pleasure (Bentham) or happiness (Mill).

As Bentham formulated it, the principle of utility states that an action is right if it produces the greatest balance of pleasure or happiness and unhappiness in light of alternative actions. Bentham's form of consequentialism is often referred to as hedonism, which holds that the basic human values are pleasure and pain (sometimes simply referred to as the absence of pain). According to this view, everything that people desire, want, or need can be reduced in one way or another to pleasure or pain.

Mill supported a principle similar to Bentham's, using what he called the "proof" of the principle of utility—namely, the recognition that the only proof for something's being desirable is that someone actually desires it. Since everybody desires pleasure or happiness, it follows, according to Mill, that happiness is the most desirable thing. The purpose of moral action is to achieve the greatest overall happiness, and actions are evaluated in terms of the extent to which they contribute to this end. The most desirable state of affairs, the greatest good and the goal of morality, said Mill, is the "greatest happiness for the greatest number" (Donaldson & Werhane, 1999).

Utilitarianism is concerned with the greatest good for the greatest number (*summum bonum*). The objective is to measure the utility of consequences of all possible alternatives to find the one that will help the group the most. Modern-day utilitarians fall into one of two groups: act utilitarians and rule utilitarians. Act utilitarianism argues that an act is ethical if its outcomes or consequences are beneficial. Therefore, the principle of utility should be applied to individual acts, and each individual act, in all its concreteness and in all its detail, is what should be subjected to the utilitarian test (i.e., measuring the consequences of each individual act according to whether it maximizes good). Rule utilitarianism argues that an act is ethical if it conforms to established rules. Therefore, instead of considering the results of specific actions, one must weigh the consequences of adopting a general rule exemplified by that action. By adopting and acting according to a general rule, an individual will maximize good. If keeping a rule produces more total good than breaking it, we should keep it. This theory can be criticized on the grounds that it might discriminate against a disadvantaged segment of society by generating rules that favor the advantaged majority. It is really a frail form of act utilitarianism, since a rule will be followed or rebuffed depending upon the consequences of the action.

Why favor the rule utilitarian rather than the act utilitarian approach? For many of today's utilitarians the answer is that adopting simplifying rules saves time and avoids the need to compute the full consequences of every decision and action. This is especially important because in practice we cannot know all the consequences of a particular act, nor can we know in advance, and with certainty, many of the specific consequences of such an act. Nor can we always determine individual and group preferences. The theory is also criticized for not allowing rights to the minority. According to Ross (1930), the "essential deficit [of utilitarianism] is that it ignores, or at least does not do full justice to, the highly personal character of duty" (p. 47). Rules such as "never renege on a contract," "always tell the truth," or "never steal" can be logically shown to lead to beneficial outcomes in all foreseeable cases, but the basis for the rules remains the balance of positive and negative consequences that come from every act or decision. The rule utilitarian approach does not require guesswork as to what will happen. As one writer notes, "The history of humankind provides the sourcebook. If we wish to see the results of murder, lying, stealing, or breaking contracts, we can easily recall the consequences of past cases" (DeGeorge, 1999, p. 62).

Deontology

The word deontological comes from the Greek *deon*, which means duty or the obligations of an individual. Deontology places an emphasis on behavior and actions based on principles, laws, and duties rather than on consequences or comparative amounts of goodness. Much deontologism comes from religious doctrine and is considered the theory of divine command, but Kant was the most prominent deontologist. Moralists in this area (Immanuel Kant and John Rawls) would never agree that the ends should be used to justify the means in a decision. They would not consider violating principles of honesty and fairness because such actions would infringe on the rights of others. No amount of end-result utility would make them proper. Deontologists argue that moral principles exist within the conscience of each person, and all humanity, therefore, has a sense of duty.

Should we not treat others as we expect to be treated by others? This thought expresses a common moral ideal. Its most familiar version is the Golden Rule, "Do unto others as you would have others do unto you." The Golden Rule contains additional ideas that may be found in a form offered by the German philosopher Immanuel Kant. Kant's central moral precept is called the categorical imperative. "So act that the maxim of your will could always hold at the same time as a principle establishing universal law" (1956, p. 60). This mode of thinking asks whether the rationale for an action is suitable to become a universal law or principle for everyone to follow. Kant's formidable phrase involves some less formidable moral ideas that express the content of the Golden Rule well. The following is an effort to state the point more simply.

By a "maxim" or a "principle" Kant simply means a moral rule. "Do not steal" is an example. What does it mean to say that a moral rule should be universal? Kant proposes a simple test to see if the principle underlying an action can be willed to be a universal law. The test for personal duty and goodwill is intended to eliminate self-interest and self-deception and to ensure regard for the moral worth of others. If you are about to apply a moral principle to someone else, are you willing to be lied to? If you steal, are you willing to be stolen from? If you are willing to lie but not be lied to, you are not willing that the principle that guides your behavior should be treated as a universal rule of human conduct.

A practical deontological question an individual might ask themselves could be, "What kind of world would this be if everyone behaved this way or made this kind of decision in this type of situation?" Kant's ideas can be understood as an attempt to tie moral actions to rational decisions, with rationality defined as being based upon consistent and universal maxims. Moral standards, according to Kant, are based upon logical consistency. Thus, for someone in the Kantian tradition, being moral is the same as being rational. Just as no one can force us to be rational, no one can force us to be moral. In this view, if we choose to be rational, we also choose to be moral.

According to Kant, the Golden Rule requires that we act in ways that respect the equal worth of moral agents. It requires that we regard human beings as having intrinsic worth and treat them accordingly. That is why we have a duty to accord others the same kind of treatment we expect them to accord us. This idea can be referred to as the principle of *equal respect for others*. The principle of equal respect involves three subsidiary ideas.

First, the principle of equal respect requires to treat others as *ends rather than means*. That is, we may not treat them as though they were simply means to further our own goals. We must respect their goals as well. We cannot treat people as though they were things, mere objects, who are valued only insofar as they contribute to our welfare. We must consider their welfare as well.

Second, we must regard all people as *free, rational, and responsible moral agents*. This means that we must respect their freedom of choice. And we must respect the choices people make even when we do not agree with them. Moreover, it means that we must attach a high priority to enabling people to decide responsibly. It is important for people to have the information and the education that will enable them to function responsibly as free moral agents.

Third, no matter how people differ, as moral agents they are of *equal value*. This does not mean that we must see people as equal insofar as their abilities or capacities are concerned. Nor does it mean that relevant differences among people cannot be recognized in deciding how to treat them. It is not, for example, a violation of equal respect to pay one person more than another because that person works harder and contributes more. That people are of equal value as moral agents means that they are entitled to the same basic rights and that their interests, though different, are of equal value. Everyone, regardless of native ability, is entitled to equal opportunity. Everyone is entitled to one vote in a democratic election, and every vote should be worth the same as every other vote. No one is entitled to act as though his or her happiness counts more than the happiness of others. As persons, everyone has equal worth.

Kant would wish to argue that all consequentialist positions end up treating some persons as though they are means to the ends of others. When we seek to maximize the average happiness, are we not saying that we may trade the happiness of some for the happiness of others so long as the average happiness increases? When we do this are we not treating the happiness of those who are made less happy as a means to the happiness of others?

The Contractarian Alternative

A different view of deontology is offered by many philosophers who focus less on the actions of individuals and more on the principles that govern society at large (Donaldson & Werhane, 1999). This view is represented by two philosophers, John Locke and John Rawls. According to these two deontological philosophers, rights and justice are not derivable from utilitarian calculations. Instead, they try to establish universal principles of a just society through what might be called "social contract thought experiments." They ask us to imagine what it would be like to live in a situation where there are no laws, no social conventions, and no political state. In the so-called state of nature, we imagine that rational persons gather to formulate principles or rules to govern political and social communities. Such rules would resemble principles derived through categorical imperative, in that they are presumably principles to which every rational person would agree and which would hold universally (Donaldson & Werhane, 1999). Locke's and Rawls's approach to establishing rules or principles of justice differ and the difference illustrates two distinct forms of contractarian reasoning.

Rights. Locke argues from a "natural rights" position. Moral rights are important, normative, justifiable claims or entitlements. The right to life (or the right not to be killed by others) is a justifiable claim, based on our status as rational beings, worthy of respect, and ends-in-ourselves (DeGeorge, 1999). In the Declaration of Independence the founding fathers spoke of natural rights of life, liberty, and the pursuit of happiness. Locke claims that every person is born with, and possesses, certain basic rights like those espoused in the Declaration of Independence. These are "natural" rights. They are inherent in a person's nature, and they are possessed by every one equally. Like other inherent traits, they cannot be taken away.

They are "inalienable" rights. According to Locke, when rational individuals meet to formulate principles for governing social and political communities, they construct a social contract that is the basis for an agreement between themselves and their government. The rules of this contract protect natural rights.

Rights can be thought of as "negative rights," such as the limits on government interference with a citizen's right to privacy or the pursuit of happiness. Or rights can be thought of in more positive terms, such as the individual's rights to health and safety. The rights of one party can conflict with the rights of another party, as when the right of a company to seek profits for its shareholders conflicts with the right of a community to have clean water and air. Furthermore, the rights of one party are generally related to the duties of another. So, if we agreed that communities have the right to clean water, businesses would have the duty to protect that right.

Justice. According to Rawls, the concept of distributive justice (that equals should be treated equally and unequals unequally) must be maintained to prevent social unrest. He also contends that social unity is dependent on maintaining just institutions. Unlike Locke, Rawls does not begin from a natural rights position. Rawls argues from a "reasonable person" position and asks which principles of justice rational persons would formulate if they were behind a "veil of ignorance"—that is, if people knew nothing about who they were. They would not know what kind of society they were to be born into, nor would they have knowledge about their own capabilities and personalities. But they would have a rational concern for their long-term perspective. That is, one would not know whether one were male or female, old or young, highly motivated or lazy, rich or poor, or anything about one's personal status in society. Unable to predict which principles, if picked, will favor them personally, Rawls argues, individuals will reason more honestly and be forced to choose principles that are fair to all.

From this initial position he develops two principles of justice. The first is the principle of equal liberty, that "each person is to have an equal right to the most extensive basic liberty compatible with similar liberty for others," and the second, that "social and economic inequalities are to be arranged so that they are both (a) reasonably expected to be to everyone's advantage, and (b) attached to positions and offices open to all" (Rawls, 1958, p. 525). This second principle, the difference principle, is intended to govern society's economic and social institutions. In a business context this demands that resources be allocated fairly and equitably among stakeholders.

The social contract approach maintains a deontological character and is used to formulate principles of justice that apply universally. In the moral evaluations of business, all deontologists, including contractarians, would ask questions such as the following (Donaldson & Werhane, 1999):

1. Are the rules fair to everyone?
2. Do the rules hold universally even with the passage of time?
3. Is every person treated with equal respect?

Virtue Ethics (Integrity)

For many philosophers and others who teach business ethics, the preceding two ethical theories or models exhaust all possible modes. That is to say that all theories can be classified as either teleological or deontological. I leave the decision as to whether this is true or not to others. However, many business ethics teachers also cover a third category—virtue ethics—which can be traced back to the Greek philosopher Aristotle. It remains a fact that individuals do meaningfully evaluate actions, and that there are many actions—such as stealing and lying—that are prima facie wrong. Yet there is a good deal to learn from an Aristotelian approach to ethics that adds to what we teach our students.

Aristotle's analysis of the moral life emphasizes the importance of judgement, virtue, and character. The character of a person is the sum of his or her virtues and vices. A person who habitually tends to act morally has a good character. If she resists strong temptation, she has a strong character. If she habitually acts immorally, she has a morally bad character. If, despite good intentions, she frequently succumbs to temptation, she has a weak character. Because character is formed by conscious actions, in general people are morally responsible for their characters as well as for their individual actions.

For Aristotle, good or virtuous people do not simply emerge or develop on their own. In virtue ethics, character is very much defined by one's community. Individuals must be raised and taught what virtue is from virtuous people. They are taught by example, by stories, by moral models. They are raised in a tradition and presented with heroes, historical or mythical. They need a society in which virtues are held in esteem and in which virtuous persons are respected and looked up to (DeGeorge, 1999). A virtue ethics perspective considers primarily the actor's character, motivations, and intentions.

The criterion for judging the goodness of any action is whether or not the action is compatible with one's inherent human capacities. Actions that enhance human capacities are good; those that deter them are bad, unless they are the best among generally negative alternatives. For example, eating nothing but starches is unhealthy, but it's clearly preferable to starving (Donaldson & Werhane, 1999).

Because of its strong social and community focus, a virtue ethics approach allows the decision maker to rely on relevant community standards without going through the complex process of trying to decide what's right in every situation using deontological or consequentialist approaches. The assumption is that the community has already done this type of thinking. However, what if the community hasn't done this type of thinking? Or what if the community is just wrong? Furthermore, the usefulness of virtue ethics in business may be limited because in many areas of business there is limited agreement about what the standards are. There is no universal code of conduct for all business managers to follow (Trevino & Nelson, 1999).

Each of these three philosophies (teleological, deontological, and virtue ethics) provides a framework for seeking to understand the ethical components of a particular issue. These approaches, developed by philosophers, have been designed to help individuals decide what they should do in response to ethical dilemmas. They are representative of what is often taught in business ethics courses to develop students' theoretical knowledge base and ability to analyze issues facing people in business situations.

KOHLBERG'S THEORY OF MORAL DEVELOPMENT

With the philosophical constructs of ethical thought understood, it is possible to move to more detailed approaches for examining business ethics in decision making. One of the most notable found in the business ethics literature and used in the teaching of business ethics is Kohlberg's theory of moral development.

It is also useful to view the development of ethical thinking as a process. Kohlberg (1969, 1984), drawing heavily on the work of developmental psychologists such as Piaget, formulated a theory of the development of moral reasoning that has substantially influenced the thinking behind many initiatives in ethics education. The stages of moral reasoning central to Kohlberg's theory are briefly summarized below.

Pre-conventional level—behavior is controlled by external rewards and punishments.

Stage 1: *punishment and obedience orientation*. The physical consequences of an act determine whether it is good or bad.

Stage 2: *instrumental relativist orientation*. Things that satisfy one's needs, and sometimes the needs of others, are good.

Conventional level—behavioral standards are moderately internalized, although the standards are still imposed by others such as parents, authority figures, and laws.

Stage 3: *"good boy/good girl" orientation*. Behavior that pleases others and earns approval is good.

Stage 4: *"law and order" orientation.* Respect for authority, order and doing one's duty determine what is right,

Post-conventional level—totally internalized reasoning, personal moral code.

Stage 5: *social contract orientation.* The consensus of society, which can change, defines what is right.

Stage 6: *universal ethical principle orientation.* Right is defined in terms of self-chosen universal principles of good and bad.

Within each of the three general levels, there are a number of stages of moral development in which right and wrong are successively defined in slightly different terms. In general, the stages proceed from self-oriented thinking and from a punishment-reward orientation to an abstract principle orientation. Each successive stage represents a higher level of reasoning regarding the definition and nature of right and wrong. A number of studies suggest that the moral reasoning of adults is similar to that described in Stage 4 of Kohlberg's theory (Colby, 1978) and that moral reasoning at Stage 5 or beyond is not common, even in educated groups such as managers (Trevino, 1986).

All individuals are not going to pass through each of the stages in Kohlberg's model. Some do not even progress past stage one. Kohlberg argues that individuals cannot move to a higher stage without first going through the earlier stages. Individuals may have difficulty seeing the logic of moral reasoning more than two stages above their own. People tend to be attracted to the reasoning of the next highest level and will move when their present level proves inadequate to handle a complex moral dilemma.

Moral judgements are social judgements and are prescriptive or normative judgements about people's rights, obligations, and responsibilities rather than their preferences. Critics, including Carol Gilligan (1982), have argued that Kohlberg's theory is a theory of "justice reasoning" rather than a theory of moral judgement. However, Colby and Kohlberg (1987) dispute this, stating that:

Although it is true that the dilemmas in the Standard Moral Judgment Interview pose conflicts of rights, the actual judgments made by respondents may focus on concern and love for another person, on personal commitments, on one's fellow human beings as well as rights, rules, and duties. As long as these concepts are used prescriptively, as defining what is morally right or good, the scope of the domain we assess is considerably broader than is conveyed by the term *justice* reasoning. (p. 11)

To understand Kohlberg's theory, you must remember that it is a cognitive theory. What counts is the reasoning processes involved in a decision, not the decision itself. So, a Stage 1 individual and a Stage 5 individual may make the same decision, but their reasons for making it are very different.

The process of developing a style of moral reasoning spans a person's entire childhood and much of adulthood. Kohlberg's theory describes a way of viewing the world that develops over a long period of time, and this certainly complicates the challenge of teaching ethics. The issue of transfer of learning is particularly relevant. Even if we succeed in teaching business students to think about moral problems in a different way, there is no guarantee that accompanying changes in behavior will result when the students enter the workforce. As Trevino (1986) points out, ethical behavior reflects both individual and situational influences and, among the individual influences, the style of moral reasoning might not be the most important factor. A variety of other individual characteristics, including locus of control and ego strength, might be important in determining whether an individual translates his or her judgement about what is right or wrong into ethical behavior at work.

Kohlberg's theory has particular relevance for business ethics education. Initially Kohlberg's framework can guide faculty in formulating goals for business ethics education. Entry-level undergraduate students may focus more naturally on ferreting out rules and discussing avoidance behavior. Graduate students and executives will be more aware of the limitations of the earlier stages of moral development. During the implementation stage, Kohlberg's framework can help guide the choice of pedagogy and the selection of materials. A stimulating ethics case may simultaneously provoke responses such as: Will I get caught? Does this break the rules? What will others say and think about me? Is this decision consistent with my personal sense of integrity?

If the mandate for business ethics education is examined in terms of Kohlberg's framework, two conclusions emerge as especially important guidelines. First, efforts to develop business ethics education at Kohlberg's conventional level are critical to the well-being of the business profession and society. Achieving this goal depends on the level of commitment, the pedagogy, and the materials selected to support business ethics education. Secondly, business ethics education efforts should be sufficient to sustain a dialogue capable of transcending the conventional level, allowing students to develop a higher level of ethical awareness.

CONCLUSION

Decisions on the scope, sequence, breadth, and depth of business ethics teaching efforts present key challenges for teachers. A radar "scope," such as those used by air traffic controllers, provides information about aircraft within a particular part of the sky. The scope contains only those things that fall within the direction, vector, and distance of the radar beam. For business ethics courses, the scope of a course may be determined by curriculum planners or those faculty responsible for teaching business ethics. Without a clear understanding of scope, the business ethics teacher can wander in many directions without a clear focus for the teacher or, of greatest importance, for the students.

Business ethics teachers must also order topics in a reasonable sequence. The sequence of topics can be determined by an inner logic growing out of the discipline or the experiences of the business ethics teacher. Sometimes the process involves an ordering of skills that requires students to master the prerequisite skills needed to perform advanced skills. With an interdisciplinary business ethics course, the rules for determining sequence of topics usually need to be created by the team.

Decisions also need to be made about the breadth of topics to be included and the depth of treatment given to each topic. This distinction is most frequently made in describing the differences between an introductory or survey business ethics course and a more advanced seminar. The survey course touches on general business ethics topics lightly, introducing students to many aspects of the subject. The seminar goes into significant depth. Because an interdisciplinary team approach to teaching business ethics consists of a team of faculty who possess a broad range of expertise, there may be a tendency to emphasize breadth and include a broad range of material because team teachers know about many things.

Pedagogical approaches used to teach business ethics can focus on developing students' theoretical knowledge base, on analyzing issues facing people in business situations, or focus equally on theory and practice. Most business ethics teachers fall somewhere between the philosophical and practical extremes of the pedagogical approaches. It is particularly important for teachers to strive to achieve a balance between an active engagement with the issues and a critical analysis of the choices in teaching business ethics.

There are a variety of philosophical or ethical theories included in business ethics teaching efforts, including the three covered in this chapter: teleologicalism/consequentialism, deontology, and virtue ethics. All of these approaches to moral or ethical reasoning can be distinguished in terms of their basic methodological elements. Kohlberg's conceptual framework of ethical development can guide both the process of establishing educational goals and the pedagogy employed to reach these goals.

REFERENCES

Beauchamp, T.L., & Childress, J.F. 1979. *Principles of biomedical ethics* (2nd ed.). New York: Oxford University Press.

Bowie, N., & Lenway, S. 1992. H.B. Fuller in Honduras. Copyrighted by Columbia University School of Business Administration. In T. Donaldson & P. Werhane (1996), *Ethical issues in business: A philosophical approach* (5th ed.). Upper Saddle River, NJ: Prentice Hall.

Colby, A. 1978. Evolution of a moral development theory. In W. Damon (ed)., *Moral development*, San Francisco: Jossey Bass, pp. 17–32.

Colby, A., & Kohlberg, L. 1987. *The measurement of moral judgment* (Vol. 1). New York: Cambridge University Press.

DeGeorge, R.T. 1999. *Business ethics*. Upper Saddle River, NJ: Prentice Hall.

Donaldson, T., & Werhane, P.W. 2002. *Ethical issues in business: A philosophical approach* (6th ed.). Upper Saddle River, NJ: Prentice Hall.

Dyck, A.J. 1977. *On human care: An introduction to ethics*. Nashville, TN: Abindgon.

Gilligan, C. 1982. *In a different voice: Psychological theory and women's development*. Cambridge, MA: Harvard University Press.

Hosmer, L.T. 1996. *The ethics of management*. Chicago: Irwin.

Hosmer, L.T. 2000. Standard format for the case analysis of moral problems. *Teaching Business Ethics* 4: 169–180.

Iyer, G.R. 1998. Integrating business ethics in classroom teaching: Some preliminary considerations. *Teaching Business Ethics* 1: 315–331.

Kant, I. 1956. *Critique of practical reason*. Indianapolis, IN: Bobbs-Merrill.

Kohlberg, L. 1969. *Essays on moral development* (Vol. 2). *The psychology of moral development: The nature and validity of moral stages*. New York: Harper & Row.

Kohlberg, L. 1984. *The psychology of moral development: The nature and validity of moral stages*, 2 vols. New York: Harper & Row.

Nash, R.J. 1996. *"Real world" ethics: Frameworks for educators and human service professionals*. New York: Teachers College Press.

Rawls, J. 1958. Justice as fairness. *The Philosophical Review* 57: 525–533.

Rawls, J. 1971. *A theory of justice*. Cambridge, MA: Harvard Unviersity Press.

Ross, W. 1930. *The right and the good*. Oxford: Clarendon Press.

Stevens, E. 1974. *The morals game*. New York: Paulist Press.

Trevino, L.K. 1986. Ethical decision making in organizations: A person-situation interactionist model. *Academy of Management Review* 11: 601–617.

Trevino, L.K., & Nelson, K.A. 1999. *Managing business ethics: Straight talk about how to do it right* (2nd ed.). New York: John Wiley & Sons.

Chapter 8

Practical Approaches to Teaching Business Ethics

INTRODUCTION

The AACSB (International Association for Management Education, formerly the American Assembly of Colleges and Schools of Business) is the major accrediting body of business schools. It has mandated the integration of ethics, social responsibility, and other related issues in the curriculum. How these issues are addressed and evaluated, however, is left up to faculty members and school administrators. In general, a college or school of business is expected to fulfill the ethics curricular obligation using techniques and approaches appropriate for its mission, student population, and educational philosophy. The types of instructional or pedagogical methods used to satisfy this obligation vary from school to school.

In previous chapters we have discussed some of the issues related to teaching business ethics, including: (1) separate business ethics or Business and Society courses or the integration of ethics across the business school curriculum and (2) interdisciplinary versus single disciplinary approaches to teaching business ethics. Another issue in the delivery or teaching of business ethics is the mode of delivery (i.e., deciding on the choice of pedagogy). In response to the continuing and growing interest in business ethics, numerous pedagogical techniques have been developed to cover the philosophical, legal, moral, behavioral, and organizational aspects of the curriculum. In the last chapter we described some of the philosophical or ethical theories used to increase students' theoretical knowledge base. In this chapter, we examine various practical approaches to teaching business ethics, including traditional techniques like lectures, case study method, guest lectures, and so forth as well as more recent approaches, including structuration theory, Freud's theory of cognitive process, the TV and significant others test, decision tree/cross-cultural model, and computer conferencing via the Internet. Many of the techniques examined in this chapter are common in both stand-alone courses and integration (LeClair et al., 1999; Sims, forthcoming).

Pedagogical approaches that I believe fall under the umbrella of experiential learning are the focus of the last section of this chapter. These experientially oriented approaches include role-playing, business simulations, and service learning. I recognize that most business ethics teachers use a combination of approaches and that not all techniques are discussed here.

CRITICISMS OF APPROACHES TO TEACHING BUSINESS ETHICS

While there is yet no strong empirical evidence identifying the preferred pedagogical approach to teaching business ethics, it is important to take a look at the approaches that have been suggested by various writers. However, before taking a closer look at some of the available pedagogical approaches, we will briefly review some of the criticisms raised about existing approaches.

The traditional approach of presenting ethical theories alone has been criticized as being too abstract and impractical for business students (Gilbert, 1992; Liedtka, 1992). For example, one writer observed that the typical pedagogical model, teaching students the process of moral reasoning by introducing principles of ethical theory and then applying the principles to the resolution of ethical dilemmas involving business situations, ignores important contextual factors (Furman, 1990). In another review, Etzioni (1991) claimed that most approaches to teaching business ethics were characterized by a "compartmentalization"—that is, an abstract, principle-based model of ethics that was divorced from the realities of the marketplace. Both Furman and Etzioni concluded that the typical principle-based approach to teaching ethics is inadequate, and they argued for a more complex approach, one that examines the theory and principles of moral reasoning firmly grounded in organizational, cultural, and/or historical contexts.

On the other hand, approaches that rely solely on mechanistic decision, rules, and policies have also been criticized as being inadequate for developing moral imagination (Strong & Hoffman, 1990). As Strong and Hoffman have argued,

Simple cookbook methods of dealing with situations do not prepare the student to deal with the organization as a whole. Using this type of mechanical decision procedure leads the student to believe that all the student need do is provide the input, run it through the formula, and out comes the answer; this method sidesteps the thinking process. (p. 604)

Thus, there appears to be an emerging consensus among writers that ethics education should combine ethical theory and principles with opportunities for students to *practice applying these principles in specific contexts* (e.g, organizational, cultural, historical) (McDonald & Donleavy, 1995).

As noted in the last chapter, writers like Iyer (1998) and Hosmer (2000) note that these two methods obviously conflict. Iyer (1998, p. 315) speaks of the "tensions between ethical theory and disciplinary applications, and between abstract reasoning and practical actions," and then confirms the bifurcated structure of the discipline in the following terms:

Business ethics are often taught through one of two dominant approaches. The first is the descriptive enterprise of outlining various ethical systems and perspectives (such as Utilitarianism, Kantian Categorical, Imperative, etc.) and providing accounts of how actions may differ within such systems. Such methods involve the a priori identification of ethical principles that could be applied to particular circumstances. The second is the argumentative approach of providing case instances and identifying the ethical decisions and guidelines as they emerge from the particulars of the case. Such methods use the case context as the ground for moral reasoning and provide the background for the emergence of particular rules and principles. (p. 327)

In reality it would be safe to say that most faculty who teach business ethics fall somewhere between the philosophical and practical extremes. It is particularly important to strive to achieve a balance between an active engagement with the issues and a critical analysis of the choices in teaching business ethics.

Practical approaches, such as the use of cases, role-plays, and so on may be effective in identifying situations for which specific ethical rules and principles have not yet been discerned. These methods are often relevant for new issues within the business discipline. For example, ethical issues surrounding the use of the Internet for business as well as various other newer business practices can be better identified and debated using case examples. However, while cases offer particular instances from which some ethical issues and principles can be identified, they appear to provide merely a sampling of ethical issues. The particular contexts of the business cases used as well as the primacy placed on "sensitizing" rather than unique reasoning detract from the effectiveness of the case method in providing a complete ethical evaluation of any decision or even attempting to formulate more general ethical principles or rules.

SOME TRADITIONAL APPROACHES TO TEACHING BUSINESS ETHICS

In this section, we examine several traditional approaches to Teaching Business Ethics. This discussion is not intended to be all inclusive but rather to provide the reader with a description of methods that were used by others to teach us and that we in turn use to various degrees in our own business ethics teaching efforts.

Lecture

The straight lecture approach affords the instructor control, although it is doubtful that students "learn much by sitting in class listening to teachers" (Chickering & Gamson, 1987, p. 3). The lecture method is efficient because it can reach a large number of people at once, and students are not required to actively participate in the process (i.e., possibly disrupt the flow) (Chism et al., 1989).

LeClair et al. (1999) note that students are usually passive learners in this context and it is doubtful that their ethical decision-making skills (which the authors view view as an important goal of most professional schools) are improved by listening to lectures. Furthermore, business ethics is the result of both personal and organizational influences, neither of which can be adequately experienced via passive learning. In addition, most lectures do not expose students to the myriad of viewpoints that can be taken in an ethical analysis.

Business ethics teachers who use lectures can obtain rapid feedback from students after each class by using the "minute paper" (in which students are asked to jot down their thoughts at the end of class about a question such as, "What unanswered question do you have about the material presented today?" or "What was the most important thing you learned today?"). Another assessment technique is called the "The Muddiest Point," in which students are asked to quickly write down a response on a half-sheet of paper or index card to the question, "What was the muddiest point in the lecture today?" (Angelo & Cross, 1993). Another mechanism is a "Critical Incident Questionnaire," which asks a few questions such as, "At what moment in the class did you feel most engaged with what was happening?" and "At what moment in the class did you feel most distanced from what was happening?" It is not essential with any of these approaches for students to sign their names.

Case Study Method

A number of writers view business ethics as applied ethics; hence, the case study method, which requires the application of ethical considerations to situations or practical concern (Beauchamp, 1998; Geva, 2000). Cases are often based on prepared written descriptions of business situations requiring a decision. Other cases are based on articles in current events periodicals, interviews with key local executives, films and videos, and experiential living events. A wide range of case-based instructional methodologies have been advocated, including oral debates, team projects, written individual assignments, role playing, and computer-based simulations.

The case study method is useful for understanding the various personal factors and organizational circumstances that lead to ethical dilemmas. Students are active learners because they read the case, analyze the issues, and make recommendations based on case facts. The most commonly invoked approaches to the case study method include:

1. Ascertaining the facts of the case.
2. Defining the ethical issues.
3. Identifying the major principles, rules, and values related to the case.
4. Selecting alternative plans.
5. Comparing values and alternatives, anticipating the consequences of the various options that might be adopted.

Yuthas and Dillard (1999) identified the following steps in the traditional process approach to case analysis:

1. Identify the ethical issue(s).
2. Determine the affected parties and identify their rights.
3. Determine the most important rights.
4. Develop alternative courses of action.
5. Determine the likely consequences of each proposed course of action.
6. Assess the possible consequences, including an estimation of the greatest good for the greatest numbers.
7. Determine whether the rights framework would cause any course of action to be eliminated.
8. Decide on the appropriate course of action.

After students recommend the appropriate course of action, the instructor may provide details of the action actually taken by the organization. Students learn from hindsight, from the instructor's critique of their approaches, and from class feedback. The case approach teaches problem solving, although some students may not be comfortable with its ambiguity. Further, this approach requires students to be able to articulate their opinions and listen to opposing viewpoints. Cases also allow students to see the reality of the situation, which enhances the believability and importance of issues presented.

Despite the importance of case studies in teaching business ethics, they tend to be narrowly focused and require little accountability on the students' part. Students may suggest solutions to an ethical issue that are unrealistic for realities of organizational life, including political maneuvering, power relationships, and profit concerns.

Case teaching has had its more specific critics, including a former president of Harvard University: "Although the case is an excellent device for teaching students to apply theory and technique, it does not provide an ideal way of communicating concepts and analytic methods in the first instance" (Bok, 1997, p. 83). It has also been noted that the case study method is deficient in promoting character development and often misses the affective aspect of learning altogether (Hill & Stewart, 1999). Critics go on to say that dispassionate critiques make for excellent critical thinking skills but may not engage students' personal values and convictions. This is perceived as being particularly counterproductive when, as is often the case, multiple ethical systems (e.g., utilitarianism, Kantianism, egocentrism) are being used simultaneously. As MacIntyre warns, the case method approach runs the risk of valuing the thinking process so highly that content, virtuous attitudes, and conduct may be given short shrift (MacIntyre, 1984).

Other writers believe that the case study method *is* adequate to foster the development of virtues. "What we see when we consider hard cases, how we respond to the moral dilemmas around which theories like Kohlberg's is built, depends on what we care about" (Meilander, 1984). In other words, motivation is every bit as important as knowledge in developing ethical character and conduct.

Games and Scenario-Based Methods

Games create a learning environment using a format all participants can relate to and find enjoyable. By creating a team learning experience, games often use common elements such as scoring, a game board, task cards, and other game pieces. The Ethics Challenge Game developed by Lockheed Martin is a scenario-based ethics training game that provides realistic mini-cases, with optional behavioral reactions from which team members may choose. The answers represent various degrees of correctness, as defined by the company's mission, values, and ethics program. Detailed feedback is provided on each alternative answer by a game facilitator. The company has generously distributed the game to other companies and universities.

Scenarios also provide students with the opportunity to engage in a decision-making exercise about a specific ethical problem and are often part of game-based methods. Most scenarios are relatively short and place the player in a specific situation that requires a decision. The scenarios expose students to ethical issues they may encounter in the business world and help them apply their values to the problem at hand. Some scenarios list a number of options from which the reader can choose. These options are useful for making class comparisons, although they force readers into pre-determined responses.

Literature/Narratives

Garaventa (1998) has suggested that many ethical challenges faced by contemporary managers are not easily resolved by existing guidelines and require managers to expand their scope of analysis in attempting to arrive at satisfactory resolutions. Like others, he suggests that literature can be an especially useful alternative source of insights, since authors are able to highlight behaviors that may not be accessible in traditional sources.

Literature and other narratives are often used as a springboard for reflection and discussion. For example, students might be asked to consider the poetry of Walt Whitman in order to understand an individualistic perspective and its attendant ethics and values. In another instance, Plato's *Protagorus* (1976) could be assigned in conjunction with the first course topic, "What is ethics?" The text provides exposure to the Platonic tradition of basing ethical decisions on dialectical reason, an approach that a faculty member may endorse as students attempt to understand, compare, and synthesize various ethical perspectives. Finally, Milan Fust's *The Story of My Wife* (1989) could be recommended to spark further reflection on self, others, and moral ways of acting and interacting.

Other writers advocate that ethical education can be enhanced by an interdisciplinary team approach (as suggested in Chapter 4), using resources from the literature department as well as from the philosophy, religion, and business departments (McDonald, 1992). One of the most widely discussed of these techniques is using fiction—for example, using *To Kill a Mockingbird* to present ethical dilemmas. Fiction engages the imagination, allowing students not only to analyze an ethical dilemma but also to discover that dilemma embedded in the context of a character's life. In addition to providing a more real-life scenario than most "real" business cases, the use of literature permits students analytical distance, which makes them feel safe in defending or condemning a character's behavior (Marini, 1992).

For some scholars, plays are more useful than novels in attempting to inculcate moral and ethical values, since they more sharply address the interactions of characters, and the reader becomes more involved in their situations. Plays such as Henrik Ibsen's *An Enemy of the People*, Arthur Miller's *Death of a Salesman*, and David Mamet's *Glengarry Glen Ross* all have intense plots and characters, which allow the reader to observe a wide range of motives, emotions, and traits (Garaventa, 1998). This untraditional approach to teaching business ethics enhances students' ability to relate to the increasingly complex ethical issues facing the individual and the organization.

Other narratives, whether in the form of books or movies, whether fiction, nonfiction, or biographies, have been identified as key pedagogical techniques useful for teaching business ethics. Hill and Stewart (1999) suggest that unlike case studies, narratives make no pretense of being morally neutral. With complex plots, characters, and outcomes, narratives provide an emotional hook for students, a story with which to resonate. Advocates of this approach suggest considering, for example, the character Atticus Finch in the novel *To Kill a Mockingbird*. A widower with two young children, he serves as a defense attorney for a black man falsely accused of raping a white woman half a century ago in the deep South. In doing so, he displays the virtues of honesty, perseverance, fairness, and compassion. The book's sustained narrative engages students at an emotional level, providing a powerful image of how professionals should comport themselves in difficult situations (Hill & Stewart, 1999; Stewart, 1997).

Vitz proposes that narratives, real or fictitious, are particularly suited to promulgating moral development in students and should therefore be rehabilitated as a valuable part of higher education (Hill & Stewart, 1999; Vitz, 1999). This could include novels such as *The Firm*, movies like *The Spitfire Grill*, and biographies focusing on well-known business figures such as Al "Chainsaw" Dunlap and Intel's Andy Grove (Hill & Stewart, 1999).

Writers who advocate inclusion of stories in university curricula (Dennehy et al., 1998; Nussbaum, 1989) suggest that if human life in general, and emotions in particular, are narrative in form, then business ethics should be concerned with such texts (Sims, forthcoming) because "literary form and human content are inseparable" (Nussbaum, 1989). Nussbaum argues that the sort of self-scrutiny required for moral development requires a narrative text for its evocation. Others support this view. Coles (1989) and Shaffer (1987), in teaching medical and legal ethics, respectively, have argued that stories are far more likely than case studies to grip students and develop their moral lives.

Movies. Connecting the ethical issues interwoven in cinematic characters, plots, and outcomes to business ethics provides students with an interesting way to learn the nuances of ethical decision making (Giacalone & Jurkiewicz, 2001). It helps to assert for the student that ethical issues in everyday life are not distinct and separate from ethical issues at work. Quite the contrary, students discover that the same core ethical dilemmas can surface in myriad of ways. It has been suggested that integrating students' values through ethical inquiry that spans personal and professional issues can serve to elevate ethical behavior in the workplace (Cooper, 1999; Van Wart, 1998).

Using movies to help students learn about ethical issues, apply ethical principles, and solve ethical problems has a number of educational benefits (Giacalone & Jurkiewicz, 2001). Movies:

- Allow students to focus on something they enjoy.
- Help students recognize that ethical issues exist within a systemic context, that they are not discrete events.
- Make ethics realistic in a way cases cannot.
- Help students develop critical and creative thinking skills.
- Demonstrate how ethical decisions, decision makers, and events are interconnected and interdependent.
- Help students see the connection between scholarship and ethical decision making.
- Provide students with practice in exploring decision-making alternatives and understanding the obstacles to ethical decision making.

Those interested in a step-by-step methodology, along with possible variations of a movie exercise, should see Giacalone and Jurkiewicz (2001).

Literature and other narratives can be a powerful force involving and moving students in ways that the current dominant pedagogies—cases and "war stories"—cannot match (Kennedy & Lawton, 1992). Literature and other narratives offer a compelling methodology which, when used alone or in combination with more traditional techniques, can enrich the teaching of business ethics. Stories can stir emotions, stimulate imagination, involve and compel us to enact for ourselves the dilemmas faced by scores of literary figures. Through this enactment, students are changed and their sense of ethical response is heightened and clarified. Narratives show the impact of business decisions on all aspects of business and personal life. Contemplation of the humanities, of novels, plays, poetry, and the like assist in the development of ethical and empathic insight because they move students to understand others and themselves in an intuitive and personal way. I have found that fiction enables students to imaginatively enter the worlds of others, see the world through their eyes, and consider their concerns and values. I believe such skills are central to good business or professional practice and that these skills can be derived from multiple insights into the human situation found in literature, narratives, and movies.

Guest Lectures

Another method that has been advocated for teaching business ethics is the use of guest speakers. The positive aspect of using guest speakers is that an appropriate speaker can bring unusual expertise to a particular subject matter discussed in the course. Guest lectures typically provide students with an individual's perspective of the ethical issues and dilemmas that occur in the business world. For example, an individual with an ethics-related experience can provide first-hand knowledge of topics like corporate fraud, insider trading and whistleblowing.

Guests are usually well-received and heighten students' interest because students enjoy hearing "war stories" and appreciate the opportunity to examine the applicability of academic concepts to business practice. In addition, guest speakers from other academic disciplines can broaden students' perspective of ethics and corporate responsibility (Nicastro & Jones, 1994). Although guest lectures are useful for sparking students' interest and demonstrating applicability of textbook concepts, they are less systematic than some other approaches for several reasons. First, it is difficult to control the content of the guest's presentation. Second, the guest may focus on stories, without providing much guidance on how students can recognize and respond to intricate ethical issues. Finally, guest lectures are a one-shot exposure to an individual's experiences and must be understood in that context. On balance, however, I advocate the use of selectively chosen guest speakers when teaching a business ethics course.

OTHER APPROACHES TO TEACHING BUSINESS ETHICS

Several suggestions for business ethics curriculum improvements have been proposed to answer criticisms like those mentioned above. Some researchers advocate creating "honorable business school communities" in which students are involved in grappling with the ethical conflicts faced in administering their own educational process (see, for example, Trevino & McCabe, 1994). These programs create situations in which students must see and define their ethical dilemmas and participate in problem resolution. Others suggest using local newspaper articles as the basis for ethical dilemmas studied in class and enriching the learning process by interviewing those mentioned in the articles (Schaupp & Lane, 1992). This methodology encourages the inclusion of a variety of points of view and focuses on real-life, current problems. Another writer advises allowing students to report their own ethical dilemmas and then using an ethics book to analyze the student-generated dilemmas, providing students with practice in applying an ethical framework to their own situations (Pizzolatto, 1993).

The premise behind these views is that business ethics courses might be best taught to encourage students to engage in the process of reasoning by including the variety of roles that employees play and the context of the ethical decision. One author has noted that the double-loop learning that most effectively stimulates ethical thinking is not the type of learning expected of students in other courses. In fact, students who are most adept at "school behaviors" and therefore the most successful students are often those who seek a single right answer and are rewarded for finding it (Liedtka, 1992). Other researchers have found that when faced with a choice of ethical problems to deal with, students chose the simpler dilemmas rather than accepting a challenge. Similarly, Liedtka found that students who are convinced of their arguments tend to be the ones who enter the discussion most enthusiastically, while those who are actually engaged in questioning their own assumptions may sit silently in confusion. The instructor in an ethics class is therefore facing multiple challenges in teaching.

Iyer (1998) suggests an innovative medium for reconciling competing justifications and ethical dimensions, while drawing benefits from alternative pedagogical tools, by including real-life experiences that go well beyond the discussion of business strategy as formulated by any business organization. For example, one could entreat students to conceptualize and evaluate business strategy as if they were consumers, or even as if they were public officials. This could be done with a separate set of questions, distinct from the normative aspects of strategy. It could be, in many cases, the precursor to any discussions of normative business strategy and descriptions of business practice. When one touches upon and draws out students' own frustrations as dissatisfied customers of organizations engaging in questionable business practices, a ready empathy for consumers may be obtained. Such empathy is often of a higher degree due to "lived experiences" than that which is obtained through role playing in some contrived case situation or from mere discussions of business strategy in a case context.

This approach to education, though seemingly rare in business fields, is the method that seems to typify much of liberal arts education and is identified by Simon (1983) as the "hot cognition" approach to learning. However, the use of such emotions in business education, especially when teaching ethics, presupposes that business faculty have understood the nature and content of ethics as applied within their respective disciplines. When students build normative models of how they should behave as informed consumers, they are able to include these crucial building blocks in formulating business strategy. The strategy so devised works better, since ethical considerations enter de facto into normative models of strategy rather than entering as post facto evaluation of strategy. Students are able to build for themselves a normative model of rational and ethical consumption through self-reflection as consumers. And subsequently, when they are exposed to normative models of business strategy, students are better able to view the responsibility of the business person as one of competitive rationality tempered with practical morality. They are also better informed about the consequences of unethical business decisions. When ethics is approached from different angles, students are soon able to realize more precisely how various unethical strategies can negatively impact consumers, employees, shareholders, and the general public as well as how such strategies may be detrimental to entire ecological and socioeconomic systems.

The remainder of this chapter takes a look at some other pedagogical approaches to teaching business ethics, including current events periodicals, structuration theory, and Freud's theory of cognitive processes. Other frameworks used in ethical analysis are also briefly described and include the TV test and the significant others test, decision tree/cross-cultural analysis framework, and computer conferencing via the Internet.

Current Events Periodicals

Critically analyzing news and current events in the world of business is a useful pedagogical tool. By definition, current events materials are current and relevant to what modern managers are facing. The greatest strength of these materials is that they establish an immediate and obvious relevance in the classroom.

Key advantages to using current events periodicals are: they demonstrate the relevance of business ethics theory; they provide a means of testing students' knowledge of the theory; they provide immediate and current examples of theory in use; and they establish a habit of staying current with business affairs and the ethical implications thereof (Phillips & Clawson, 1998). In using current events periodicals the issues, managers, and organizations in question may be as current as that morning, and periodicals like the *Wall Street Journal* are an excellent and readily available source of classroom examples of situations high in ethical content. A consistent review of current periodicals can illustrate dramatically what kinds of issues arise and how they arise in the business world.

One potential disadvantage of using current events instead of prepared cases lies in the richness and depth of the data. Well-researched and well-written cases are likely to contain more detail than the average newspaper or magazine article. Newspaper reporters may not have access to the kind of data given to a more trusted case researcher, who has promised confidentiality until the final right of last review. This need not necessarily be the case, however, depending on the variation of current events pedagogy used.

Demonstration of the usefulness and relevance of a theory can also be highly motivational for students. Observing a given theory in practice has a tendency to encourage learning in a way that dry and impersonal theoretical lectures or descriptions may not. As Knowles suggests (1996, p. 36), adults are motivated to learn primarily after having noted a need to learn. Hence, the use of business periodicals has the "andragogical" effect (contrasted with "pedagogical" by Knowles to indicate the differing demands of adult learning) of stimulating learning by demonstrating the current events usefulness of the theory or issue in question (Phillips & Clawson, 1998).

But the only way this approach will succeed is if students adequately understand the theory or point in question and have to some degree internalized it. In this instance, then, the teacher would have some method for judging the extent to which a theory has been so internalized. Current events may provide the means for doing this. (Note that current events in my opinion provide an excellent means for going through the experiential learning stages suggested by Kolb's experiential learning theory.)

Analyzing current events periodicals requires students not only to memorize and recite the model but also actually to *use* the model or theory. That is, recognizing the nature of a problem from a newspaper story—one that was not written with any pedagogical presuppositions in mind—demonstrates the ability to cut through the inevitable noise surrounding a business decision to find out just what kinds of problems there are. Then, if the student is able to appropriately employ a particular framework or model to a current business issue—an issue that was not designed to demonstrate the use of that particular model—it is clear that the student understands and can generalize the model to actual managerial or business situations. According to Kolb's experiential learning model, individuals have learned when they can demonstrate their ability to apply theories to real life situations (i.e., individuals learn when they go through the process of concrete experience, reflective observation, abstract conceptualization, and active experimentation).

Another important advantage of using current events periodicals in teaching business ethics is that they provide concrete examples as points of reference for material. Business ethics teachers can use current events periodicals once per semester, weekly, or during each class meeting. According to proponents of this pedagogical tool, it will be time well spent. Based on their own experiences, Phillips and Clawson (1998) note that the use of current periodicals as a pedagogical tool brings the material closer to the hearts and minds of students, creates an avenue for retention, makes students more current in their conversations and insights, develops consistent reading habits that keep students current, and adds energy and depth to the business classroom.

Structuration Theory

Yuthas and Dillard (1999) have suggested in their analysis of traditional philosophical theories (i.e., utilitarian and deontological analyses) that these theories tend to treat individuals as autonomous, possessing the free will to formulate and carry out actions. The unit of analysis is the individual, and the analysis begins at the point when the ethical dilemma arises and ends when action is taken and consequences are realized. They propose the use of structuration theory (Giddens, 1984) as a framework for expanding traditional approaches to ethical decision making (Yuthas and Dillard, 1999). Contrary to traditional approaches (for example, utilitarian and deontological approaches), which focus on an individual decision maker facing an ethical dilemma and on his or her ability to decide ethically, the structuration approach highlights the dynamic nature of organizational ethics. Advocates suggest that this approach helps students recognize how strong structural forces operating in an organization can influence the thoughts and actions of individuals and how the actions of those individuals can have an ongoing affect on the ethical climate of the organization (see Yuthas and Dillard, 1999, for more information on structuration theory).

The primary purpose of the structuration perspective is not to provide specific guidance in resolving a particular ethical dilemma. Rather it provides a framework through which the antecedents and consequences of the dilemma can be explored. The structuration approach is primarily concerned with the development and transformation of ethical norms. It can be used to evaluate the moral climate of an organization before ethical dilemmas arise and to guide action toward creation of climates that support ethical behavior.

The structuration approach analyzes a case by examining structures (rules and resources that drive the thoughts and actions of agents) operating within an organization, their interactions, and how they evolve through the actions of agents (individuals who are capable of thinking and acting). The approach requires students to think about how they evolve through the actions and about what individual agents can do to help create a desired moral climate within an organization. The specific steps in the structuration theory process approach are:

1. Identify the agents.
2. Identify current structures and structural conflicts.
3. Explore actions and interactions that created the current structures.
4. Explore potential consequences of alternatives.

According to its advocates the structuration approach helps students understand how structures of power and meaning are tightly interwoven with structures of morality and how changes in one will lead to changes in the others. The approach also helps students think about how the organization's moral climate influences the actions of employees within the organization.

Some of the potential benefits to adding a structuration perspective to traditional analysis of ethical cases are:

1. It can help students appreciate the dynamic nature of organizational ethics. That is, the structuration perspective recognizes that the actions of agents construct and reconstruct the structures that influence ethical behavior in organizations.

2. Another benefit of the structuration perspective lies in its treatment of agents. For example, rather than treating the individual faced with an ethical dilemma as an autonomous decision-making unit that can exercise free will in resolving the dilemma, it recognizes that human action is constrained and guided in ways by structural conditions.

3. The structuration perspective also contributes to understanding ethical cases by providing a framework through which students may not only develop a better sense of what to do when faced with an ethical dilemma but also acquire an understanding of how their actions can affect the ethical "climate" of the organization.

Freud's Theory of Cognitive Processes

Waldmann (2000) has suggested that most of the approaches taken in ethics education concentrate on (conscious) reasoning and decision making (see Gilbert, 1992). Waldmann contends that an understanding of Freudian psychology would help students develop a greater awareness of the unconscious mechanisms that sometimes come into play when an individual is faced with a stressful ethical dilemma.

This approach to teaching business ethics recommends that various defense mechanisms would be of particular interest and relevance to business ethics education (i.e., denial, projection, repression, rationalization, and reaction formation). Waldmann believes that an understanding of these mechanisms would enable faculty to incorporate them into case studies, simulations, and other pedagogical techniques. Waldmann further suggests that the topic of ego defense mechanisms and its relevance to ethics is best dealt with towards the latter part of the course and introduced as a psychological perspective on ethical dilemmas. Further, a brief introduction to Freudian psychology, together with explanations of ego defense mechanisms, should be provided.

This teaching method involves asking students to imagine what kind of rationalizations, denials, and so forth are likely to occur in a number of selected cases. Waldmann notes that students can then assume that this occurs during self-debate or justifications made to another individual. This exercise is best done as a group activity, using small groups of four or five. Students should be encouraged to exercise their imaginations and extend the case study if they so desire. Students are to assume that the individuals involved are basically ethical in their behavior but face a strong conflict between their moral beliefs and their personal desires.

The goal of this approach is to help students see that ethical reasoning does not necessarily fall into neat, logical patterns when stressful ethical dilemmas are involved. An understanding of defense mechanisms will also enable students to identify cognitive processes in others and gain insight into their own thinking.

The TV and Significant Others Tests

These two tests share common threads. Both specify that the decision should be made in light of imagined public evaluation of the decision. In the TV test, the evaluation is made by an unknown media audience, while in the significant others test the evaluation is made by a known audience—the family, friends, and colleagues of the individual.

The essence of the TV test is that to judge whether a proposed decision is moral, the individual should imagine its being reported on a news program. In some versions of the TV test the criterion upon which this judgement is based is straightforwardly what the individual believes his/her emotional reaction would be if the decision were reported. This guideline has two salient features. The first is public disclosure of the decision. The second is using one's own predicted emotional response to the disclosure as the basis for deciding the morality of a proposed action.

The essence of the significant others test (O'Connor & Godar, 1999) is that to judge whether a proposed decision or action is moral, one should imagine it being disclosed to people with whom one has a significant personal or professional relationship. In one version of this test the criterion invoked to decide the question is one's imagined emotional reaction to the disclosure (as in the TV test). In another version the criterion is left unspecified, but the question one is to ask is: "Would I disclose to my boss or family what I'm going to do?"

O'Connor and Godar (1999) suggest that both the TV test and the significant others test suffer from numerous severe deficiencies:

Regarding the approval of the general public as a barometer for ethics is based on fallacious reasoning; regarding the approval of the members of a reference group as signifying the morality of actions is bad reasoning. Moreover, this guideline is even less satisfactory than the TV test because it assumes that the standards of the reference group are morally correct. (p. 80)

The authors suggest that these two guidelines are based on a thorough misunderstanding of what ethics is and of the process used in making ethical decisions. Further, the instruments not only "convey inaccurate information but substitute emotional or approval-seeking 'tools' for ethical ones, and certainly do nothing to enhance the moral decision-making of the new generation of managers" (p. 84). O'Connor and Godar suggest ways in which four stakeholders—authors of management textbooks, publishers, instructors, and business schools—can address the deficiencies of these two tests. See O'Connor and Godar (1999) for an excellent critique and discussion of the various formulations of these guidelines or tests, as discussed in leading management textbooks.

Decision Tree/Cross-Cultural Analysis Framework

Several writers have stressed the need for some mechanism to determine appropriate actions in international business situations in which ethics collide (Kohls et al., 1999). They have suggested using a decision-tree model for managing situations involved in cross-cultural ethical conflicts. The model, based on previous theory and research on conflict resolution (Thomas, 1990) and international ethics (DeGeorge, 1993; Donaldson, 1996), is intended to provide a conceptually sound yet pragmatic aid to decision makers faced with such conflicts. Kohls et al. (1999) note that while the model can be useful in addressing any ethical conflict, it can be especially useful in the case of conflicts across cultures.

The decision tree model asks the decision maker to evaluate the cross-cultural conflict using three questions based on an assessment of the moral significance, power, and urgency of the issues. The three questions are:

- Is this situation high in moral significance?
- Do I have a high level of influence over the outcome of the situation?
- Is there a high level of urgency to resolve the situation?

Based on this assessment, the model points to feasible sets of conflict-resolution strategies (avoiding, forcing, education, negotiation, accommodation, and collaboration).

According to Kohls et al. (1999), the strength of the decision tree approach is that it encourages contingency thinking and points to plausible courses of action. It provides a guide that the decision maker can use to help to find his/her way through the decision-making process. While useful as a guide, it is not intended to replace careful consideration of additional factors in the situation, evaluation of likely consequences, and the moral imagination to find win-win solutions (Buller et al., 1997).

To date, Kohls et al. (1999) have found that students trained in the decision tree model demonstrate more flexibility in their responses to case situations involving cross-cultural ethical conflict and recommend solutions more consistent with expert opinions. The writers note several potential dangers in using the decision tree, however. For example, it has the potential to become a substitute for critical thinking and moral imagination, since some students may be inclined to answer the questions mechanistically and uncritically accept the strategies suggested by the decision tree. Additionally, the model can become a way to rationalize preferred strategies, since it is relatively easy to choose the yes or no answers to the three questions, misusing the model to give desired strategies. See Kohls et al. (1999) for more information on this model.

Computer Conferencing via the Internet

The Internet opens new horizons of learning experience. It expands the framework of the case analysis, which traditionally focuses on the application of accepted rules to a given difficult business problem, in two opposing directions: backward and forward. Instead of providing students with a description of a concrete business situation and a common set of data as the basis for analysis and discussion, the Internet invites them to take an online voyage of discovery through the chaotic environment of the information superhighway, requiring them to confront multiple perspectives on a live topic, identify a problem (if one exists at all), and spot the relevant facts. Only after this preliminary task of acknowledging and identifying a moral problem is completed is the stage set for ethical analysis.

The Internet offers opportunities to develop and examine new creative solutions by facilitating the pursuit of additional information. Because access to information and resources is so easy in the online environment and live topics characteristic of Internet debates are continually developing rather than being accomplished facts, students are stimulated to use creative moral imagination in coping with ethical issues. Moral imagination and creativity involve the ability to reframe the ethical problem from various perspectives, the ability to envision new options for fruitful action, and the ability to change the conditions of the moral agency (Werhane, 1998). The Internet, which carries a message of endlessly available information, may contribute to the use of creative imagination in solving business ethical problems.

Geva (2000) suggests computer conferencing as a framework for exercising reflective equilibrium, which links the explicit and implicit messages of books, on the one hand, and the Internet, on the other. The central idea behind this framework is that the combination of the Internet and books in networking learning technologies is not only a matter of methodology but also a matter of educational message. The concept of reflective equilibrium underlies the curriculum of a one-semester course in business ethics. The phase model of moral decision making presents a systematic process of moral decision making developed through reflective equilibrium. Each phase outlines the framework of the "class" discussion as the course progresses. Geva notes that experience in using this framework demonstrates that networking may enrich both individual and group learning processes and advance the growth of business leadership capable of incorporating moral considerations within managerial decisions.

EXPERIENTIALLY ORIENTED PEDAGOGICAL APPROACHES TO TEACHING BUSINESS ETHICS

Experiential learning exercises span a wide variety of functional areas and formats. Indeed, the variety of exercises available and the creativity involved in developing them is amazing. Any experienced teacher typically relies on a variety of different methods in their teaching endeavors: lecture, case study, role-play, behavioral modeling, and simulations. This sequencing reflects the theory that active experience facilitates learning better than passive techniques and that participants learn better through interactive methodologies that are action oriented.

Moral judgement is action oriented. Business students should participate in experiential (learning) exercises that require them to ask themselves: What is the right thing to do, or what is the wrong thing to do? Experiential exercises that expect students to respond to moral questions that are personal in nature and involve interpersonal relations require normative responses to determine the appropriate course of action (Sims & Sims, 1991). In this age of moral relativism, business school curricula should provide students with continuous experience in examining the underlying moral issues. What are a managers' or employees' responsibilities or obligations to an organization, a work group, themselves, their families, and society? And what will be the possible consequences of a particular action if they make an immoral decision and knowingly harm others?

Many ethical problems do not have specific "correct" solutions like the problems presented in a number of courses and examinations in business schools (i.e., accounting, operations, statistics, etc.). Furthermore, an emphasis on factual rules, which are important to success on professional examinations, can create a classroom expectation that is especially unwelcoming to the unstructured and ill-defined ethical problems that students will face. Thus, the problem is twofold: (1) the emphasis on mastery learning of facts to produce correct solutions to examination problems is too narrow a focus; and (2) the pedagogy customarily applied to analyze ethical issues is not the right approach when the objective is to develop the ability to make independent ethical judgements.

To address these two problems, business students need to have an experiential awareness of the types of ethical dilemmas they will face (i.e., relevancy), and they need to be able to evaluate and identify possible courses of action when confronted by ethical dilemmas. As noted by Maglagan and Snell (1992), reliance on information-transfer approaches to ethics should be complemented by experiential methods. The use and value of experiential methods or exercises as a teaching medium are well recognized and have been widely reported (Sanyal, 2000). For example, Hemmasi and Graf (1992) show that experiential exercises have the following positive attributes: students retain material longer over time, students are actively involved in the learning process, actual work environments are simulated, and students enjoy them. Sanyal (2000) notes that experiential exercises serve as an effective training and teaching tool to prepare students to understand and cope with the ethical minefields that they are likely to encounter.

Black and Mendenhall (1989) have noted that experiential training methods such as simulations, field trips, and role-plays are more rigorous and engage the participants more fully than methods such as lectures and videotapes. Simulations, for example, can provide students with hands-on experience and a better understanding of the concepts discussed in the classroom. In simulations designed for teaching business ethics, students can be faced with ethical dilemmas that encourage them to react as though they were in a real-life situation. Role playing also provides students with the opportunity to participate with a high level of personal involvement. Students could be asked to develop a code of ethics for an organization. Similarly, field trips can provide another pedagogical vehicle to actively engage students in analyzing ethical problems and identifying creative resolutions. Finally, Lampe (1997) has noted that requiring students to provide some form of community service also offers the potential for personal and emotional impact that may be difficult to capture through traditional classroom learning. The movement toward experiential service learning has gained considerable momentum in business education since the early 1990s (Zlotkowski, 1996). These pedagogical approaches all emphasize high participation and active rather than passive learning. Several of these approaches are described below.

Role Playing

A common characteristic of many business ethics teaching initiatives is the use of business-related scenarios, statements, or case studies. In most of these instances, students are asked to assume the roles of various key stakeholders—an executive, a manager or even a company president—and make ethical decisions relating to the stakeholders' positions. Role playing is one of the techniques advocated for teaching about ethical issues (Baetz & Carson, 1999). In particular, it has been noted that role playing might help students transfer their ability to reason ethically into the business context (McDonald & Donleavy, 1995). Role playing leaves a memorable impression and actively engages all players in the learning process. One way to understand role playing is to compare it with the case study method.

Role Playing versus Case Study. Role playing is a cross between the case method and an attitude development program. Each person is assigned a role in a situation (such as in a case) and asked to play the role and to react to other players' role playing. The player is asked to pretend to be a focal person in the situation and to react to the stimuli as that person would. The players are provided with background information on the situation and the players. Usually, a brief script is provided for the participants. Sometimes, the role playing is videotaped and reanalyzed as part of the development situation. Sometimes, the role playing is done in small groups of a dozen or so. The success of this method depends on the ability of the players to play the assigned roles believably. If done well, role playing can help an individual become more sensitive to the feelings of others.

Although role playing is a cross between the two, comparison of the general forms of role playing and the case method suggests a few differences between them:

Case Study	Role Playing
1. Presents a problem for analysis and discussion.	1. Places the problem in a real-life situation.
2. Uses problems that have already occurred in the company or elsewhere.	2. Uses problems that are now current or are happening on the job.
3. Deals with problems involving others.	3. Deals with problems in which participants themselves are involved.
4. Deals with emotional and attitudinal aspects in an intellectual frame of reference.	4. Deals with emotional and attitudinal aspects in an experiential frame of reference.
5. Emphasis is on using facts and making assumptions.	5. Emphasis on feelings.
6. Trains in the exercise of judgements.	6. Trains in emotional control.
7. Provides practice in analysis of problems.	7. Provides practice in interpersonal skills.

By design, role-plays reflect reality but provide the participants only limited details about the hypothetical situation. Because of this, the range of behaviors that might unfold during the exercise is almost unlimited. Responding appropriately to whatever evolves, using the knowledge gained, is an inherent part of the exercise.

In role playing, participants are required to respond to specific problems they may actually encounter in their jobs or real-life situations. Rather than hearing about how a problem might be handled or even discussing it, they learn by doing. Role playing is often used to teach such skills as interviewing, grievance handling, performance appraisal, group/team leadership, team problem solving, effective communication, and leadership style analysis. As a rule, role-plays are most useful for practicing interpersonal skills: conflict management, negotiation, team building, influencing, active listening, giving and receiving feedback, and communication.

Sanyal (2000) describes a recent example of a role playing exercise, Self-Interest, used in teaching business ethics. Self-Interest is a role playing experiential exercise that uses role playing to enable participants to confront and understand ethical dilemmas that arise while conducting international business. The exercise can be used by itself or as a complement to other teaching methods such as lectures or case studies. Through an interactive dialogue and debate, Self-Interest emphasizes the multifaceted approach to any ethical issue—an approach grounded in the self-interest, experience, and values of the various players (employers, employees, customers, and the society at large). While the game is designed to address issues in the international business setting, with slight modification, ethical dilemmas in a wide variety of fields can be easily accommodated (see Sanyal, 2000 for more information on this exercise).

As an adragogical approach Sanyal suggests that the Self-Interest exercise is superior to lectures, assigned readings, or case studies. This view is consistent with that of Black and Mendenhall (1989), who have noted that experiential training methods like role-plays are more rigorous and engage participants more fully than methods such as lectures and videotapes.

Service Learning

Service learning is an experiential learning tool that combines community service, readings, and reflection. Students participate in organized, voluntary service, read relevant literature, and take the time to reflect upon it. The idea is that the readings and service create challenges for the students, which they realize and address in reflection. The goal for students in service learning courses is to learn to serve and serve to learn. They learn to serve by actually serving and through reflection come to value the service. They serve to learn by using the service experiences to better understand their own personal paradigms and the course material.

The pedagogy underlying service learning is firmly based on that of experiential learning. Kolb's learning cycle model provides a useful framework for understanding the power of service learning. This four-stage process model begins with "concrete" experiences, resulting in reflective observations, whereby abstract conceptualizations are developed to make sense of the world newly experienced. These processes then lead to active experimentation or concept testing before the individual repeats this learning cycle. Service learning expands the repertoire of "concrete" experiences necessary to fully develop as a manager. These contacts with the community-at-large form the basis of many new explanations, justifications, and behavioral concepts for the participating students and faculty. Outside of the "safe" zone of traditional business school programs, students are called upon to construct new concepts of reality and make adjustments to ineffective personal concepts and models of the past. It is here where the real potential for personal learning arises.

Service learning provides a means through which ethical theory and moral convictions are translated into action. Service learning projects can be simple or complex. They can be built into one class or extend over entire universities or colleges. For example, at one university accounting students prepare tax returns for low-income individuals and conduct audits for charitable organizations. Entrepreneurship and marketing students prepare business plans for small businesses and marketing plans for nonprofit organizations, respectively. Faculty responsible for teaching business ethics can make service learning the primary pedagogical tool or include service as a component in the classes they teach. (For examples of different service learning projects and more information about them, see the January 1996 issue of the *Journal of Business Ethics*, which was devoted to service learning in business ethics courses; Graham, 1996; Kohls, 1996.)

While most business schools have housed service learning in their ethics courses, others have attempted to expand it across the curriculum. At Bentley College, for example, over 25 percent of full-time faculty integrate service learning into their courses (Hill & Stewart, 1999; Kenworthy, 1996).

Behavioral Simulations

Several writers have proposed using simulations to improve learning of skills and concepts in business ethics (LeClair et al., 1999). Those advocating the use of simulations suggest that although traditional teaching tools have their strengths, none provide the organizational context and degree of accountability that represents how ethical decisions in business are actually made.

Behavioral simulations can provide students with hands-on experience and a better understanding of the concepts discussed in the classroom. In a simulation designed for business ethics courses, students are faced with ethical dilemmas that encourage them to react to the problems as though they were in a real-life situation. Simulations give students the chance to explore their attitudes, feelings, and communication skills. Advocates of this approach note that after participating in a simulation, students become more open minded, or at least more cognizant of important ethical issues. They also get a better picture of the complexity involved and how individuals in organizations work through ethical dilemmas (LeClair et al., 1999). Simulations can incorporate various perspectives on business ethics because they allow for decision analysis, an organizational experience, and the opportunity to observe human behavior.

The Soy-DRI simulation is an example of an ethics education tool developed for use in business courses. It is a simulation of a complex, realistic, and value-laden business situation that requires a timely response. The simulation has been used in undergraduate and graduate business classes. LeClair et al. (1999) note that this simulation enhances traditional approaches to teaching and learning business ethics and allows students to experience ethical conflict and problem solving. (For more information on the Soy-DRI simulation see LeClair et al., 1999.)

The Lewinian Experiential Learning Model (Kolb, 1984) forms the foundation upon which most simulations are based. With an experiential approach that closely simulates the kind of situations managers may face on the job, business students can be taught to engage in decision-making behaviors elicited in the simulation. The "right decisions" are not taught; rather, the process of making decisions is the fundamental experience and goal of the simulation.

Learning from experience involves changing both how people see things (i.e., interpretation of a situation) and what they do (i.e., behavior). The intent of simulations is to offer multiple perspectives on complex situations and opportunities to explore behavioral alternatives. The focus is on response learning, that is, a change in the way participants "are prepared to respond in a certain situation" (Cell, 1984).

Self-Reflection

Self-reflection encourages change by providing opportunities for individuals to consider their own behaviors in light of their espoused theories and commitments. Thus, it takes as a starting point personal experiences and assumes that these provide a foundation for learning. In doing this, a reflective approach differs from one that is grounded on conceptual frameworks and theory-based empirical evidence as the necessary material for productive business or professional preparation experiences. Like others, I contend that experiences are good fodder for ethical growth and personal and professional development. As noted earlier, experiential learning theorists, including Dewey, Lewin, Piaget, and Kolb maintain that learning is most effective (i.e., most likely to lead to behavioral change) when it begins with experience. They are joined by Knowles (1996), McCarthy (1990), and others, who also point out that learning grounded in the realities of students' lives is quite consistent with insights derived from the growing body of research on adult learning. Because reflection invites—and indeed often depends upon—a consideration of actual experience, its use as a pedagogical strategy suggests that the knowledge of practice is considered a valid and important part in teaching business ethics.

A number of writers believe students should be encouraged to examine their attitudes and convictions via journals, reaction papers, and reflection assignments like personal application assignments (PAAs) (Kolb et al., 1995), which are an important component of experiential learning theory.

These are particularly appropriate in relationship to strategies like teaching business ethics via narratives and providing service learning opportunities.

Various approaches have been used at different colleges and universities to provide opportunities for self-reflection. For example, students at Gonzaga University who engage in service learning must keep a journal, draft a paper evaluating the experience, and make a class presentation. At Wheaton College in suburban Chicago, one professor goes so far as to require students to experience and reflect upon a "voluntary displacement experience" by spending a night in jail or temporarily living on the streets of Chicago (Holmes, 1984). Students at North Central College in Naperville, Illinois, may take an elective reflection seminar while performing their internships. Among other assignments, they are required to keep journals, draft cases about ethical issues in their work settings, and lead class discussions (Smith, 1996).

One instructor lauds the experience of self-reflection because "lessons are arrived at inductively from personal experiences and observations." While acknowledging this method to be "slow and less efficient than readings and lectures," he notes that it is "less abstract, provides connections between life problems and academic concepts, and motivates lasting learning by providing concrete examples of theories." Perhaps most importantly, he observes that the project's biggest success is in moving the hearts of students" (Kohls, 1996, p. 56).

CONCLUSION

As should be evident from the descriptions of the pedagogical approaches and techniques highlighted in this chapter, instructional style in business ethics teaching efforts is no different from the teaching tools employed in other courses. Lectures, case analysis, and guest lectures are still very much in use, along with techniques such as the use of fiction and more recent innovative techniques like computer conferencing. These and the many other approaches create both an opportunity and a challenge for business ethics teachers. On one hand, there appear to be unlimited pedagogical approaches or techniques available to business ethics teachers that can be used in accomplishing the objectives of business ethics education. However, the challenge remains to ensure that the pedagogical approaches used reflect the kind of experiences students are likely to encounter in real-world situations. Thus, business ethics teachers must continue to strive to increase the relevance of business ethics education by choosing materials and pedagogies that emphasize active rather than passive learning for students. Activities like role-plays, business simulations, and service learning can help better address the relevance challenge that we encounter in teaching business ethics.

While we may all have a bias towards certain pedagogical approaches (mine just happens to be experiential approaches), the reality is that effective teachers use all or some combinations of the available approaches in their teaching efforts. A multimethod approach is always preferable, for it is more attentive to differences in learning styles and thus, in my view, has a greater likelihood of maximizing the teaching and learning of business ethics.

REFERENCES

Angelo, T.A., & Cross, K.P. 1993. *Classroom assessment techniques: A handbook for college teachers* (2nd ed.). San Francisco: Jossey-Bass.

Beauchamp, T.L. 1998. *Case studies in business, society, and ethics* (4th ed.). Englewood Cliffs, NJ: Prentice Hall.

Black, J.S., & Mendenhall, M. 1989. A practical but theory-based framework for selecting cross-cultural training programs. *Human Resource Management* 28(4): 511–539.

Bok, E.L. 1997. *Selected speeches (1979–1995)*. Princeton, NJ: The Carnegie Foundation for the Advancement of Teaching.

Buller, P.F., Kohls, J.J., & Anderson, M.S. 1997. A model for addressing cross-cultural ethical conflicts. *Business and Society* 36(2): 169–193.

Cell, E. 1984. *Learning to learn from experience*. Albany: State University of New York Press.

Chickering, A.W., & Gamson, Z.F. 1987. Seven principles for good practice. *American Association of Higher Education Bulletin* 39: 3–7.

Chism, N., Jones, C., Macce, B., & Mountford, R. 1989. *Teaching at the Ohio State University: A handbook*. Columbus: Ohio State University Center for Teaching Excellence.

Coles, R. 1989. *The call of stories*. Boston: Houghton Mifflin.

Cooper, T.L. 1999. *The responsible administrator*. San Francisco: Jossey-Bass.

DeGeorge, R.T. 1993. *Competing with integrity in international business*. New York: Oxford University Press.

Dennehy, R.F., Sims, R.R., & Collins, H.E. 1998. Debriefing experiential learning exercises: A theoretical and practical guide for success. *Journal of Management Education* 22(1): 9–25.

Donaldson, T. 1996. Values in tension: Ethics away from home. *Harvard Business Review* (September–October): 47–62.

Etzioni, A. 1991. Reflections on the teaching of business ethics. *Business Ethics Quarterly* 1(4): 355–365.

Furman, F.K. 1990. Teaching business ethics: Questioning the assumptions, seeking new directions. *Journal of Business Ethics* 9: 31–38.

Fust, M. 1989. *The story of my wife: The reminiscences of Captain Stoerr* (I. Sanders, trans.). London: Cape. (Original work published in 1957.)

Garaventa, E. 1998. Drama: A tool for teaching business ethics. *Business Ethics Quarterly* 8(3): 535–545.

Geva, A. 2000. The Internet and the book: Media and messages in teaching business ethics. *Teaching Business Ethics* 4: 85–106.

Giacalone, R.A., & Jurkiewicz, C.L. 2001. Lights, camera, action: Teaching ethical decision making through cinematic experience. *Teaching Business Ethics* 5: 79–87.

Giddens, A. 1984. *The constitution of society: Outline of the theory of structuration.* Berkeley: University of California Press.

Gilbert, J.T. 1992. Teaching business ethics: What, why, who, where, and when. *Journal of Education for Business* (September–October): 5–8.

Hemmasi, M., & Graf, L.A. 1992. Managerial skills acquisition: A case for using business policy simulations. *Simulation & Gaming* 23(3): 298–310.

Hill, A., & Stewart, I.C. 1999. Character education in business schools: Pedagogical strategies. *Teaching Business Ethics* 3: 179–193.

Holmes, A.F. 1984. *Ethics: Approaching moral decisions.* Downers Grove, IL: Intervarsity Press.

Hosmer, L.T. 2000. Standard format for the case analysis of moral problems. *Teaching Business Ethics* 4: 169–180.

Iyer, G.R. 1998. Integrating business ethics in classroom teaching: Some preliminary considerations. *Teaching Business Ethics* 1: 315–331.

Kennedy, E.J., & Lawton, L. 1992. Business ethics in fiction. *Journal of Business Ethics* 11: 187–195.

Kenworthy, A. 1996. Linking business education, campus culture and community: The Bentley service learning project. *Journal of Business Ethics* 15: 121–131.

Knowles, M. 1996. *Teaching management.* Houston, TX: Gulf Publishing Company.

Kohls, J. 1996. Students' experiences with service learning in a business ethics course. *Journal of Business Ethics* 15: 45–47.

Kohls, J., Buller, P.F., & Anderson, K.S. 1999. Resolving cross-cultural ethical conflict: An empirical test of a decision tree model in an educational setting. *Teaching Business Ethics* 3: 37–56.

Kolb, D.A. 1984. *Experiential learning: Experience as the source of learning and development.* Englewood Cliffs, NJ: Prentice Hall.

Kolb, D.A., Osland, J.S., & Rubin, I.M. 1995. *Organizational behavior: Instructor's manual.* Englewood Cliffs, NJ: Prentice Hall.

Lampe, M. 1997. Increasing effectiveness in teaching ethics to undergraduate business students. *Teaching Business Ethics* 1: 3–19.

LeClair, D.T., Ferrell, L., Montuori, L., & Willems, C. 1999. The use of a behavioral simulation to teach business ethics. *Teaching Business Ethics* 3: 283–296.

Liedtka, J. 1992. Wounded but wiser: Reflections on teaching ethics to MBA students. *Journal of Management Education* 16(4): 405–416.

MacIntyre, A. 1984. *After virtue.* Notre Dame, IN: University of Notre Dame Press.

McCarthy, B. 1990. Using the 4MAT system to bring learning styles to school. *Educational Leadership* (October): 31–37.

McDonald, G.M. 1992. The Canadian research strategy for applied ethics: A new opportunity for research in business and professional ethics. *Journal of Business Ethics* 11: 569–583.

McDonald, G.M., & Donleavy, G.D. 1995. Objections to the teaching of business ethics. *Journal of Business Ethics* 10(1): 829–835.

Maglagan, P., & Snell, R. 1992. Some implications for management development research into managers' moral dilemmas. *British Journal of Management* 3: 157–168.

Marini, F. 1992. Literature and public administration ethics. *American Review of Public Administration* 22(2): 111–125.

Meilander, G.C. 1984. *Theory and practice of virtue.* Notre Dame, IN: University of Notre Dame Press.

Nappi, A.T. 1990. Teaching business ethics: A conceptual approach. *Journal of Education for Business* (January): 177–180.

Nicastro, M.L., & Jones, D.C. 1994. *Cooperative learning guide for marketing.* Englewood Cliffs, NJ: Prentice-Hall.

Nussbaum, M. 1989. Narrative emotions: Beckett's genealogy. In S.M. Hauerwas and L. Jones (eds.), *Why narrative?* Grand Rapids, MI: Eerdmans, pp. 216–248.

O'Connor, P.J., and Godar, S.H. 1999. How not to make ethical decisions: Guidelines from management textbooks. *Teaching Business Ethics* 3: 69–86.

Phillips, R.A., & Clawson, J.G. 1998. Current events periodicals and business ethics. *Teaching Business Ethics* 2: 165–174.

Pizzolatto, A.B. 1993. Ethical management: An exercise in understanding power. *Journal of Management Education* 17(1): 107–109.

Plato. 1976. *Protagorus* (C.C.W. Taylor, trans). Oxford: Clarendon.

Sanyal, R.N. 2000. Teaching business ethics in international business. *Teaching Business Ethics* 4: 137–149.

Schaupp, D.L., & Lane, M.S. 1992. Teaching business ethics: Bringing reality to the classroom. *Journal of Business Ethics* 10: 211–219.

Shaffer, T.L. 1987. *Faith and the profession.* Provo, UT: Brigham Young University Press.

Simon, J.A. 1983. *Reason in human affairs.* Stanford, CA: Stanford University Press.

Sims, R.R. Forthcoming. Business ethics teaching for effective learning. *Teaching Business Ethics.*

Sims, R.R., & Sims, S.J. 1991. Increasing applied business ethics courses in business school curricula. *Journal of Business Ethics* 10: 211–219.

Smith, D. 1996. Ethical reflections and service internships. *Journal of Business Ethics* 4: 13–19.

Stewart, I.C. 1997. Teaching accounting ethics: The power of narrative. *Accounting Education* 2(2): 173–184.

Strong, V.K., & Hoffman, A.N. 1990. There is relevance in the classroom: Analysis of present methods of teaching business ethics. *Journal of Business Ethics* 9: 603–607.

Thomas, K.W. 1990. Conflict and negotiation process in organizations. In M.D. Dunnette (ed.), *Handbook of industrial and organizational psychology* (2nd ed.). Chicago: Consulting Psychologists Press, pp. 752–777.

Trevino, L.K., & McCabe, D. 1994. Meta-learning about business ethics: Building honorable business school communities. *Journal of Business Ethics* 10: 211–219.

Van Wart, M. 1998. *Changing public sector values.* New York: Garland Publishing.

Vitz, P. 1990. The use of stories in moral development. *American Psychologist* 45(6): 709–720.

Waldmann, E. 2000. Incorporating Freud's theory on cognitive processes into business ethics education. *Teaching Business Ethics* 4: 257–268.

Werhane, P.H. 1998. Moral imagination and the search for ethical decision making in management. *Business Ethics Quarterly*, Special Issue 1: 75–98.

Yuthas, K., & Dillard, J.F. 1999. Teaching ethical decision making: Adding a structuration dimension. *Teaching Business Ethics* 3: 339–361.

Zlotkowski, E. 1996. Opportunity for all: Linking service-learning and business education. *Journal of Business Ethics* 15(1): 5–19.

Chapter 9

Moving into the Classroom: Developing the Climate for Teaching and Learning Business Ethics

INTRODUCTION

Developing the climate for learning when teaching business ethics requires careful attention by the faculty. The purpose of this chapter is to build on the discussion of learning environments introduced in Chapter 6 and focus on several models that will help business ethics teachers to actually create learning environments that facilitate a productive learning climate. More specifically, this chapter discusses the importance of the "psychological contract" in the effective development of learning climates during business ethics teaching efforts. A basic premise of this chapter is that business ethics teachers must work to create the kind of learning environment most responsive to their own need and to their students' needs. A model for managing student and faculty expectations and contributions during business ethics teaching efforts is presented. The model creates learning environments that facilitate shared responsibility for the learning process between the business ethics teacher and the students.

DEVELOPING THE CLIMATE FOR TEACHING AND LEARNING BUSINESS ETHICS

Business ethics teachers are responsible for managing the content, process, and learning environment of all the efforts intended to teach ethics. Content refers to the material to be covered and to the general sequence in which it will be presented. Process encompasses the approaches by which that content is delivered. Environment is the physical and psychological surroundings for the learning initiatives.

Like other teachers, I often spend the first hours of a business ethics teaching effort trying to develop a sense of community and deciding how to use experience and the interactions of students for maximum learning. For me the business ethics teaching effort becomes a *learning community*— a community in which students support one another, are open with one another about their feelings and opinions during discussions, and are willing to confront or compare different opinions, responses, insights, and experiences. Learning to learn is important enough (and difficult enough) for students to spend time building such a climate systematically. A key aspect of this sort of learning environment in business ethics involves learning how to use one's experiences and those of others effectively.

Characteristics of a Classroom Learning Environment

As highlighted in Chapter 6, a crucial component of teaching business ethics is considering the learning environment the instructor wants to create. Hiemstra (1991) defined a learning environment as "all of the physical surroundings, psychological or emotional conditions, and social or cultural influences affecting the growth and development of an adult engaged in an educational environment" (p. 8). Different writers have focused on different aspects of the environment that promote and encourage learning. Some have stressed the importance of the physical setting. For example, Vosko (1991) described the impact of seating arrangements, sight lines, and equipment on learning. Other writers have emphasized the importance of psychological or interpersonal variables related to learning environments. Still others have suggested that business ethics teaching efforts should "take place in a setting conducive to safe, honest interpersonal exchanges, to uninhibited self-exploration, and to hopefulness that the desired change can be made" (Sims, forthcoming). Knox (1986) highlighted the need for a balance between support and challenge and defined a challenging environment as one that "is problem-centered, is neither boring nor threatening, promotes worthwhile educational achievement, and helps participants [students] understand the problem situation, as well as the problem, and strategies for formulating effective solutions" (p. 132). Knowles (1980) suggested that an educational environment should include "respect for personality, participation in decision making, freedom of expression and availability of information; and mutuality of responsibility in defining goals, planning and conducting, activities, and evaluating" (p. 67).

The learning environment model discussed in this chapter differs in some key respects from the stereotype of the traditional business course or program. First, it is based on a psychological contract of reciprocity. Reciprocity is a basic building block of human interaction which emphasizes that relationships based on a mutual and equal balance of giving and getting thrive and grow, whereas those based on unequal exchange very quickly decay. This process of reciprocity is particularly important for creating an effective learning environment when teaching business ethics because many initial assumptions about learning run counter to it. Learning is most often considered a process of getting rather than giving.

The process of getting rather than giving is most evident in conceptions of students' and faculty members' roles. Traditionally, faculty members give and students get. Yet, for successful learning, both giving and getting by faculty members *and* students is critical. In getting, there is the opportunity to incorporate new ideas and perspectives. In giving, there is the opportunity to integrate and apply these new perspectives and to practice their use.

A second characteristic of the learning environment model discussed in this chapter is that it is experience based. The motivation for learning comes not from the faculty member's dispensation of rewards but from problems and opportunities arising from the student's own life experience. Third, this learning environment emphasizes personal application. Since students' learning needs arise from their own experience, the main goal of learning about ethics is to apply new knowledge, skills, and abilities to the solution of the kinds of business situations students will encounter in the real world.

Fourth, the learning environment is individualized and self-directed. Just as every student's experience is different, so are each student's learning goals and learning style. A major concern in the management of learning environments in business ethics teaching efforts is to organize resources in such a way that they are maximally responsive to what each student wants to learn and how he or she learns it. Essential to achievement of this kind of learning environment is students' willingness to take responsibility for the achievement of their own learning objectives. Perhaps the most important of the students' responsibilities are evaluating how well they are getting the learning resources they need to achieve their goals and alerting the learning community (faculty members and other students) to problems when they arise, since they are in the best position to make this judgement.

Finally, it is important that students integrate learning and living. There are two goals in the learning process. One is to learn the specifics of a particular subject matter like business ethics. The other is to learn one's own strengths and weaknesses as a learner (i.e., learning how to learn from experience). When the process works well, students finish their ethics learning experience with not only new intellectual insights but also an understanding of their own learning style. This understanding of learning strengths and weaknesses helps in the application of what has been learned to real-world situations and provides a framework for continued learning. In this instance, learning is no longer a special activity reserved for the classroom; it becomes an integral and explicit part of the work world business students will encounter upon graduation.

The remainder of this chapter is designed to help business ethics teachers form contracts with students to build effective learning environments and to share responsibility for the learning process during the business ethics teaching effort. In a sense, faculty members should use the model as a catalyst for conversations among students and all those responsible for teaching business ethics and that are directed toward building and maintaining a highly effective learning community.

Psychological Contracts

In order to build an effective learning environment, it is important for faculty members to understand the nature of the psychological contract and how they influence student functioning in learning initiatives. A psychological contract is implicitly formed between students and the course or class of which they are members. The contract involves instructor's expectations of students and students' contributions to meet those expectations. It also deals with students' expectations of the course or instructor and the contributions to meet those expectations. However, first it is important to more clearly define the psychological contract in the context of teaching business ethics.

When students decide to participate in any business ethics teaching endeavor, they enter into a psychological contract with the business school and faculty member(s). A psychological contract is a set of unwritten reciprocal expectations between the student and the instructor or course. It is the bedrock of the student-instructor link because learning is based upon an implicit exchange of beliefs and expectations about the actions of the student vis-à-vis the course/instructor and the course/instructor vis-à-vis the student. As such, psychological contracts usually involve expectations about learning conditions, requirements of the course itself, and the level of effort (participation) to be expended by the student in the course.

Unlike a legal contract, a psychological contract in a business school course defines a dynamic relationship that may continually change and be renegotiated. Often both parties to the contract may have different levels of expectation clarity, since some of the items may have been explicitly discussed and others only inferred. Important aspects of the contract are not always formally agreed upon.

Expectations are sometimes implicit premises about the relationship. Faculty or business school contributions, such as a sense of challenge in the business ethics course, and student contributions, such as active participation, are expected and in some instances are not consciously weighed. Yet this contract is a reality that has many implications for the productivity of the ethics course and student satisfaction. A business ethics teaching effort that is filled with students who feel "cheated" and expect far more than they get is headed for trouble. Students who feel the ethics program does not meet their expectations becomes a stumbling block to a productive learning environment. On the other hand, a business ethics teaching effort that demands total compliance to peripheral norms, such as manner of dress or dedication to one particular ethical theory that is in favor with the faculty member, will stifle student creativity and participation.

Expectations and Contributions

The dynamic quality of the psychological contract developed in a business ethics teaching effort means that students' and instructor's expectations and contributions usually influence one another. Students entering into the psychological contract contributes their productive and participative capacity directed towards achieving the course's purpose. High expectations on the part of the instructor outlined in the course syllabus can produce increased student contributions (i.e., class participation), and great contributions will likewise raise expectations. From the teachers responsible for teaching business ethics the questions become, "How can we teach the students so that we can maximize their individual contributions?" and "How can we create a learning environment that meets students' expectations and our norms?" For students the question is, "How can this business ethics course increase my knowledge or performance, personal growth, and development?"

Entering a business ethics course the first time is very much like the first day on a new job. In my experience, the typical orientation program in a business ethics, or most any other, business course is one-sided. Most communication flows from the faculty member to the student: "These are our policies, procedures, and expectations as outlined in the syllabus."

One effect of this one-sided process is to cause students to feel that the faculty member is much more powerful than they are. So instead of trying to formulate and articulate their own expectations, students often say what they think the faculty member wants to hear. Another effect is the tendency to oversocialize students. Students' feelings of powerlessness often lead them to be more passive than they might ordinarily be in the situation, and this can contribute to many of the fears students may already bring to business ethics courses, as described in Chapter 3.

Unfortunately, in many instances the faculty member may read passivity as a sign that students want and need more direction and control. This can create a feedback cycle that in the long run operates to the detriment of the relationship between students and faculty. Maintaining a balanced psychological contract is necessary for a harmonious relationship. Since psychological contracts are entered into as students enter the ethics course, whether or not their expectations about the contract are met is crucial to the tenor of their relationship with the faculty member or course. For example, if students take a business ethics course with the expectation that their psychological contract includes some input in evaluating the instructor's performance only to find out that the instructor's views differ, then the students are likely to suffer considerable dissatisfaction with the course, based primarily on the perception that their psychological contract has been violated.

Violation of the psychological contract can signal to students that the parties no longer share (or never shared) a common set of values or goals. Once this happens, one can expect a breakdown of communications among the parties, a failure in mutual understanding, increasing levels of frustration (and subsequent emotional responses) on the part of both parties, and a learning climate less conducive to learning.

Students may find learning environments they encounter in business courses in general dull, boring, and unexciting. They may sit passively in class, uninvolved in their own learning, and work half-heartedly to meet the course's expectations. Their own expectations for learning, involvement, and stimulation may go unsatisfied, in large measure because they never get the opportunity to make such expectations explicit. This, of course, need not be the case. If students and faculty can initially share their expectations and goals and can establish a climate where a shared responsibility is maintained, then it becomes possible to better meet everyone's objectives or learning needs.

A Dynamic Process

It is important, however, to recognize that the psychological contract is not set forever in the initial business ethics class meeting. As mentioned at the outset, the initial class meeting represents a starting point for a dynamic learning process that will necessitate continued discussion and updating of mutual expectations throughout the life of the course. The remainder of this chapter will introduce two models for thinking about the learning process that should help create an "early warning system" for the identification of problems and reinforce a set of norms for the learning community that will encourage students to evaluate their own learning progress and to sound alarms for the faculty when learning objectives are not met. The psychological contract may be the central determinant in whether a business ethics education effort is effective, generating student commitment, loyalty, and enthusiasm for the effort and its goals. This may depend to a large measure on two conditions: (1) the degree to which students' expectations of what the course will provide them and what they must give to the course match the expectations of the faculty member and the course and what they will give and get; and (2) assuming there is agreement on expectations, what is actually exchanged? An example of such exchanges include active participation and commitment by students during the course in order to enhance their personal growth and development. Figure 9.1 illustrates the importance of the match between expectations and contributions for a business ethics course. The more students establish psycho-

Figure 9.1
The Importance of the Match between Business Ethics Teaching Contributions and Inducements in the Psychological Contract

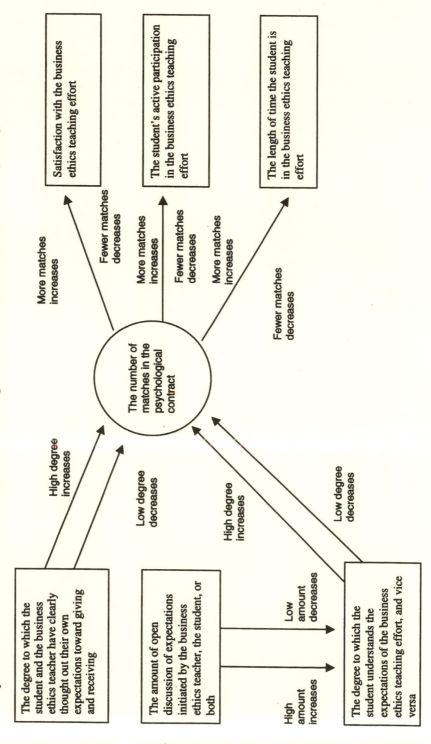

logical contracts that are made up of matches in expectations, the greater will be their satisfaction with the business ethics course.

Often students are not clear about what they want or need, or what they are capable of contributing during a business ethics course (this is often the result of the failure of the teacher to show any interest in students' expectations). Unfortunately some business ethics teachers, like a number of their colleagues, are not always as clear about their expectations of students as they should be. As a result, they don't talk about many important areas or pay sufficient attention to them. Mismatches can occur by accident or out of neglect.

What is needed then is for students to carefully consider all areas of expectations in order to overcome the problem of clarity. Too often this step does not occur because the business ethics teacher and students do not consider it to be important. The effectiveness of business ethics education can be enhanced if those responsible for designing, implementing, and evaluating these efforts attempt to increase the number of matches in the psychological contract depicted in Figure 9.1.

A MODEL FOR MANAGING PSYCHOLOGICAL CONTRACTS

Sherwood and Glidewell (1971) have developed a simple but powerful model, the pinch model, which describes the dynamic quality of psychological contracts and suggests ways of maintaining the potentially dysfunctional consequences of shifting expectations (Figure 9.2). This model provides a framework for the continuous management of the psychological contract in the day-to-day work or classroom setting. The model, which has often been referred to as the "pinch model of contract negotiation," is cyclical and includes four phases that can be applied by business ethics teachers to the development of more matches in the psychological contract within their business ethics teaching efforts. The four phases adapted by the author for the development of effective learning environments in business ethics teaching efforts are:

1. Phase 1 involves sharing learning information and negotiating expectations by faculty and students during open discussions.
2. When properly conducted, Phase 1 leads to mutual commitment to defined roles by both the faculty and students.
3. With commitment and role definition by both the faculty and students, actual implementation of the course results in stability and productivity.
4. Often the emergent and individualized nature of the learning process in the course will inevitably lead to a new state of disruption.

The first stage of the learning relationship should be characterized by open discussion between the faculty and students through sharing of in-

Figure 9.2
Model for Managing Psychological Contracts in Business Ethics Teaching Efforts

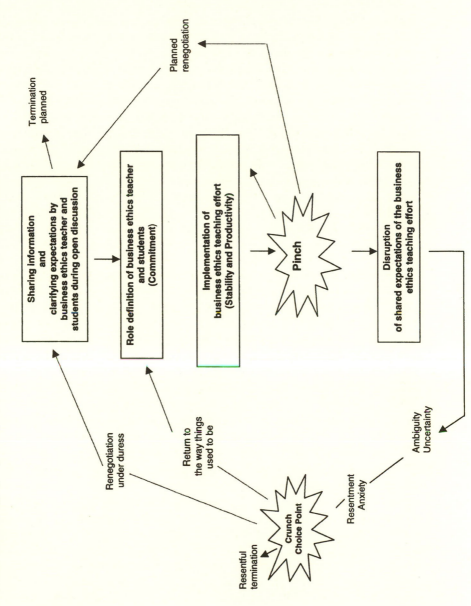

formation and a negotiation of expectations. A simple way to understand the first stage is to consider the following: Suppose that students taking a business ethics elective course were informed by the teacher on the first day of the course that there would only be two written assignments. Students expect two written assignments. However, at the end of the third class the teacher informs students that she has decided that a third written assignment will be required. If this difference in expectations cannot be resolved at this point, the teacher and students may part ways. They have found out immediately that they may have an irresolvable mismatch. Or suppose students are expecting a business ethics course that relies primarily on the instructor giving lectures only to find out on the first day of the class that an experiential learning approach will be the predominant pedagogical approach used in the course. This presents an immediate mismatch that may be further compounded by the fact that active participation by students in class discussions and a service learning component are key components of successful performance in the course.

Assuming that both parties hear enough of what they expect to hear from the other, they will work towards making a joint commitment. If commitment and an understanding of roles and ground rules occurs, faculty and students can both expect to move into a period of stability and productivity as they get down to work during actual implementation of the course.

Even with the best of intentions, assuming full sharing of initial expectations (which is often unlikely), changes are likely to occur over time. These changes can and do take a variety of forms, but the consequence is the same—there is a disruption of shared expectations. Since the "rules" that were agreed to initially have been upset, faculty and students, or both, experience heightened uncertainty, which invariably results in heightened anxiety. Human nature being what it is, the business ethics teacher and students invest energy in reducing this anxiety. Typically, what should happen at this point is an effort to return to the way things used to be. This may require the business ethics teacher to attempt to clarify the misunderstanding, resolve the conflict, and renew the commitment. To the extent that both teacher and students remain unsatisfied in this cycle, the result is invariably some form of termination—psychological (i.e., apathy: "I'll be darned if I'm going to do any more than I'm required to do for the remainder of this course") or physical (i.e., students no longer actively participate in discussions or actually withdraw from the course).

At the point of anxiety, it is much more productive if the business ethics teacher cycles back to the starting point and tests whether or not any new information is now available. Given the dynamic, changing nature of most relationships, it is very likely that a new psychological contract is appropriate and realistic. If the business ethics teacher discovers that new, changed expectations cannot be successfully negotiated, termination is still a possibility, but in my experience this is an extreme response and should be avoided at all costs. The critical difference, in this condition, however, is that the termination is an agreed-upon, joint decision rather than a unilateral decision based upon untested assumptions.

Business ethics teachers must realize that this disruption, depending on its seriousness, inevitably leads to some degree of uncertainty, anxiety, and discomfort. The discomfort can in turn lead to a number of possible outcomes, depending on how it is handled. It can lead to termination, withdrawal, or avoidance of the business ethics course altogether. It can lead to a kind of conservative return to the way things were at the price of avoiding new learning opportunities and resources. Or it can lead to a renegotiation by a resharing of the new information and expectations that have been generated as a result of the disruption.

Sherwood and Glidewell (1971) point out that there is a natural tendency to ignore a host of early warning signs ("pinches") that signal a potentially disruptive situation. "I don't have time to test this issue with students." "If I raise this issue with the instructor, he'll think I'm just complaining so I'll ignore it." But there is a way to achieve stability in the psychological contract without all the unpleasant side effects of disruptions. This approach is called "planned renegotiation," and it is based on the development of group norms that allow members to announce signs ("pinches") that they feel signal an imminent disruption. These signs, when noted during the beginning of a business ethics course (the stage of stability and productivity), for example, can provide data that the business ethics teacher can use for preventative renegotiation of expectations, which may avoid costly disruption of a productive learning process. Examples of "pinches" that may signal the need for renegotiation in business ethics courses include the following:

- Students feel bored or tuned out of a discussion.
- A business ethics teacher senses that preparation assignments haven't been completed.
- Classes don't start on time or go past the designated end time.
- Students are not actively participating in experientially oriented business ethics activities, sharing personal experiences, or speaking up in discussions.
- Students feel pressured to share an ethically related experience before they are ready.

Dealing with the pinches allows both the business ethics teacher and the students to conduct the renegotiation process in a planned manner, without the heat of emotion that can accompany a disruption. (It's like an automatic safety valve on a boiler.) If students and the business ethics teacher let each other know when they feel these subtle pinches, it becomes possible to make changes and minor adjustments without pressure, anxiety, and a crisis atmosphere.

CLARIFYING THE PSYCHOLOGICAL CONTRACT

Creating a safe and trusting environment where students are willing to share their experiences is essential for the depth of personal learning that can occur when one grapples with ethical issues. The next few sections offer an example of how I have tried to clarify the psychological contract and create a classroom climate conducive to sharing beginning with the first class.

Developing the Classroom Climate with the First Class

Once business ethics teachers decide that they want to create a learning environment conducive to sharing, it is important to start the first class with in-class and independent experiences to support their activities. In my own business ethics teaching efforts, the activities I plan directly coincide with the kind of environment I am hoping to create. For example, one of the ways I begin the first class is with a familiar exercise of introducing classmates, which I have incorporated into an ethics theme. I ask students to think of a situation in which they were confronted with an ethical dilemma and give them about five minutes to jot down some notes about their experience and their feelings. I then ask them to pair with someone they do not know (the instructor also pairs up with one of the students). Their task is to introduce themselves to their partner and to describe their experiences and feelings related to the ethical dilemma they identified. When they have each told their stories, we convene as a large group and each person introduces their partner and describes the partner's ethical dilemma. This is followed by the person being introduced responding to questions about the experience that group members ask.

This exercise sets the stage for many aspects of the learning environment we are trying to create. It engages students in active participation, self-disclosure, and especially, reciprocity, or sharing responsibility for talking about experiences. It provides an opportunity for students to begin to understand their own experiences with ethics (ethical dilemmas in this situation) and to learn about the experiences and feelings of others. It sets the tone in the class for openness, trust, and interest in one another. And it creates the beginning of feelings of community within the class.

As I continue in the course, I design several types of opportunities for students to be actively involved in the class sessions. They discuss issues and experiences in dyads, trios, small groups, and as a large group. I usually mix students each time so that they interact with, learn from, experience themselves with, and, we hope, learn to trust a variety of people. Occasionally I group people by like characteristics—for example, by sex, by major, or by occupation—especially when self-understanding and specific group learning are important.

When I select topics for discussion, I usually integrate or build on to issues raised in reading assignments with experiences from students' personal and working lives. For example, after reading about cross-cultural ethics, I ask them to discuss, in groups representing various countries or cultures, questions concerning ethical conduct for individual decision makers in multinational corporations. An example of such a question is: "When ethical perspectives, values, and behaviors conflict, whose ethics are right, and how does one resolve the differences?" Students are expected to discuss their responses to the question from both the perspective of the host country and their own home country. This compare-and-contrast design supports openness and trust among the students. I then have each group provide a summary of their discussion and feelings to the other groups. This enhances disclosure and risk taking. It also develops an understanding of the experiences of another group. I also discuss the implications of cross-cultural ethics for the workplace in general and changes that they might need to make in current and future jobs.

An alternative to the first class exercise presented above is suggested by Fort and Zollers (1999) and is provided here for your consideration. Like others, Fort and Zollers acknowledge that there are many stakeholders in the education "business," including accrediting organizations, colleagues, deans, alumni, and future employers (Fort & Zollers, 1996). Because students are affected by academic action and have some insights about how they can best learn, it is important to tap into that insight. Fort and Zollers suggests using a Total Quality Management (TQM) survey that can show what things are most important to students as they begin the class. The following is an adaptation of the introduction to and the actual survey (those interested in the full text should see Fort & Zollers, 1999):

We need to establish your expectations/requirements currently and periodically to see if they are being met throughout the course as well as at the conclusion of the course. You are one of the stakeholder groups whose requirements and expectations must be met. The other groups' requirements are partially reflected in the materials and topic coverage described in the syllabus. What remains to be communicated are your requirements/expectations for this learning process. To stimulate your thoughts and ideas, I have a basic framework in which you can capture your requirements.
  I.   Requirements of the Professor
  II. Requirements of your Fellow Students
  III. Requirements of the Material
  IV. Requirements of Yourself
  V.   Requirements—Others (pp. 286–287)

The survey is distributed to the students on the first day of class. The instrument allows students to bring their concerns into the class. The survey asks students to list their requirements for their professor (such as being energetic, responsive to students' learning needs, available, and prompt about returning assigned work), for the course material (such as being relevant, a resource for later thinking, and manageable in length), for each other (mutual respect, openness, attentive, prepared, and willingness to challenge perspectives), and a final miscellaneous category (such as meeting the ethics requirement for the school!).

The professor then tabulates the results and at the next class meeting informs the students of the most central concerns. Students and the professor learn what requirements are most important to the group as a whole. These then become the requirements for the course. Like Fort and Zollers, I have found that in the three times I have used the TQM survey to date, the technique has three immediate benefits:

First, the exercise provides very helpful information to me about what is important to students. If there are particular things that are helpful to students, I can make adjustments to make sure the class learns in the most effective way. Getting this information early is especially important, given my commitment to an experiential learning approach to teaching business ethics. This way, I am able to get an early indication of students' receptiveness to this pedagogical approach and the degree to which I will need to supplement the approach with other approaches.

Second, occasionally a student requirement cannot be met. Discussing this right away with students is much appreciated and can resolve misunderstandings about the course immediately. For example, it is not unusual for students to come to class believing that by the end of the course they will be able to consult a list of simple do's and don'ts to handle ethical dilemmas. I find that it is important to quickly dispel this belief and reinforce my belief that ethical dilemmas are far more complicated than that. I also use such opportunities to explain that we will be using codes of ethics mainly as broad (and suggestive) normative guidelines for behavior, not as definitive specifications for ethical decision making. Related to this is the expectation that I will be foisting upon them my moral biases and expecting them to adopt my ethical views. As with the issue of ethical do's and don'ts, such misunderstandings must be handled early in the course.

Third, the survey sends an early message about the importance of student involvement to the success of the class. That message is emphasized by the respect I show for students' ideas, as evidenced by using the instrument.

Fort and Zollers (1999) suggest as a follow-up technique the appointment of a group of four or five randomly selected students to conduct an oral in-class assessment of how well the requirements are being met. (I have found it useful to appoint other groups of students to take on this responsibility one-third and two-thirds of the way through the course. This way more students are involved in the class assessment effort). This group assessment activity also promotes trust in the classroom and sends a valuable message to the students about the professor's respect for and commitment to them.

I encourage you to take the time to read Fort and Zollers's article, which offers other valuable insights on (1) "nominating" and "electing" class virtues and telling personal stories of moral action and (2) how classes can be organized to operate by leading business ethics theories (i.e., social contract, rights, stakeholder, and virtue) that can lead to a "community" seeking and discovering moral truth, which in turn can help build a climate of trust in the classroom.

Another option I have found useful in my efforts to develop the psychological contract in my business ethics teaching efforts is an experiential exercise called "Instructor/Student Interview" adapted from Kolb et al. (1974). It is offered here for your consideration in the form I actually use.

INSTRUCTOR/STUDENT INTERVIEW: DEVELOPING THE PSYCHOLOGICAL CONTRACT

Total time suggested: 1 hour

A. PURPOSE

The goal of the exercise is to make explicit and share some of the major expectations and obligations between students and instructors. It provides an opportunity for the instructor to find out what the class expects and for the students to learn what the instructor expects.

B. PROCEDURES

Part A: Instructor's Interview of Students

Step 1: The class forms into groups of four to five persons.

Step 2: Each group elects one person as representative.

Step 3: Each group prepares its representative for the interview and should be sure that the representative understands the group's position. (See the Suggested Question Guide for Instructor's Interview of Students.)

Time suggested for Steps 1 to 3: 15 minutes

Step 4: The representatives, one from each group, meet with the instructor. The instructor interviews them about their expectations while the rest of the class observes.

Time suggested for Step 4: 20 minutes

SUGGESTED QUESTION GUIDE FOR INSTRUCTOR'S INTERVIEW OF STUDENTS

1. What are your objectives for this course?
   a. To learn theories?
   b. To reach some desired level of knowledge?
   c. To learn new skills?

    d. To gain new behaviors?

    e. To get a good grade?

    f. To get required credit hours?

2. How can the instructor best help you to achieve your goals?

    a. By giving lectures?

    b. By assigning and discussing readings?

    c. By giving exams?

    d. By leading seminar discussions?

    e. By relating personal experiences?

    f. By letting you work on your own?

    g. By being a stern task master?

    h. By being warm and supportive?

3. How can other class members help you achieve your goals?

    a. By sharing prior experiences?

    b. By participating in group discussions?

    c. By coming to class prepared?

    d. By sharing educational background?

    e. By doing nothing?

    f. By being enthusiastic and supportive?

    g. By being critical?

    h. By being flattering?

    i. By giving honest appraisals?

4. How should class members be evaluated?

    a. By quizzes, exams, and tests?

    b. By written assignments (essays, journals, PAAs)?

    c. By instructor?

    d. By peers?

    e. By quantity and quality of work?

5. How should the class be motivated and how would you in reality act toward this motivation?

    a. By self-motiavtion?

    b. By peer pressure?

    c. By instructor pressure?

    d. By class interest?

    e. By grade pressure?

6. What is the best thing that could happen in this class?

Part B: What Do I Want from This Course?

A. PURPOSE

1. To focus on key goals for this course.
2. To share expectations of what you want from this course.
3. To form a psychological contract for the class.

B. PROCEDURES

Step 1: Individually complete Column 1 of the Psychological Contract Worksheet.

Step 2: In small groups, exchange views, achieve consensus in completing Column II of the Worksheet, and develop group responses to the questions.

Step 3: Each group discusses any questions it would like its representative to ask the instructor. The representative should be sure to understand the group's questions and concerns. (See the Suggested Question Guide for Students' Interview of Instructor.)

Time suggested for Steps 1 to 3: 15 minutes

Step 4: The representatives, one from each group, interview the instructor to clarify the instructor's expectations of the class.

Time suggested for Step 4: 20 minutes

It might be helpful to incorporate into Step 4 the following: The representatives and the instructor should write on the blackboard a consensus of course objectives. This will not only reaffirm and support objectives listed in the syllabus (by allowing the class to come up with the objectives) but will also allow the students and instructor to delete or add other objectives that they feel may be important to the learning process.

The Psychological Contract Worksheet

Issues	Column I Individual Responses	Column II Group Responses
1. What were your expectations of this course when you enrolled in it?	_____	_____
2. What do you expect to get out of this course?	_____	_____
3. What will be the most enjoyable part of this course?	_____	_____
4. What skills must you work on?	_____	_____

SUGGESTED QUESTION GUIDE FOR STUDENT'S INTERVIEW OF INSTRUCTOR

You may ask the instructor any questions you feel are relevant to effective learning. Some areas you may want to discuss are:

1. How do people learn?
2. What are expectations about attendance?
3. What is the philosophy of evaluation? How are students evaluated?
4. What is the instructor's role in the class?
5. What stereotypes about students are held?
6. Is there anything else that you feel is important?

Part C: Identifying and Establishing Norms

Step 1: Meeting in the class session, discuss the following:

1. What are the pivotal and peripheral norms that are being established?
2. Which of these norms are functional or dysfunctional to the class?
3. Which of these norms would you like to change?
4. Do you have any additional behaviors you would like to see become norms?
5. How much trust is being developed among students, and between students and instructor?

Step 2: For the norms you would like to change, make some specific plans for the changes.

Time suggested for Steps 1 and 2: 15 minutes

Creation of a classroom climate that encourages students to share experiences is important for developing trust and also for setting the groundwork for dialogue, good moral conversation, conversational learning, and debriefing the business ethics education experiences. Debriefing is discussed in Chapter 11. The "Instructor/Student Interview" exercise will also be used to demonstrate debriefing in action in Chapter 11.

It is important for business ethics teachers to understand that there are times when student and faculty expectations are congruous. To communicate expectations, teachers should spend time discussing with students and other key stakeholders the objectives or purpose of the business ethics teaching effort, learning needs, and the strategies to be used to develop students' knowledge, skills, abilities, and attitudes. This means that business ethics teachers must go beyond simply including their expectations in the syllabus. Typical questions that business ethics teachers might ask students to help identify expectations throughout a business ethics teaching effort include:

1. What two or three things are most important to you in this business ethics course or class?
2. Do you feel that your learning needs are being fully addressed in this course? Previous courses? Why or why not?
3. If you had complete freedom to reconstruct this course, what changes would you make?

4. How would you describe the positive and negative aspects of this or previous business ethics classes, courses, or exercises?
5. How well does/has the business school course(s) meet/met your personal needs?
6. What do you think this course expects of you at this point?
7. What are the objectives of this class or course?

While not all encompassing, these questions can help define changing expectations and current fit between faculty and the student expectations. Consider the question "How well does the course meet your personal needs?" If the answer is primarily negative, modification of the course, improved management, or some change in teaching/learning methods may be necessary. However, a positive answer may indicate that faculty and students should move on with the learning effort.

CONCLUSION

The psychological contract is an implicit, yet important agreement among students, business ethics teachers, and a business school. It should specify what each expects to give and receive from the others in the learning relationship. The process goes to the heart of motivation, productivity, learning program satisfaction, involvement, and the management of the learning environment. There are a number of general points that result when business ethics teachers take the time to develop the learning climate in their business ethics teaching efforts. First, the development of a psychological contract early in the learning process is very important and as such is worth managing carefully. Second, what you don't know *can* hurt you. A clear understanding of one's own expectations as well as the other parties' will help form better contracts. Third, the key to contract formulation is achieving a match or a fit, *not* getting more, or the best, or whatever. Fourth, if students and the business ethics teacher have one or more very central basic mismatches, it may be counterproductive for all involved in the teaching and learning effort. Finally, with the development of matches in the psychological contract, students can begin the process of self-directed learning throughout their business ethics education and overall experience.

Business ethics teaching efforts that have clearly defined objectives should come close to meeting the expectations of students. Likewise, business ethics teachers should have the knowledge, skills, and abilities to help create sound psychological contracts that will develop the learning climate and improve the teaching and learning of business ethics. In the final analysis, the payoff for business ethics teachers depends on their awareness of the importance of psychological contracts and on their creativity in finding solutions for better management of the learning environment. The business ethics teacher, the students, and the business school all stand to gain.

REFERENCES

Fort, T.L., & Zoellers, F.E. 1996. Total quality management in the classroom. *Journal of Legal Studies Education* 14: 1.

Fort, T.L., & Zoellers, F.E. 1999. Teaching business ethics: Theory and practice. *Teaching Business Ethics* 2: 273–290.

Hiemstra, R. 1991. Aspects of effective learning environments. In R. Hiemstra (ed.), *New directions for adult and continuing education: No. 50. Creating environments for effective adult learning.* San Francisco: Jossey-Bass.

Knowles, M.S. 1980. *The modern practice of adult education: From pedagogy to andragogy* (rev. ed.). New York: Cambridge University Press.

Knox, A.B. 1986. *Helping adults learn.* San Francisco: Jossey-Bass.

Kolb, D.A. 1974. *Organizational Psychology.* Englewood Cliffs, NJ: Prentice Hall.

Kotter, J.P. 1973. The psychological contract: Managing the joining-up process. *California Management Review* 25(3): 91–99.

Sherwood, J., & Glidewell, J. 1971. Planned renegotiation: A norm OD intervention. Paper No. 338, Herman C. Krannert Graduate School of Industrial Administration, Purdue University, Lafayette, IN.

Sims, R.R. Forthcoming. Business ethics teaching for effective learning. *Teaching Business Ethics.*

Vosko, R.S. 1991. Where we learn shapes our learning. In: R. Hiemstra (ed.), *New directions for adult and continuing education: No. 50. Creating environments for effective adult learning.* San Francisco: Jossey-Bass.

Chapter 10

Teaching Business Ethics: Dialogue, Good Moral Conversation, and Conversational Learning

INTRODUCTION

"We have cast our own lot with learning, and learning will pull us through. But this learning must be reimbued with the texture and feeling of human experiences shared and interpreted through dialogue with each other" (Kolb, 1984, p. 2). Business ethics education requires attitude and behavioral change—an unprecedented and daring undertaking for the classroom. Teaching and learning about ethics evoke high anxiety and often fear in their most seasoned citizens—teachers, students, and administrators alike. As a subject matter, ethics education has few equals in terms of uncertainty of outcome. Awareness of the strong tone of beliefs and emotion generated when ethical issues are discussed leads to expressions of dismay at a trend that focuses on course content in business ethics education without attending to issues of process. It has been my experience that it is very difficult to talk about ethics, values, beliefs, morals, virtue, integrity, and so forth in a meaningful way without also talking and learning about values, beliefs, morals, virtue, integrity, and so forth. The introduction to these and other ethically related issues often generates powerful emotional responses in students, ranging from self-doubt and shame to frustration and confusion. These emotional responses, if not addressed, can result in student resistance.

Feeling safe in the classroom takes on an added significance in business ethics education. Students must feel supported and believe that they can make choices about the process of learning as they venture into what for many is unchartered territory. New experience is the foundation of learning; however, a sense of security must be attained before learners can begin

to consider the unfamiliar (Fry & Kolb, 1979). Trust is critical and enhanced by guidelines and group norms that encourage participation, risk
taking, self-disclosure, mutual support, and dialogue (Schor, 1993).

This chapter takes a closer look at building a classroom learning environment. More specifically, the chapter discusses the importance of dialogue, good moral conversation, and conversational learning to teaching
business ethics for effective learning.

DIALOGUE

Business ethics education without dialogue is programmed for failure.
Providing a forum for dialogue is one of the most proactive gestures educators can make to enhance business ethics teaching efforts. Business ethics
is a source of learning and good conversation is a means of acquiring learning from business ethics. Ideal speech, ideal listening, discourse in relationship, and promotion of the different voices on ethics are necessary
components of a good conversation among students who are learning about
business ethics.

The greatest merit of a dialogue is its practicality. Dialogue, however,
must subscribe to what is termed "the new decorum," which requires us
to listen to others and engage in a moderate tone of conversation. Dialogue
plays a role in identity formation. Self-awareness is facilitated by self-
disclosure and interaction with others (Jourard, 1971). When in the process
of dialogue, each party recognizes the identity of the other, both are then
able to understand better their individual identities. Through dialogue we
create a broader horizon that serves as the backdrop against which we
operate in the world. This broader horizon results from the "fusion of
horizons"—situating one possibility, our usual standard, along side other
possibilities, new and unfamiliar standards (Taylor, 1992).

Experiential learning theory insists that genuine learning only occurs
when students are engaged in "praxis"—political action informed by reflection (Freire, 1973). A fundamental aspect of praxis is the process of
"naming the world." Naming the world is achieved through dialogue
among equals, a dual process of inquiry and learning. Progressive business
ethics education rejects the banking concept of teaching, where students are
passive receptacles for deposits of fixed content from teachers. The idea is
to instill "critical consciousness" in students through dialogue among peers
in which the meaning of abstract ethical concepts is explored. Dialogue is
key to human emancipation of the oppressed (Freire, 1974).

Dialogue is good conversation. It must adhere to rules of the new decorum. Dialogue serves many purposes. It facilitates self-awareness and
awareness of others. It is a source of learning. It is liberating, and it lends
itself to the creation of safety for teaching about business ethics.

Experiential learning theory supports knowledge in business ethics education through the provision of a holistic model and process of learning, a structure and tool for assessing learning preferences, a framework for creating effective learning environments, and dialogue as a vehicle for creating psychological safety in the classroom. Psychological safety opens the door for good moral conversation in business ethics teaching efforts.

GOOD MORAL CONVERSATION

I have found Nash's (1996) approach to ethics discussion very useful for helping me and my colleagues better understand the importance of establishing a classroom climate in which students talk freely and understand the importance of taking risks and sharing their experiences and views with others during the course. According to Nash, a conversation is

literally a manner of living whereby people keep company with each other, and talk together; in good faith, in order to exchange sometimes agreeable, sometimes opposing, ideas. A conversation is not an argument, although it can get heated. A conversation is at its best when the participants are not impatient to conclude their business, but wish instead to spend their time together in order to deepen and enrich their understanding of an idea, or, in our case, the ideas in a text, or of a possible solution to a difficult ethical case. (p. 24)

A conversation that is moral, from the Latin *moralis* (custom), is one whose conventions emphasize the fundamental worth and dignity of each participant in the exchange, and this includes the authors of texts (Nash, 1996), other reading materials, and experiential exercises. Using Nash's view of moral conversation, the best way to get a student to talk openly in class about ethical or other concerns is to treat that student with utmost respect. It is important that we always try to treat students with the highest regard in our role as teachers in the sense that we believe all of them have a share of moral truth. That is, that no one of us has a corner on the market of ethical or other insight. No one of us inhabits the moral high ground a priori. Nash (1996) suggests that we are all moral *viators* (travelers with a purpose) on a journey to find meaning in the work we do (and in our personal life beyond work), and because our journey is our own, it possesses intrinsic worth and is to be respected.

The primary purpose of engaging in moral conversation in teaching business ethics efforts is to test, expand, enrich, and deepen students' understanding of business ethics so that each student can better apply general ethical theories, principles, rules, virtues, structures, moral ideals, and background beliefs to problems encountered in business. With the ideal of the moral conversation in mind, Nash (1996) suggests that students (and the instructor) can be genuinely respectful of one another's efforts as they work through difficult readings, scenarios, and exercises; find common classroom language to express individual interpretations of the readings, scenarios and exercises; and take conversational risks in constructing a more cogent moral discourse.

In brief, then, good moral conversation in any business ethics teaching effort starts with (adapted from Nash, 1996, p. 25):

1. An honest effort to come to class prepared (i.e., having read and come to some understanding of the material, completed pre-work on experiential learning exercises, etc.).
2. An acute awareness that we all have moral biases and blindspots.
3. An open-mindedness about the possibility of learning something from both the assigned readings and one's peers in conversation.
4. A willingness to improve current moral language.[1]
5. A conscious effort to refrain from advancing one's own current moral language as if it were best.
6. An inclination to listen intently in order to grasp the meaning of other people's languages for expressing their moral truths.
7. An agreement that clarifying, questioning, challenging, exemplifying, and applying ideas are activities to be done in a self- and other-respecting way.
8. A realization that we will frequently get off course in our conversations because a spirit of charity, intellectual curiosity, and even playfulness will characterize many of our discussions and because, as David Bromwich (1992) says: "The good conversation is not truth, or right, or anything else that may come out at the end of it, but the activity itself in its constant relation to life" (pp. 131–132).
9. An appreciation of the reality that it will take time for us to get to know one another and a realization that eventually we will find ways to engage in robust, candid, and challenging conversation about ethics without being so "nice" that we bore each other to death, or without being so hostile that we cripple each other emotionally and intellectually.

It is one thing to speak of the importance of dialogue and good moral conversation and another to bring it to fruition. One way of doing this is to focus on conversational learning in business ethics teaching efforts.

CONVERSATIONAL LEARNING IN TBE

Addressing potential and existing ethical problems, challenges, or decisions in today's world of work requires one to recognize that *conversations* among a variety of stakeholders with vastly different views are imperative. According to Alan Webber (1993), formerly a managing editor/editorial director of the *Harvard Business Review* and a founding editor of *Fast Company*, "The most important work in the new economy is creating conversations. . . . But all depends on the quality of the conversations. . . . Conversations—not rank, title, or the trappings of power—determine who is literally and figuratively 'in the loop' and who is not" (p. 28). The new economy is dependent upon the ease, frequency, and quality of conversations within and among organizations and communities. It is also dependent, in my view, on the successful teaching of business ethics and the creation of a classroom climate conducive to good moral conversation and effective ethics learning.

Building upon the work of many people, including Alan Webber (1993) and David Whyte (1996), a poet who consults with many of the most successful global organizations, I think it is important that we call for a new kind of conversation in the business ethics classroom—*conversational learning*. Because the quality of conversations is so critical, the nature, intentions, and contexts surrounding conversations need to improve, leading to a new role for the business ethics teacher vis-à-vis the increasing demands or pressures to teach business ethics and prepare students for the ethical challenges presented by changes in the new economy.

A conversational learning approach is especially advantageous for business ethics teaching efforts that so often involve:

- Recognition of student differences as essential for the continuous learning required.
- Collaborative learning among students with differing ethical backgrounds, worldviews, skills, areas of expertise, vocabularies, and so on.

There are many unexamined assumptions that could limit the capacity for the kind of learning needed among students. Some of these include: their varying preferences and expectations about how ethical decisions should be made; appropriate styles for speaking and presenting themselves; who, if anyone, in the classroom can be trusted enough to take risks with and share their thoughts, feelings, and/or opinions with on complex and sensitive ethical or moral issues; whether the total class should get down to the business of tackling complex ethical theories and issues immediately or should spend some time getting to know one another first; and who has power and who does not have power as well as perceptions about sources of power (i.e., positional, personal, authority, influence, etc.). For example, some students may have no difficulty jumping in and sharing their views or participating in experientially oriented exercises and other activities. On the other hand, other students may initially be reluctant to speak.

Given the fears, challenges, and opportunities that come with any business ethics teaching effort, how is conversational learning relevant? How can a conversational learning approach contribute to the business ethics teacher's capacity to possibly reframe student perceptions of business ethics, in general, and ways of responding to ethical situations differently, in particular? What is involved in conversational learning in a business ethics teaching effort?

The concept of learning used in this chapter is grounded in experience and is described by Kolb (1984) as "a process whereby knowledge is created through the transformation of experience" (p. 41). Conversational learning eludes precise definition. Yet, some parameters may be helpful as a guide. Much of the spirit of conversational learning rests in this message from Howard Stein (1994):

To listen is to unearth rather than to bury. It is to feel rather than to be compelled to act. It gives us all greater liberty and responsibility in our actions. . . . The heart of listening deeply . . . is attentiveness to others' voices . . . the capacity for surprise in the face of any and all planning. Serendipity is readiness and playfulness in the face of surprise . . . incorporation of the astonishing into the ordinary, the refusal to hide behind a shield of routine. It is a willingness to be moved, changed . . . letting go of control. (p. 111)

To support the kind of listening that Stein is describing, the creation of receptive spaces for conversations is essential in business ethics teaching efforts. When these safe, receptive spaces in the classroom are created and held sacred, students can learn to listen deeply to their own inner voices and to the voices of others—to listen in the spirit of learning, of being surprised, of being willing to slow down and reflect upon new possibilities, and of letting go of control.

These kinds of conversations are essential to create a classroom climate in which students are open to listening and learning and to facilitate the reframing of how students conceive of and encounter business ethics. Conversational learning requires many substantial shifts in thinking for most students, including:

- Listening to others with the intention of learning with them.
- Reflecting intentionally to gain more understanding of the complexities of organizational life, using Schon's (1983) model of the reflective practitioner.
- Moving away from the assumption that there is one way of thinking (either/or) toward the assumption that there are multiple legitimate and viable perspectives and possibilities in any situation.
- Moving away from the assumption that there is a right answer or a right approach in each ethical situation toward placing more value on trying to learn from the multiple perspectives of as many other people as is reasonably possible.
- Avoiding reactive behavior by becoming highly proactive in anticipating potential ethical or moral dilemmas and finding different ways to learn from different perspectives about how one might address such dilemmas.

THE BUSINESS ETHICS TEACHER'S ROLE IN A CONVERSATIONAL LEARNING APPROACH

Now let's consider the implications for the teacher who must create this new kind of conversation among students in business ethics teaching efforts. How would the business ethics teacher's work look different? What competencies and skills would be necessary? The intent in this section is to list some especially relevant implications.

While in no way conclusive, some of the implications for the role of the business ethics teacher include things that typically apply in all teaching engagements but have a special slant when the primary intention is to create a new kind of conversation that promotes learning and sustainable change. These include:

- Doing one's own personal work first.
- Preparing the soil (i.e., the context, the space, the students) to build as much psychological safety as possible.
- Attending with special care to *beginnings*.
- Broadening and sharing views and experiential histories (ethical or moral stories) among students who participate in the business ethics teaching effort.
- Emphasizing reflection as an essential part of learning, and working to improve the quality of reflection.
- Emphasizing the relational, social dimensions of learning in the classroom, thus, transforming the notion of conversations and relationship building as essential to the learning rather than as a divergence from learning.
- Building competence and confidence among students so that they will ask questions that delve below the surface, grapple constructively with ethical or moral issues and conflicts, stay engaged with differing perspectives even when their instincts are to avoid or react, and be able to recognize when and how to allow differences to emerge and be explored and when and how to set appropriate boundaries.
- Proactively creating new patterns and routines with students that will anticipate personal learning (and change) opportunities and will enable and support continuous conversational learning.

Many of these approaches function like overlapping layers of a textured fabric and serve to make it more durable, since the use of one will often reinforce or strengthen the intentions of several others. Therefore, many of the descriptions that follow are grouped by similar content and also highlight some of these overlapping uses. For example, I have used many of the illustrations of ways to broaden and share views and experiential histories at the beginning of business ethics teaching efforts to prepare the context and prime students to learn together collaboratively.

Self. "Doing one's own personal work first" is one of the guiding principles of responsible, professional teaching. In other words, knowing our strengths and shortcomings, being honest with ourselves, continuously striving to increase our ethical (and other) self-awareness, seeking and listening to feedback from responsible peers and colleagues, knowing our own personal "hot buttons" and how to anticipate and deal with them responsibly, being able to work from a centered place of a commitment to guide students to find their own paths forward rather than falling into the pattern of imposing our ways upon them are all part of "doing one's own work." Yet, to be able to create a climate conducive to learning, to model conversational learning, to guide students toward developing their own competence in conversational learning, and to authentically prepare them for the possible tumultuous short-term educational consequences and resistance to this approach requires business ethics teachers to be on a lifelong journey of doing their own personal work. This approach is not "business as usual" because it calls for *listening to learn* and *ongoing changes*, not just in students, but also within each of us as business ethics teachers.

Without having a fairly well-developed ethical self-awareness and acceptance of one's own self, it is difficult to listen deeply to others in ways that are open to surprise and hearing new possibilities. Without the calming effect of an authentic acceptance of multiple perspectives, it is difficult to help students create safe learning environments that seek alternative and perhaps competing ethical and other perspectives. Without openness to learning from the differences in others, it is difficult to get students to embark upon conversations that raise differing perspectives and to remain engaged with them when the inevitable tension surfaces. Without an understanding that remaining engaged constructively with differing perspectives is an essential part of a classroom climate conducive to learning about business ethics, it is difficult to stand shoulder to shoulder with students and interact with them in developing their skills of constructive engagement in conflict in general and even more so in conflict involving ethical, moral, or related "hot button" issues.

Preparing and Beginnings. "Preparing the soil" is a metaphor that may be the quintessential image that encompasses the message of this chapter. Whether in initial interactions with the whole group of students, with individual students, with groups of students assigned to work together during the business ethics teaching effort, or with external associates (i.e., colleagues, potential employers, etc.), the preparation of the soil—the context, the space, the people—may be the most indispensable part of the process.

Without a receptive space to hold and sustain conversational interactions and relationship building, the question asking and risk taking associated with learning will be curtailed. Without a strong sense of psychological safety (Edmondson, 1999; Schein, 1999), risk taking, sharing, and differences will not surface directly in ways that catalyze learning. Instead the results typically will covertly lead to destructive behavior such as:

• Avoidance
• Reactions
• Alienation
• Passive-aggressive behavior

All of these drain energy and resources from the objectives, primary missions, and tasks at hand in the business ethics teaching effort.

While trust and safety are easy to destroy by a judgmental comment, a broken promise, or a lie, rebuilding that trust and sense of safety can take endless energy and time. On the other hand, attending in the beginning of new business ethics education efforts to carefully and consistently creating a shared sense of trust and psychological safety takes far less time and effort in the long run. Furthermore, acknowledging and taking responsibility for less constructive behavior and talking about it in the group can make the inevitable human foibles much less destructive and offer potent teachable moments. Thus, from the first contact with student groups to each additional new beginning of the teaching initiative, the business ethics teacher has powerful opportunities to model and help others recognize the potential of being able to venture into conversations and relational interactions that can create new ways of knowing and understanding, which would never have been possible without trust, safety, and those connections (Gadamer, 1994).

As highlighted in previous discussions on my efforts to create a certain kind of classroom climate in my business ethics teaching efforts, I begin during the first or second meeting with the students to try to establish a relationship of trust and respect by being very candid about my values and approach as a teacher (i.e., my bias or comfort with an experiential learning approach to teaching).

I also make it a point to let students know that I am there to learn from them and that I am committed to building a relationship with each of them based on mutual trust and respect. I assure them that whenever any of them ask to speak to me in confidence, I will respect their wish for confidentiality. I also stress the point that I hope to be perceived as an independent neutral in the volatile or conflictual situations that often arise between students.

At the first class meeting, the important part of the syllabus is covered and every effort is made to prepare the context and to begin the learning process in ways that would most likely support collaborative conversational learning. I introduce myself and have students introduce themselves by sharing a bit about their hopes and expectations for our time together (i.e., during the course, workshop, etc.). I pay close attention to the words that are said and the possibilities that are raised as well as those that were not expressed. I make careful mental notes to revisit themes that I want to reinforce and comments that I think might need to be unobtrusively re-framed later.

I also talk very briefly about my hopes and expectations with the intention of beginning to help students develop some jointly shared superordinate goals that would call forth the most generous and community-minded intentions, using what I refer to in the next section as a brief (not more than 10 minutes maximum) lecturette given in a conversational manner without notes and using frequent examples that students can relate to easily.

As part of the first two class meetings, I also ask students to imagine the ideal kinds of conversations that the group might have together and to jot down some of the characteristics of what those conversations might sound like. I suggest that we do some brainstorming (offering ideas without evaluation or discussion until all ideas are on the blackboard or flip chart paper) to generate together possible norms for us to use in all of our subsequent conversations. I also come prepared with ideas that I feel are important and add suggestions for possible norms. After ideas are captured in writing, we talk collectively about the items on the list and gradually work toward a consensus—an understanding that while each item might not be shared by everyone with the same enthusiasm, each item remaining on the list is one that people can "live with" as a shared norm. This consensus is usually reached fairly quickly. A large poster of the list is printed and posted in all subsequent meetings of the group, and copies are given to each student at the class meeting. The list of norms are often revisited and slightly modified in light of student reflection after the first class meeting. This list, developed by this particular group of students, serves as the guide for appropriate ways of communicating during the business ethics education effort.

Broadening and Sharing. One way that student views can be broadened is by asking them to listen carefully to other people's stories of their experiences (i.e., ethical, moral, etc.), expanding the range of authentic possibilities. Stories, unlike the abstract declaration of ideas, can engage people in the possibilities of varied ways of growing up and developing and do so in ways that may generate more empathetic and careful consideration and attention. For some people, it is difficult to imagine how abstract ideas separated from personal experience would manifest in actual behavior. Also, especially when abstract ideas are presented, unless a speaker is especially attuned to the choice of words, tone of voice, verbal and nonverbal attitude, and so on, listeners may feel that they are being preached to, generating a reaction against the content and interfering with possible new learning and reflections. This distinction between ideas and stories is exquisitely illustrated in the following quote from Alice Walker's novel, *By the Light of My Father's Smile.* The quote is from a conversation between two of the characters in the book, one of whom is a Mundo, an indigenous population in Latin America:

No one among the Mundo believes there is anyone on earth who truly knows anything about why we are here, Senor. To even have an idea about it would require a very big brain. A computer. That is why, instead of ideas, the Mundo have stories.

You are saying . . . that stories have more room in them than ideas?

That is correct, Senor. It is as if ideas are made of blocks. Rigid and hard. And stories are made of a gauze that is elastic. You can almost see through it, so what is beyond is tantalizing. You can't quite make it out; and because the imagination is always moving forward, you yourself are constantly stretching. Stories are the way spirit is exercised.

But surely your people have ideas, I said.

Of course we do. But we know there is a limit to them. After that, story! (1998, pp. 193–194)

Thus, the story can stir the listener's imagination, tantalize the listener to stay engaged, offer an elastic gauze-like frame within which the listener's own world views can be seen and perhaps expanded. Obviously, the format and the timing for sharing stories in a business ethics teaching effort need to be contextually appropriate and relevant, but often the business ethics teacher's all too frequent assumption is that students just want specific information, a rational approach, the most "efficient" use of time, and so forth. This emphasis, however, usually precludes time for storytelling, when storytelling can serve multiple purposes simultaneously and become a high point early in the business ethics teaching effort. The teaching and organizational learning and change literature (Brown & Duguid, 2000; Schor et al., 1996; Wenger, 1998) is filled with confirmation of the substantial wealth of learning potential that can emerge in the wise use of shared stories and narratives. (See Chapter 8 for more discussion on stories and narratives.)

A few other ways to broaden student views include: brief, easy-to-understand pre-readings to prepare them for group conversations about the readings; brief, easy-to-understand lecturettes by the business ethics teacher or by a highly regarded person who has credibility (guest lecturer) either from within the school of business or from outside; and spontaneous strategic inclusion of the ideas and examples of varied philosophical or business ethics views in group conversations, especially when connections are made as examples to illustrate how differing views are filters through which the world is seen and understood.

In one business ethics teaching effort, after dividing students into groups during the first class and having them develop a list of concerns/fears they had in taking a business ethics course, one member of each group and a colleague did a thematic analysis of the data and then shared during the next class common and unique themes that emerged in the group meetings. A commonly shared theme that ran throughout the group data was the lack of trust students had of each other and the lack of willingness to share. Yet, another common theme was the skepticism they had about the possibility of "really" learning anything about business ethics.

Differences, Reflection, and Learning. Generally, it has been my experience that when students reflect upon their differences on ethics-related issues with other people, the potential for learning from the differences is increased. The likelihood for learning is further increased when the quality of reflection improves. One of the first people to write about organizational learning, which I view as relevant to learning in the business ethics classroom, was Donald Schon (1983), who also has written extensively about practitioners who reflect on their experiences and "stay in conversation" with organizational situations. These reflective practitioners, like effective business ethics teachers, are able to observe and listen intently to recognize how a unique situation is similar and different from previous ones. They are able to reflect upon intended and unintended changes to let each new situation in the organization "talk back" to them and serve as a possible source of learning. Schon, as many others after him, recognized that it is in the differences among people and in the unexpected and unintended changes that the greatest potential for learning can often be found. And yet, it is also in these very circumstances that breakdowns can occur that not only impede business ethics learning but also often lead to misunderstandings, distractions, and lost energy and productivity.

In my view, business schools' students and business teachers typically have limited skills for and little experience with constructive engagement with differences and the surfacing of conflict. The more limited these skills and experiences are, the more likely people are to avoid letting differences come to the surface and be talked about, the more likely people are to avoid others whom they perceive as different, and the more likely people are to become alienated from individuals and parts of the organization (i.e, classroom) that they perceive as different. For example, we all are aware of those courses in which there is a diverse mix of business and nonbusiness majors, who, like our colleagues, often do not talk to one another, may not be open to hearing one another's views, or have misperceptions about one another (i.e., nonbusiness majors often view business majors as "money hungry" and only concerned about the bottom line, while business majors often view liberal arts students as mainly concerned with social issues). This leads to a lack of coordination, at the least, and a lack of potential collaborative energy that could become an invaluable learning resource in business ethics teaching efforts.

It has been my experience that often students from "opposing camps" on various moral or ethical issues, cases, and so forth seldom listen calmly to others who have opposing points of view on these issues. Preparing students to trust that there will be civil conversation, that everyone will be treated with respect, that each person will have a chance to be heard, and that this will not be a futile waste of their time is a challenge that requires the kind of preparation by business ethics teachers described above.

Much of the preparation comes from trying to listen carefully to the unique experiences and perspectives of each student or group and trying to address their concerns. For example, in reference to student fears about sharing and risk taking, I had to assure them that this educational effort or experience would be different, putting my own reputation on the line and activating my own adrenalin at the same time—an effective stimulus for many of us as teachers, but one that creates the kind of stress we know too well.

I strongly believe that the initial class meetings (the beginnings) are always critical for helping business ethics students learn new ways of engaging so that they can *listen to learn* from their individual perspectives or differences. The jointly created norms of conversation provide the framework for a new kind of conversation. I find it very useful to gently intervene when norms are not observed (for example, asking students if they feel we are following our own agreed-upon norms and in some cases naming aggressive behavior when a more gentle approach is not effective). As mentioned earlier, I think it is very important to create a safe, receptive space for conversation by letting students know up front that I will intervene whenever necessary to assure that each student is treated with respect. I ask questions and bring up topics to encourage students to share their views, take risks, and respect one anothers' differences. I also try to model a new kind of conversational interaction in my own behavior. This kind of work requires business ethics teachers to have had training and experience in conflict resolution, facilitation, and group dynamics; to have sensitivity to the experiences of each student in the course or class; and to be open to various moral and ethical views and the need to allow differences to surface to challenge the status quo. For example, those of us who may espouse certain ethical theories or teaching approaches need to grapple extensively with our own biases and the views that we typically have taken for granted if we are going to have any credibility and viability in teaching business ethics and creating a new kind of conversation among diverse students.

Relational and Proactive. When business ethics learning is happening in or out of the classroom, it is taking place at and across multiple levels (i.e., at the individual level, the group level, the course level, and the business school level). As a business ethics teacher, being able to be proactive, rather than reactive, at each level to the dynamics of ethical and moral situations, challenges, opportunities, dilemmas, and so forth demands a relational orientation to the learning process. While an emphasis on relationships and social interactions is embedded in the business education and training of most students, the pervasiveness of relational dynamics is intensified in today's increasingly global world of work (a world that exposes employees to increasingly diverse ethical or moral views) where "conversation" and collaboration are the essence of the work.

In teaching business ethics, the preparation and beginnings elements must be interwoven with the ever-changing work environment that confronts students. Recognizing and being able to track the relational dynamics that are occurring on all levels simultaneously is in my view one of the biggest challenges, requiring me to structure my own frequent reflection upon the business ethics teaching effort to learn from the "talk back" or debriefing of each unique situation. Spending structured and unstructured time in the first few meetings to help students begin to build new relationships is critical.

For example, in one second class meeting, we did a visioning exercise. Each student wrote words on index cards that described their ideal images for the ethical organization. These cards were then posted on the walls of the room. Students were then asked to walk silently around the room reading all the cards. This was followed by time for group reflection, during which the conversation brought out what students noticed as they silently read the cards. Overwhelmingly, the main impression was the similarity of the images of what they wanted for an ethical organization—a transformation from seeing themselves as having very different views into a growing recognition that they shared more common ground than they had imagined. I have found this frequently to be the case, given the number of business and nonbusiness majors that are in the same business ethics or Business and Society course.

The instilliation of practical discourse or what has been referred to in this chapter as conversational learning is key to teaching business ethics and developing integrity in our business students (see Chapter 3 for more on open communication). Business ethics teachers must give voice to all relevant constituents, and especially students in the classroom. Further, as one author suggests, and I wholeheartedly agree, "The disposition to hear and be concerned for others is something that must be learned and cultivated, preferably throughout one's entire education, but certainly it needs to be encouraged and reinforced in the business curriculum" (Carroll, 1998).

As business ethics teachers we have a responsibility to create classroom learning environments that value the ideas others have to offer. This means providing students with the information they need to make informed decisions and to assess various ethical theories or philosophical approaches. It also demands open-mindedness and an intense respect for what others may view as the truth, even when it may be counter to our own view. The very act of participating in conversational learning suggests that in some instances there can be genuine consensus and that this can be distinguished from false consensus. We must make sure that the classroom environment is free from constraint and that every student has an equal opportunity to be heard. This means each student has the same chance to command, to oppose, to permit, or to forbid, and to express his or her attitudes, feelings, and intentions.

Conversational learning should be built into the curriculum itself and developed as a skill at the pre-professional level. Teaching business ethics efforts as well as all other business education efforts should be geared to consciously and sincerely taking into account what others have to say. This is essential to the integration of ethics into business education and teaching business ethics for effective learning.

CONCLUSION

By building the capacity for a new kind of conversation, the possibilities for enhancing learning and the ability to carry skills from the business ethics classroom to the business world are limitless. To be most effective as business ethics teachers, I believe we must help our students develop a new kind of conversation in the classroom. It is also important for us to be on a personal lifelong journey of increasing ethical self-awareness, to collaboratively reframe perceptions of teaching and learning business ethics, to develop increased skills in conflict resolution, and to collaboratively create with our students receptive conversational spaces imbued with psychological safety.

With the increasing complexity of business ethics and knowledge-intensive work in a pluralistic world, the nature, intentions, and contexts that surround conversations need to be given considerable attention—leading to an important role for the business ethics teacher vis-à-vis building continuous learning opportunities in the classroom. Classrooms that encourage dialogue, good moral conversation, and conversational learning contribute to business ethics teaching for effective learning.

NOTE

1. Nash (1991) suggests that there are three different kinds of moral language: background belief, character, and principle. When he uses the term language he is referring to a certain mode of moral discourse, one which features a particular type of vocabulary that both reflects and shapes a particular sociocultural context and professional organization and that prescribes and proscribes certain kinds of virtuous and vicious behaviors as well as certain kinds of judgements and decisions.

REFERENCES

Bromwich, D. 1992. *Politics by other means: Higher education and group thinking.* New Haven, CT: Yale University Press.

Brown, J.S., & Duguid, P. 2000. *The social life of organization*. Boston: Harvard Business School Press.

Carroll, R.F. 1998. The integrity factor—critical to accounting education. *Teaching Business Ethics* 2: 137–163.

Edmondson, A. 1999. Psychological safety and learning behavior. *Administrative Science Quarterly* 44: 350–383.

Freire, P. 1973. *Education for critical consciousness*. New York: Continuum.

Freire, P. 1974. *Pedagogy of the oppressed*. New York: Continuum.

Fry, R., & Kolb, D.A. 1979. Experiential learning theory and learning experiences in liberal arts education. *New Directions for Experiential Learning* 6: 79–92.

Gadamer, H.G. 1994. *Truth and method* (2nd rev. ed.). New York: Crossroad. (Originally published in 1989.)

Jourard, S.M. 1971. *The transparent self*. New York: Van Nostrand Reinhold.

Kolb, D.A. 1984. *Experiential learning: Experience as the source of learning and development*. Englewood Cliffs, NJ: Prentice Hall.

Nash, R.J. 1991. Three conceptions of ethics for teacher educators. *Journal of Teacher Education* (May–June): 163–172.

Nash, R.J. 1996. *"Real world" ethics: Frameworks for educators and human service professionals*. New York: Teachers College Press.

Schein, E.H. 1999. *The corporate culture survival guide*. San Francisco: Jossey-Bass.

Schon, D.A. 1983. *The reflective practitioner: How professionals think in action*. New York: Basic Books.

Schor, S.M. 1993. Understanding and appreciating diversity: The experiences of a diversity educator. In R.R. Sims & R.F. Dennehy (eds.), *Diversity and differences in organizations: An agenda for answers and questions*. Westport, CT: Quorum Books, pp. 73–92.

Schor, S.M., Sims, R.R., & Dennehy, R.F. 1996. Power and diversity: Sensitizing yourself and others through self-reflection and storytelling. *Journal of Management Education* 20(2): 242–257.

Sims, R.R. Forthcoming. Business ethics teaching for effective learning. *Teaching Business Ethics*.

Stein, H.F. 1994. *Listening deeply: An approach to understanding and consulting in organizational culture*. Boulder, CO: Westview Press. On-line version, PSOL CD, George Mason University.

Taylor, C. 1992. *Multiculturalism and "the politics of recognition": An essay by Charles Taylor*. Princeton, NJ: Princeton University Press.

Walker, A. 1998. *By the light of my father's smile*. New York: Ballantine Books.

Webber, A.M. 1993. What's so new about the new economy? *Harvard Business Review* (January–February): 24–42.

Wenger, E. 1998. *Communities of practice: Learning, meaning, and identity*. New York: Cambridge University Press.

Whyte, D. 1996. *The heart aroused: Poetry and the preservation of the soul in corporate America*. New York: Doubleday.

Chapter 11

Debriefing: Completing the Learning Process in Experiential Learning Exercises

INTRODUCTION

My interest in Kolb's (1984) experiential learning theory and my experiences over the years in using experiential learning exercises as techniques for promoting learning have caused me to reflect on the nature of learning. This has been reinforced as I have worked with fellow teachers and trainers to understand something of the nature of learning and of the possible role that experiential learning exercises might play in the promotion of learning. This understanding has been promoted particularly in my business ethics teaching efforts through the use of experiential learning exercises.

An experiential learning exercise is a complex event in business ethics education. It needs to provide students with the basis for understanding why and how the new knowledge they acquire is related to what they already know. It must convey to students the notion that they have the capability to use this new knowledge not only in the classrooms in which they learn it but also in other settings (Lederman, 1992b).

When rigorously administered, experiential learning exercises can be a powerful form of teaching in which participants acquire new knowledge, skills and abilities by internalizing theory through guided practice. Of crucial importance in experiential learning is the often neglected processing stage of an experiential learning exercise known as *debriefing*. The significance of the debriefing in the use of experiential learning exercises to promote learning became more and more evident as I became increasingly familiar with and practiced in the use of its techniques. For our purposes, debriefing refers to the post-experience analysis designed to provide insight into the cases, journalizing, role-plays, or other experiential learning approaches used in teaching business ethics. The purpose of this activity is to use the information generated during the experiential activity to facilitate learning for students. After students have engaged in an experiential learning activity, the debriefing provides insight into the activity. This chapter will focus on the process of debriefing and the post-experience analysis of experiential learning exercises in ethics education. The chapter provides a conceptual model for debriefing using Kolb's (1984) experiential learning cycle and model of the learning process in teaching business ethics and offers practical ideas for applying the model to debriefing experiential learning exercises used in ethics courses. Special attention is first given to a brief discussion of experiential learning exercises as a teaching tool. The importance of the business ethics teacher's role in providing structure and ambiguity in the experiential learning exercises so that learners can personalize the learning is also discussed.

TEACHING VIA EXPERIENTIAL LEARNING EXERCISES

The use and value of experiential learning methods or exercises as a teaching medium are well recognized and have been widely reported. For example, as noted in Chapter 8, in business ethics simulations designed, students can be faced with ethical dilemmas that encourage them to react to problems as though they were in a real-life situation. Role playing also provides students with the opportunity to participate with a high level of personal involvement. Students can be asked to develop a code of ethics for an organization. Similarly, business cases and field-based applications can provide another pedagogical vehicle to actively engage students in analyzing ethical problems and identifying creative resolutions. Providing business students with problems involving improper gifts, kickbacks, and conflicts of interest will develop their ability to analyze unstructured ethical dilemmas and discern alternative courses of action. Requiring students to participate in some form of community service also offers the potential for personal and emotional impact that may be difficult to capture through traditional classroom learning.

Another familiar experientially oriented pedagogical approach that I have found to be highly effective is scheduling discussions about current events that have ethical ramifications. Reports and individual journals can be prepared from current periodicals based on recent headline-making fraud and embezzlement cases, and the class discussion can focus on how these problems could have been avoided (this also opens the door to a discussion of white-collar crime). It is equally valuable to ask undergraduate business students to examine the ethical code of their college and student body (e.g., honor code, harassment policies) and query graduate business students on the ethical codes of their current or former employers.

The pedagogical approaches presented above all emphasize experiential learning, high participation, and active rather than passive learning. It is critical that experiential learning exercises are carefully designed and thoughtfully executed to include time for debriefing what actually occurred during the exercise.

DEBRIEFING DEFINED

While a number of authors have written about the debriefing process, not all use the term "debriefing" to mean the same thing. We have defined debriefing as the post-experience analysis designed to provide insight into the cases, journalizing, role-plays, or other experiential learning approaches used in teaching business ethics. Pearson and Smith (1986) offer the following insight into the relationship between the experience of learning and the debriefing phase: the "active experience is involving and interesting, even exciting. Debriefing means the cessation of this experiencing and the deliberate decision to reflect on action" (p. 156).

In his model of experiential learning, Thatcher (1986), drawing on the earlier work of Kolb (1984), emphasizes that reflective observation (debriefing) is the crucial link between experience and the process of change that makes the elements of the experience a part of the conceptual foundation of the learner. Thatcher (1986) notes: "Debriefing is the part of the process in which the reflection takes place and from which the change in the person will occur, because it is the part of the activity which focuses on the complex processes which took place in each individual and in the group as a whole" (p. 151).

Debriefing has always been a key component of successful experiential learning exercises. The link between objectives, course materials, and the experiential learning exercise seems rarely, if ever, crystal clear to the participants. In the organizational world, this is even more relevant because some participants resist experiential learning exercises or games when they're "played" with Tinkertoys, Lego blocks, or other related activities.

DEBRIEFING IN BUSINESS ETHICS TEACHING EFFORTS

Every business ethics teaching activity needs a closing. And experiential learning exercises are no exception. Students typically finish some business ethics education activity—a case, role-play, or simulation, for example—and then what? What you do with the final few minutes of each class, module, or experiential learning activity is very important.

Reasons the Last Minutes Are Important

The closing portion of an experiential learning exercise in a business ethics teaching effort usually serves at least three purposes, and sometimes has a fourth as well. The final minutes can serve to:

1. *Relieve Emotional Intensity.* Experiential learning activities can be stressful. Students can be put into new, artificial, and somewhat uncomfortable roles. Often, the experiential learning activities involve competition (even if it is only a matter of two groups playing a game and then reporting their results, or two groups working through a number of issues and decisions on a particular ethical problem. Many students take any form of experiential learning exercises seriously. Furthermore, most experiential learning exercises—no matter how enjoyably designed—deal with serious issues. Individual and organizational performance and success or the future mission and course of the organization may be on the line. Emotions will surface as students grapple with personal values, beliefs, and morals. They need to be acknowledged and aired.

Even if the experiential learning exercise doesn't seem to involve stressful activities or highly personal issues, emotional release is needed. I have found that people have the urge to share, to tell others what they did (or did not do), thought, and felt during the experiential learning exercise. Everyone needs the relief of debriefing, which means that all students should have the chance to comment if they wish.

2. *Solidify the Learning.* During the experiential learning exercise, students will have tried out a new idea, ethical framework, behavior, or skill. Having tried it, they may have questions that didn't arise earlier. Those questions should be answered now so that the students are ready to move on to the next exercise, discussion, or other activity. Once questions are answered, learning can be reinforced by comparing and contrasting the experiences of individual students or groups. Discussing the differences and similarities, linking students' experiences to the intended objectives for the experiential learning exercise or the ethical focus for the day's class, highlights any new insights and draws lessons or conclusions.

3. *Give Immediate Feedback.* By listening to students' comments and questions, the teacher knows whether the intended learning objectives for the exercise or for the day were achieved. In short, you'll learn whether or not students are "still with you." Any concerns can be handled now, before they disrupt the flow of the class, module, or course.

4. *Bring the Class to a Decision by Consensus.* Two points need to be made about consensus. First, not all experiential learning exercises in business ethics teaching efforts lead to decisions, and not all decisions are reached by consensus. Nevertheless, consensus is most consistent with the business ethics teaching goal of concluding the class with an agreed-upon ethical principle, guideline, or major learning to build on for the future. Ideally, there are times when the whole class should be in accord, or at least the majority of students should agree while the minority accepts the outcomes, direction, or key ethical learnings.

Second, consensus is not necessarily needed at the end of each business ethics class. Consensus may sometimes be important at appropriate times during an experiential learning exercise, at the close of an exercise, at appropriate midpoints, or at the end of a series of closely interrelated exercises that focus on particular ethical issues or themes.

For these reasons, not every debriefing of an experiential learning exercise has consensus as one of its purposes. If, however, decision by consensus is a goal for closing or debriefing a class or activity, then I have found that it is best to set expectations at the outset of the class or exercise. In short, I tell students that we will be carrying out exercise X, with the goal of reaching consensus on Y. Or, if necessary, I tell them how a decision will be reached if other than by group consensus.

Hunsaker (1978) provides the following standards for debriefing:

The main function of the facilitator during the debriefing is to insure an integration of the experiences with concepts and applications to outside situations so that appropriate generalizations can be made. It is also important that the facilitator encourage participants to exchange feedback and clarify strengths and weaknesses in their interpersonal behavior. Consequently, the facilitator should direct attention to both the content and process of the exercise with respect to both conceptual and personal learnings. (pp. 3–4)

The debriefing phase can be conceptualized as a dialogue or conversation between the instructor (debriefer) and the students. For example, consider the case of a guest speaker who views environmental pollution and adherence to legal restrictions as an economic problem of profit maximization. The event of the speech provides the opportunity for a follow-up session involving role playing to make certain the issues focused on by the speaker were well understood. A debriefing phase following the speech and subsequent role playing provides the opportunity to address questions such as: "Is there a difference between legal authority and moral authority?" "What is the role of business in society?" "Should the university have censored the speaker's remarks?" "Now that the point of view of the speaker is known, should he be invited to speak again?" "What are the costs to society?" "What if all businesses followed the same practices?" A structured dialogue following such an activity offers valuable opportunities for students to learn and apply this learning to other situations. However, such dialogue can only occur if the teacher takes the time to plan for debriefing.

Planning for Debriefing

The debriefing stage must be planned so that it provides students with continuity of the experience. Without planned debriefing students may lose the learning because they have not had a chance to experience and understand its application. For the experience to be maximally effective for students, therefore, the debriefing must be allocated an adequate amount of time or much of the potential richness of the experience is lost. No exact amount of time for the debriefing is recommended. The faculty member can decide upon the length of the debriefing session. Some of the factors teachers may want to consider when determining the length of the debriefing session include the purpose, complexity, and level of intensity of the exercise; the responsiveness of students; and the format of the debriefing session (e.g., shared work experiences, debriefing game, etc., as discussed later).

A CONCEPTUAL MODEL FOR DEBRIEFING IN BUSINESS ETHICS TEACHING EFFORTS

In order to achieve a level of learning in which students not only absorb the knowledge presented but also apply this learning in practice, it is helpful to consider the entire process of learning and then to apply this learning process specifically to the debriefing session. Therefore, Kolb's experiential learning model will be used to inform and direct our considerations.

As discussed in Chapter 4, the heart of Kolb's model is a cycle of learning. The underlying premise of Kolb's cycle, or learning sequence, is that learners learn best when they are active, take responsibility for their own learning, and can relate and apply what they have learned to their own context. Kolb's cycle of learning proposes four learning modes: concrete experience, reflective observation, abstract conceptualization, and active experimentation. Learning occurs most effectively when all four modes in the cycle of learning are completed.

According to Kolb, we all learn from the experience of doing a task, and the results of that learning can be used constructively and even assessed. But it is not sufficient simply to have an experience in order to learn. Without reflecting on this experience or discussing it with others, it may be rapidly forgotten or its learning potential lost. The feelings and thoughts emerging out of this reflection can fit into a pattern that starts to make sense so that generalizations and concepts can be generated and relationships made with existing theories. And it is generalizations and theories that give the learner the conceptual framework with which to plan and tackle new situations effectively.

What has this to do with the process of debriefing? Debriefing is the part of Kolb's learning cycle in which reflection takes place and from which learning and change in individuals will occur, because it is the part of the activity that focuses on what took place in each individual and in the group as a whole. The debriefing is an important point of learning from Kolb's experiential learning cycle. It is the process by which the experience of an experiential exercise is examined, discussed, and turned into learning.

Kolb et al.'s model of adult learning (1995) defines each stage of the learning process and is presented here for application to debriefing. For each stage, key questions are provided that may help the faculty member progress through the stages, applying each to the debriefing of experiential learning exercises in their business ethics teaching efforts (see Table 11.1). Additional questions are offered by Gaw (1979).

Although students may naturally proceed through some of the stages in Kolb et al.'s (1995) model during a debriefing exercise, often the progression does not result in active experimentation (doing). For example, the faculty member's goal may be to ultimately motivate students to use learned ethical concepts or theories in new situations. Yet, some students may merely conceptualize and not chance practice, while others may try different methods of practice without integrating learned concepts in a meaningful fashion. Through applying Kolb et al.'s model to the debriefing session, however, the teacher can guide students through the stages to achieve active experimentation.

What should occur during the application and transfer stage seems more clearly found in the active experimentation stage as described by Kolb et al. (1995). The focus in the debriefing is to influence people in an active way and to transform situations in a dramatic fashion. It emphasizes practical applications as opposed to reflective understanding, a pragmatic concern with what works as opposed to what is abstract, an emphasis on doing as opposed to observing. Here, the focus is on getting things accomplished and achieving objectives. Impact and influence on the environment are valued. Active experimentation allows for testing the implications of ethical concepts and theories in new situations. These hypotheses are tested on future action, which in turn leads to new experiences.

THE DEBRIEFING MODEL IN ACTION

The following is an example of how I used the debriefing model to debrief a modified version of the experiential learning exercise "Instructor/ Participant Interviews" (Kolb et al., 1995), used in the first two classes of an undergraduate Business and Society course. Briefly, the modified goal of this experiential exercise was for the instructor to learn from students what their expectations for the course are and what they hope to learn; any concerns or fears they might bring into the class; and the virtues, values, or characteristics that they admire and would like an organization (i.e., course) of which they are a member to be guided by. An additional goal was to try to learn what students feel they can contribute to the achievement of their expectations and to the learning process.

During the exercise the instructor first interviewed students. Then representatives of the class interviewed the instructor. Finally, before the debriefing discussion, the whole group compared the interviews and identified potential pinches (differences that will influence the learning process). It should be noted that the exercise was preceded by reading, lecture, and in-

Table 11.1
Debriefing Experiential Learning Exercises by Using the Kolb Model

Stage in Kolb's Model of the Learning Process	Description of Kolb's Stage	Questions for Application of Learning Stage to Stages in Debriefing Session
Concrete Experience (Feeling)	Students objectively describe the experience in terms of who, what, when, where, and how. They also subjectively describe their feelings, perceptions, and thoughts that occurred during (not after) the experience. They tell their story. If the event is stressful, emotional, or disturbing, students can gain composure.	• Did you complete your assignment? • Were the objectives of the assignment clear? • How did you feel?
Reflective Observation (Watching)	At this level, the experience is viewed from different points of view that add more meaning and perspectives to the event. This approach values patience, impartiality, and considered, thoughtful judgement.	• Did you make assumptions about X, Y, Z? • What was happening for you during the exercise? • What did you observe in others? • What did the exercise mean for you and in relation to others? (Clarify differences of opinion.)
Abstract Conceptualization (Thinking)	The debriefing relates ethical concepts, theories, or models from the readings and lectures to the experience in the activity. An original model or theory can be created.	• What policies/rules could you make based on your experience in this exercise? • With what variables would the rules/policies not apply? • Given such variables, what would be a better rule or policy?
Active Experimentation (Doing)	Students apply what has been learned in the experience of the activity to the parallel world outside the classroom. "What if" scenarios may be explored.	• How would you change aspects of the experience for a better outcome? What new strategy would you use? • In what real-world/practical work situations could this new strategy be utilized? • What situations would call for a backup or alternative strategy?

class discussion on Kolb's (1984) experiential learning model and Sherwood and Glidewell's (1972) psychological contract and pinch model discussed in Chapter 6. In preparation for the first two classes, students also read a summary paper on traditional and contemporary ethical theories and models. All of these were intended to begin to develop a classroom climate of trust, openness, and sharing.

In the first step (concrete experience) of debriefing the exercise, students were asked to take three to five minutes to write down their individual feelings, perceptions, and thoughts that occurred during the exercise. The instructor also completed this task at the same time. Students were then asked to take 10 minutes to share their work with other members of the groups in which they were working during the exercise. Following the group discussion, the instructor asked members of each group to share with the whole class some of the information gathered in their group discussion.

Some of the comments generated by students were, "We weren't sure what we were supposed to learn from the first two classes and we all agreed that these classes were very different from other classes we had taken here at the college." "We weren't sure whether or not you really care about our fears, concerns, and expectations, but time will tell!" At this stage of the debriefing process it is important to remember that as the instructor I was concerned with getting as many students' feelings, perceptions, and thoughts expressed as possible. To accomplish this goal I asked students, "Are there any more questions?" and, "Did other groups have similar feelings or thoughts?"

After spending about 10 to 15 minutes on the first stage of the debriefing process, I made a transition to the reflective observation stage by asking students to take a few minutes as a group to look back over what had occurred during the exercise and to reflect on the questions they raised during the first stage of the debriefing process. In particular, I asked them to think about what ways their group's concerns, fears, virtues, values, or characteristics for an organization and the group's expectations and contributions agreed or disagreed with mine. Key questions I posed to students during this stage were: "In looking back over today's exercise and your group's discussion, what did you observe?" "Did you make any assumptions about what I and your other class members expect of you, of this course, of the virtues, values, or characteristics that they admired and would like an organization (i.e., course) to be guided by?" "What did the exercise mean for you and others?" With these questions I tried to concentrate on encouraging students to reflect on their experiences during the exercise and articulate their perspective so that the whole class could explore these understandings and learn from them.

Some points that came out of this reflective observation stage of the debriefing were: "No course we had ever taken had asked us questions like: 'What were my learning objectives for this course?' 'Was I willing to participate actively in the setting of those objectives and in their attainment?' 'What values or norms did we want to use to guide this course?' Several of us think this is what the exercise was all about."

As I reflected upon the comments made by students not only in this course but also in previous courses, I recognized that students have been conditioned to listen and accept objectives, to take a passive role in the learning process, and to not be expected to share their concerns (or fears). Thus, when they were asked during my first class to participate actively in setting objectives and in an active learning process, many of them were unprepared to respond in a meaningful way. As a result, I have found that I have become increasingly sensitive to the need for me, in my role as an instructor, to recognize and appreciate how much diversity there is within the class in students' ability to understand and respond to a different learning expectation and environment. More will be said about the importance of understanding student differences at the end of this chapter.

In the next stage of the debriefing process (abstract conceptualization), I asked the students to first individually think about and then discuss in their groups the following question: "What ethical theories/models or course concepts that you heard about in the lecture or read about in preparation for class relate to your understanding of today's exercise?" While all the groups seemed to respond effectively to the question once the full class discussion began, one group's comments (with a little prodding from me) were clearly on target with the learning and insight I wanted to come out of the exercise and the first two classes. The following comments highlight the result of this debriefing stage: "First, this is to be an active learning experience. This sounds almost trivial but it is the basis of the psychological contract between you (the instructor) and the class (the organization) and furthermore is fundamental to learning in this course." A member of another group followed with: "To be active learners means that I and the rest of the class will learn about business ethics by not only reading but by also actively experiencing situations that require some ethical decision making, etc. We must scrutinize the functioning of individuals, groups, and organizations of which we are members, observe important situations, behaviors, etc., make hypotheses about these interactions, and actively test these hypotheses within the group in order to learn." Finally, after some generous discussion among the students, I pointed out that these comments almost directly flowed from the first element (students are active learners) and the second element (a psychological contract between me as the instructor and them as students).

Not only would conversations be enhanced during the course through dialogue, but students would also have opportunities to apply various ethical theories themselves. Finally, working through the direct application of various ethical theories or models provided a challenging learning experience for the students and the instructor. Students and faculty who seriously work through the application of the material together discover new insights. The elements directly concerned the learning process in which I would engage them in this course and foster the substantive learning and teaching of business ethics itself.

My comments were intended to make a transition in the debriefing discussion from relating concepts and theories of the experience in the activities to focusing on the specifics (or rules of thumb) for students to be active learners in the remainder of the course. Both my own and the students' comments about active learners in my course were the main focus of the active experimentation stage of the debriefing model for the first two classes.

To continue our discussion on active learning, I asked students, "What will you need to do in future classes to meet your own and my expectations for this course?" I specifically asked the students to think about and generate rules of thumb or action resolutions. In response, one group commented, "In the future you [as the instructor] and we as students must take responsibility for raising a pinch [a point of disagreement in the model of psychological contracts] if and when it develops. We thought that pinches could either be raised via written comments or informal discussion, say, at the end of class."

As evidenced in this debriefing example, the richness and strength of using the debriefing model presented above can be enhanced if debriefing proceeds through all of the stages: from concrete experience to reflective observation to abstract conceptualization and, ultimately, to active experimentation. The model allows for testing implications of course concepts and theories in new situations, which, in turn, leads to new experiences and learning.

It is important to note that in the above example two elements in combination led to a higher motivation to learn and provided students with a much better grasp of how the course would be conducted, and that knowledge allayed students' fears (i.e., uncertainty as to material, what is expected of students, and the invasiveness of dealing with "personal" values) often brought into an ethics course. Those two elements are: (1) the psychological contract between the instructor and students and (2) the fact that students have some responsibility for setting the learning objectives. Additionally, when a class agrees to the specific virtues relevant to the conduct of the course, students are provided with assurances of which norms are prescribed and what kind of classroom conduct is expected. Finally, the foundation is established for building a climate of trust and sharing in the classroom. In point of fact, I have found that both my attitude and student attitudes toward learning and our subsequent behavior have reflected these efforts. As a result of using the debriefing model, I believe students are more inquisitive, more committed to learning, and more open to learning about business ethics. In short, they are more involved in the learning process. It has been my experience that this involvement results in large rewards for both the instructor and the students.

DEBRIEFING: COMPLETING THE ENTIRE LEARNING EXPERIENCE

Equally important to the effective planning of a debriefing exercise is providing an environment that is conducive to completing the entire learning experience. I think it is helpful for business ethics teachers to understand the need for ambiguity and the need for structure in the experiential learning exercise. Finally, providing ground rules in which students will be able to experience all phases of the experiential learning cycle is helpful for keeping the classes focused and effective.

Encouraging an Environment of Ambiguity

As mentioned earlier, skills and knowledge gained from the exercise will differ for each student. Thus, the debriefing session will be perceived with some degree of ambiguity. For example, in the debriefing model in action just discussed, many of the students were unprepared to respond to an objective setting and active learning process. The questions made no sense to some of the students! Ambiguity is necessary so that individual's minds are stretched to apply ethical concepts and theories to real-world situations. It may seem paradoxical that the pursuit of a conceptual model for debriefing is urged, yet ambiguity is also urged to meet the subjective needs of individuals and the reality of the ethical situations they will encounter outside of the classroom. Both requirements (structure and ambiguity), however, can be met if the faculty member is cognizant of each of the steps of the debriefing model and uses it as a road map to facilitate discussion so that all learning stages are experienced.

When adult learners reach the level of active experimentation (doing), they will use new skills, having experienced their usefulness/meaningfulness, and will feel capable of using the skills, having experienced the competency to do so (Bandura, 1977; Kolb et al., 1995). The challenge for business ethics teachers is to encourage the necessary amount of ambiguity in the experiential learning exercise so that students can apply theories in practice. Faculty must provide guidance, helping students to keep focused and effectively translating abstract conceptualization (theory) into active experimentation (practice). For example, in the debriefing model in action, students generated rules of thumb, or action resolutions, as part of the psychological contract. In the end, working through the direct application of ethical theories/models provides a challenging learning experience for both the students and the professor.

This is similar to the notion of self-efficacy in Bandura's social learning theory, which states that human beings acquire new skills vicariously. Bandura (1977) argues that human beings think about and interpret their experiences as opposed to absorbing blindly. From self-directed learning experiences, one gains a sense of self-efficacy in which new skills are used because the individual (1) has experienced their usefulness/meaningfulness and (2) feels capable of using the skills, having experienced the competency to do so. The instructor must encourage individuals to give and to get so that they develop their own meaningful applications of theory and will be more likely to experience their usefulness (Kolb et al., 1995). You will recall that in the example I gave, students soon recognized my role in the debriefing as a facilitator, even though some had not experienced this situation in other classes.

To provide ambiguity, it is necessary to create an environment of *mutuality* (two-sided exchange) in which learning is self-directed. Although there is no set method of creating such an environment, it may be helpful for business ethics teachers to remember that the lecture-oriented environment is typically one-sided, with teachers giving and students getting. In contrast, adult learning needs are best fulfilled in an environment conducive to two-sided exchange. As Kolb et al. (1995) state, "In adult learning both giving and getting are critical. In getting, there is the opportunity to incorporate new ideas and perspectives. In giving, there is the opportunity to integrate and apply these new perspectives and to practice their use" (p. 58).

Thiagarajan (1992) recommends as a general rule that instructors take on a cooperative role (as opposed to hierarchical or autonomous) in which the balance of power is equal between instructor and students. This mutuality allows for the fulfillment of the "contract of reciprocity" (Kolb et al., 1995) in which students take an active role, responsibility, and interest in their learning.

Finally, Gunz (1995) suggests that the instructor provide a great deal of tutorial support. A tutor with a good understanding of the exercise can ask appropriate questions of the participants, guiding them to appropriate observations from which they can build more helpful hypotheses. If this is not done, there is a risk that students will not make any successful circuits of the Kolb (1984) experiential learning cycle, and learning will not take place.

Providing Structure for the Exercise: The "Game Plan"

Once the format for the debriefing session (i.e., discussion, game, constructive feedback, etc.) has been decided upon, business ethics teachers must explain the game plan and ground rules for the session to students. By game plan, I mean a specific description and sequence of events to take place during the session. In terms of the game plan, faculty may choose to describe the game or discussion format to the group and explain how it will play out in the context of the stages. For example, if a constructive feedback session is used within the framework of Kolb's model, the business ethics teacher could explain that the experience will be discussed (concrete experience), followed by feedback from group members (reflective observation), followed by a conceptualization of rules that may apply to other situations (abstract conceptualizations), and concluded with practical applications of the concepts to work situations (active experimentation). In describing the stages, the business ethics teacher can set a time limit for discussing each to ensure that there is ample time for all stages. If the group becomes lost in a digression, the instructor can refocus the debriefing by redirecting the group back to the game plan that had been previously articulated. The business ethics teacher can ensure focus by asking the types of questions for each stage provided earlier in Table 11.1. Table 11.1 provides the teacher with a tool for guiding the experiential learning cycle at the pace, depth, breadth, and intensity that seems appropriate.

Following the explanation of the game plan, it is important to set ground rules for the debriefing session, since it will involve discussing the actions of others, especially during the concrete experience (feeling) stage. Specifically, the business ethics teacher should state that feedback should be descriptive (as opposed to evaluative), nonjudgmental, and noncritical. The constructive (as opposed to destructive) purpose of the exercise must be underscored (Borisoff & Victor, 1989).

PRACTICAL SUGGESTIONS AND CAUTIONS FOR FACULTY TEACHING BUSINESS ETHICS

The goal of the experiential learning exercise is to ensure that it has provided valuable learning that is practical for the individual. To assist in the application of debriefing concepts, the following suggestions may be implemented in business ethics teaching efforts.

Shared Work Experiences

In this activity students discuss scenarios from their work experience in which the newly acquired learning would be/would have been helpful.

Instructions. Ask students to think of a situation in which they were confronted with an ethical dilemma, and give them about five minutes to jot down some notes about their experience and feelings. After students finish sharing their stories with another student or a group, start the debriefing phase of the exercise by asking questions relevant to the concrete experience and reflective observation stages. Students can also respond to questions about their experience from other class members as means of further reflection.

During the abstract conceptualization and active experimentation stages, invite students to share previous or potential work experiences in which the ethical concepts or theories/models learned would be/would have been beneficial. For example, in the abstract conceptualization stage, ask, "Think about work experiences you have had that are similar to the situation you experienced in the exercise. Based on both experiences, what rule (i.e., ethical decision-making principle or guideline) could you follow that would be beneficial to both situations?" In the active experimentation phase, ask, "Can you think of other work situations in which this rule would apply? How about situations in which it would not apply? In situations where it would not apply, what would be an alternative?"

What This Exercise Achieves. It brings to life the ethical theories or concepts learned and offers practical data for analysis (concrete experience) and ideas for applying concepts (abstract conceptualization). It encourages active experimentation.

The Envelope Game

This game was developed by Thiagarajan (1992). In it, each group has the opportunity to explore what might have occurred during the exercise given different variables. Each group's questions are answered by other groups, inviting views from diverse perspectives. It provides the grist for lively classroom discussion. I use a version of the envelope game combined with an experiential learning activity, "Winning an International Contract." Briefly, the exercise poses the following question to participants: "What if the only way you could win a much coveted and career-enhancing contract in a foreign country was by paying a bribe?"

Instructions. Start the debriefing phase of the exercise by asking questions relevant to the concrete experience and reflective observation stages. During the abstract conceptualization and active experimentation stages, students are divided into groups. Each group passes around an envelope that contains a "what if" exercise question, which is written on the outside of the envelope. For example, "What if awarding of the contract is determined by which bidder pays the highest bribe? "What if some companies encourage their bidders to do 'whatever' is necessary to win the contract (including paying a bribe)?" "What if you, as the company bidder, were informed by your immediate boss that failure to be awarded the contract would result in your dismissal?" Once groups have finalized their responses to the "what if" questions, they then answer questions posed by the other class members (based on their experience and learning), which are then inserted into the appropriate envelope. As group responses are read, ethical rules or guidelines are formulated and summarized on a chalkboard to engage learners in the abstract conceptualization stage. The business ethics teacher can then conclude with a discussion of the rules and how they apply to other settings (both from the resulting "what if" scenarios and other discussion).

Using the "Winning an International Contract" theme as part of the envelope game can also be debriefed from the perspective of host- and home-country individuals or managers, governments, and so forth. Thus, by writing various generalizations from the game, students can develop rules of thumb for various current and future real-world applications.

What This Exercise Achieves. It invites many different questions that help to personalize learning. It provides ideas for practice from many different perspectives that may not have otherwise been discussed. It provides an opportunity for active experimentation.

Journal Writing

With journals, a student writes about personal experiences, problems, and growth. Journal writing significantly extends the learning process in the experiential learning exercise. The writing not only substantiates learning, but it also enhances analytical learning.

Journal writing provides quiet students with a mode of communication. They are able to share thoughts and ideas that they feel are private. For the shy student, and sometimes the foreign student who is not use to the active and aggressive dialogue that one sees in U.S. business schools, writing may be a better means of communication.

In my experience, through journal writing each student (and especially some foreign students) relates many more personal experiences from the experiential learning exercises than are shared in oral discussion. Students bring their own backgrounds and cultures to their perceptions of the experiential learning exercise. The journal allows for an in-depth analysis from each student's perspective. In the end, journal writing allows students to record their experience, the relevant concepts, and future application of concepts.

Instructions. After the experiential learning exercise is completed, the business ethics teacher instructs students to write about the experience in a journal. A general guideline for journal entries might be:

1. *Experience*: Explain what happened during the exercise. Include your observations of others and how you felt about these interactions.
2. *Theory*: Based upon the ethics readings and class lectures, what theories apply or would be helpful to implement in the exercise?
3. *Application*: Considering the objectives of the exercise and your performance, how could you change the experience for a better outcome? How do you think the outcome would have changed and why? In what situations could this strategy be used? What situations could call for a back-up strategy?

The faculty member can then provide individual feedback in writing for each student.

What This Exercise Achieves. Writing allows for uninhibited expression, the opportunity to reexamine written ideas, and the ability to proceed through all learning stages in a structured manner. It also provides the opportunity for the faculty member to comment and enhance each individual's needs and goals (Petranek et al., 1992).

The three experiential learning exercises presented above set the stage for, and assist in, debriefing. The exercises engage students in each stage of Kolb's experiential learning cycle and provide for active participation, self-disclosure, and especially, reciprocity, or sharing responsibility for talking about and learning from experiences.

MISTAKES TO AVOID IN DEBRIEFING

The debriefing phase in business ethics teaching efforts is easy to design. Typically, each group (and very often each individual) reports on the process and/or the results of the experiential learning exercises. The business ethics teacher (or one of the students) as facilitator captures key points on a flip chart or on the blackboard, then leads a discussion.

Although this process sounds simple, I have found that four common mistakes are made in debriefing experiential learning exercises:

1. *Rushing.* Under pressure to stay within the confines of a scheduled class period, a business ethics teacher hurries through the debriefing and fails to give the class enough time to explain what happened and what they learned. Obviously, the debriefing phase cannot run indefinitely, and every ethics class or exercise does not need to tell every detail of its experience. There are ways to eliminate repetition. For example, after two groups of students have reported in, you might ask later groups if they had a similar experience and encourage them to add to or contrast with (rather than repeat) what has already been said. Techniques to keep the debriefing phase well paced will work as long as everyone feels she or he has had the chance for self-expression.

To avoid rushing, schedule adequate time for debriefing. If the experiential learning exercise is simple and the class is small, five minutes may suffice. Larger classes and more complex exercises may take 20 minutes or more.

2. *Forgetting to Give Credit.* I have found that students learn best and are more committed to ethical reflection and learning when they have made the discovery themselves. When summarizing, it often helps to point out what students have contributed and learned. Give credit for their insights rather than making them feel they have "gotten the right answer" by reaching one of the ethical or other insights you expected.

For example: Instead of saying, "As I explained at the beginning, one of the keys to effective ethical decision making is . . . ," try saying, "As group A discovered when it played the negotiation game, one of the keys to effective ethical decision making is . . ." Or instead of saying, "One of the conclusions from our discussion is that unethical behavior in organizations depends heavily on . . . ," try saying, "During our discussion, Rachel and Jermaine pointed out that unethical behavior in organizations depends heavily on . . ."

3. *Suppressing or Ignoring Emotions or Feelings.* Experiential learning exercises used in teaching business ethics bring forth emotions. Because emotions make some people uncomfortable, students may try to rein in their feelings, and business ethics teachers may be content to pretend those emotions don't exist. But they do exist and, left unaddressed, they can pull the class off track. I recall one ethics course for graduate business students during which students played a two-day business game that included a major focus on sexual harassment. Pressed for time, we didn't adequately discuss the class's emotional responses. Instead, when the day's class ended, some students refused to speak to others, and the atmosphere became increasingly hostile through the evening. Talking about those emotions and feelings became the next order of business before we began the second day of the game.

You should be sure that emotions and other feelings are expressed. I have found that if you sense that the class is tense, hostile, frustrated with one another, or in any way "charged," open the door for a discussion by saying something like: "When I've used this exercise with other classes, people sometimes have been frustrated by how difficult it can be to find a really good solution. Are any of you feeling frustrated?" Or, "I'm sensing a little anxiety here. Are you comfortable in the roles we've been practicing? Are some of you uneasy?" Or, "When other students played this game, everyone was very competitive and some people were angry with some of the ways others played their roles. How do you feel?" The goal is not to avoid students' tense or uncomfortable feelings but to be sensitive to the fact that sometimes intervention in the form of a mini-debriefing might be necessary on your part to increase the overall learning for the ethics exercise.

4. *Forcing Consensus.* Some experiential learning exercises I use in teaching business ethics generate a lively, interesting discussion but no clear-cut conclusion. A business ethics teacher who tries to force consensus risks alienating the students.

When planning an experiential learning exercise, it has been my experience that you should anticipate the likely findings, insights, lessons, and conclusions. Consider these likely outcomes to be written in pencil, not carved in stone. During the actual debriefing phase, listen carefully and be sure your comments reflect what the class really experienced, learned, and concluded. It is better to reach partial agreement or to "agree to disagree" than to force a conclusion or consensus.

How can you design a debriefing when so much depends on students' actual experience in the ethics class and the experiential learning exercise? There are limits to how much you can plan an "online" event. Nevertheless, you can:

- Be sure you have scheduled adequate time for debriefing.

- Mentally practice some of the comments you might make to be sure that you give credit to students for their insights (and in my experience they will have many) and that you encourage them to express their thoughts, feelings, and other reactions.

- Imagine how you will handle the situation if the class does not readily reach consensus on an important ethical point or issue or if it draws conclusions that are different from those you anticipated. How can you acknowledge the outcome, keep the class in a positive frame of mind, and move forward to the next ethics class or activity?

CONCLUSION

Debriefing is a necessary part of the experiential learning process. It is crucial to completing learning in business ethics teaching endeavors. Kolb's model of the learning process is offered as a conceptual model for achieving the ultimate goal of active experimentation from experiential learning exercises.

Business ethics teachers must provide an environment in which learning can occur and be transferred to real-world situations. To meet these goals, structure is required. It is also necessary, however, to allow ambiguity so that students can personalize the learning and experience meaningfulness (usefulness) in its application so that learning is relevant to the individual.

REFERENCES

Bandura, A. 1977. *A social learning theory*. Englewood Cliffs, NJ: Prentice Hall.

Borisoff, D., & Victor, D. 1989. *Conflict management: A communication skills approach*. Englewood Cliffs, NJ: Prentice Hall.

Gaw, B.A. 1979. Processing questions: An aid to completing the learning cycle. In J.E. Jones & J.W. Pfeiffer (eds.), *The 1979 annual handbook for group facilitators*. La Jolla, CA: University Associates.

Gunz, H.P. 1995. Realism and learning in management simulations. *Journal of Management Education* 19(1): 54–74.

Hunsaker, P.L. 1978. Debriefing: The key to effective experiential learning. In D.C. Berenstuhl & S.C. Certo (eds.), *Exploring experiential learning: Simulations and experiential exercises*. East Brunswick, NJ: Nichols.

Kolb, D.A. 1984. *Experiential learning: Experience as the source of learning and development*. Englewood Cliffs, NJ: Prentice Hall.

Kolb, D.A., Osland, J.S., & Rubin, I.M. 1995. *Organizational behavior: An experiential approach* (6th ed.). Englewood Cliffs, NJ: Prentice Hall.

Lederman, L.C. 1983. Intercultural communication, simulation and the cognitive assimilation of experience: An exploration of the post-experience analytic process. Paper presented at the 3rd Annual Conference of the Speech Communication Association of Puerto Rico, San Juan.

Lederman, L.C. 1992a. After the game is over (Guest Editorial). *Simulation & Gaming* 23(2): 143–144.

Lederman, L.C. 1992b. Debriefing: Toward a systematic assessment of theory and practice. *Simulation & Gaming* 23(2): 145–159.

Pearson, M., & Smith, D. 1986. Debriefing in experience-based learning. *Simulation/Games for Learning* 16(4): 155–172.

Petranek, C., Corey, S., & Black, R. 1992. Three levels of learning in simulations: Participating, debriefing, and journal writing. *Simulation and Gaming* 23(2): 174–185.

Sanyal, R.N. 2000. Teaching business ethics in international business. *Teaching Business Ethics* 4: 137–149.

Sherwood, J.J., & Glidewell, J.G. 1972. Planned renegotiation: A norm setting OD intervention. In W.W. Burke (ed.), *Contemporary organization development: Orientations and interventions*. Washington, DC: NTL Institute.

Thatcher, D. 1986. Promoting learning through games and simulations. *Simulations/Games for Learning* 16(4): 144–154.

Thiagarajan, S. 1992. Using games for debriefing. *Simulation and Gaming* 23(2): 161–173.

Chapter 12

Assessing the Impact of Business Ethics Teaching Efforts: A Total Quality Management and Student Outcomes Assessment Approach

INTRODUCTION

While questions about whether or not ethics can or cannot be taught still exist, the nature, content, and scope of business ethics is of considerable interest to ethical theorists and practicing managers. For business ethics teachers the lack of a ready consensus on such matters as assessment is often a thorny issue. One writer notes that issues such as pedagogical methods and their effectiveness require considerable thought. For this reason, many business school professors often show a distaste for teaching business ethics, even though they may acknowledge the subject matter to be important (Iyer, 1998).

It is not hard to understand concerns about teaching ethics when the results of efforts to teach business ethics continue to get mixed reviews. For example, as noted earlier in this book, some scholars still argue that ethics courses cannot be effective because values are formed early in life and because "honesty is not a course to be taught," (Miller and Miller, 1976; Weber & Glyptis, 2000). Furthermore, it is not unusual to find that students who are tested on ethical choices at the end of MBA programs or courses show no improvement, whether they have taken an elective ethics course or not. However, other research shows that business ethics courses have a more positive impact on students' decision-making and reasoning abilities (see, for example, Adams, et al., 1999; Weber & Glyptis, 2000). In spite of the mixed results, it is important to continue efforts to assess the impact of teaching business ethics.

Assessing student learning is an important step. As soon as the goals of business ethics teaching efforts are clearly articulated, business ethics teachers and the other key stakeholders must spend the time agreeing on how to assess student learning (outcomes assessment). The methods used to assess student learning in business ethics education will vary with the kind of learning that is taking place and the teaching strategies employed.

Improvement in business ethics teaching is facilitated by feedback. We need ways to find out how we are doing. Data about teaching effectiveness may also be used by our departments in decisions about salary and promotions.

This is the first of two chapters devoted to the topic of outcomes assessment. This first chapter is primarily concerned with offering an answer to the question: *How* do we assess the impact business ethics teaching efforts have on students? The chapter will first offer a definition of outcomes assessment and then briefly discuss assessment in teaching business ethics. Next, Total Quality Management (TQM) is introduced as a broader framework for managing the outcomes assessment process of ethics education efforts in business schools. The chapter concludes with a look at some of the issues business schools and even the broader institution must consider when deciding to move towards institutionalizing assessment and getting faculty buy-in to outcomes assessment initiatives. The next chapter provides a narrower discussion on outcomes assessment and in particular on why business ethics teachers should measure or evaluate their teaching performance.

ASSESSMENT AND ACCOUNTABILITY IN INSTITUTIONS AND BUSINESS SCHOOLS

The concern about assessing student learning is part of a larger movement called "the quest for quality," which reaches beyond colleges and universities to many other institutions that provide products and services to the public. With the passage of Public Law 101–542, The Student Right-to-Know and Campus Security Act of 1990, colleges and universities are required to track students' progress toward meeting degree requirements within the "normal time" and to report "graduation rates" (Erwin, 1991, Seymour, 1993).

Although the merits of the "quality movement" have been debated for the past decade (it is surely not all good or all bad), there continues to be an emerging awareness that assessment of student learning is no longer a luxury but a necessity on every campus.

This poses an interesting set of measurement problems for colleges and universities and their faculties. On the one hand, individual faculty members, like those who teach business ethics, are expected to focus their efforts more on describable student learning and need to develop more sophisticated methods of assessing that learning in their classes. On the other hand, the departments, programs, and colleges within which business ethics teachers teach and the institutions as a whole, need to devise methods of assessing the cumulative effects of teaching on students. Thus, student learning outcomes may be thought of as existing at certain levels or in tiers:

- Classroom or structured out-of-class learning outcomes that result from students being registered in particular courses.
- General learning outcomes, such as growth in certain skills in written and spoken communication, ethical reasoning and reflective skills, and core knowledge growing out of enrollment in general education programs.
- Discipline-based learning in specific domains of knowledge and/or development of professional competencies resulting from enrollment in specific programs and concentrations (i.e., accounting, marketing, etc.).
- General student development outcomes such as cognitive development, maturity in moral judgement, historical (or ethical) awareness, problem-solving ability, and critical thinking, which result from the cumulative experience of going to college.

Assessing these outcomes is no easy task and requires efforts to measure learning that cut across conventional institutional structures and employ innovative methods of gathering and synthesizing data about student learning. Because this kind of assessment focuses on growth and institutional impact—what Alexander Astin refers to as "talent development"—it is necessary to do much more than most institutions have historically done to obtain entry-level, base-line measures of students in order to assess progress and demonstrate "value added" through the educational experience (1988, 1991).

Business schools and their faculties (including business ethics teachers), like their larger institutions, have witnessed an increased interest in assessment and accountability. In recent years, the term assessment has come to be related to the evaluation of educational institutions and their programs. However much one might wish to divorce academic assessment of student learning from assessment of institutions and business school programs, this cannot be done without prejudice to the problems which assessment creates. Assessment is as much concerned with the experience of the business school, the effects of grades on subsequent careers, and the effects of instruction on learning as it is with the technique. Fortunately, the same model may be applied to the larger institution and business schools as well as to assessment and learning of business ethics. To do so requires business schools and ethics teachers to have a clear idea of their aims or goals for teaching business ethics (as discussed in Chapters 1 and 2) because it is the extent to which business ethics achieves its aims that is the primary measure of accountability.

Subsequently, the term quality was introduced into the dialogue but with little fundamental appraisal about what quality is. Quality assessment focused on the delivery of academic programs, and a search began for performance indicators with which to measure quality.

There is a danger that business schools may become overburdened by the sheer volume of data they are supposed to collect and that they may not make effective use of the data they have. To avoid this problem, business schools should choose a small number of indicators that will help them focus on key issues. Part of the problem is that many of those who demand such indicators have little understanding of the complexity of the broader institutional and business school process. Those concerned with business school effectiveness need, in particular, to understand how institutional and business school structures can enhance or impede learning.

Accreditation programs, like the International Association of Management Education (formerly the AACSB), have also come in for a lot criticism in the United States. A particular concern is that some of them demand so many outcomes that the process may become trivialized. For change to take place, the larger institutions and business schools need to have a whole-hearted commitment to the process as something they themselves require internally. Without this, change is unlikely to take place.

It is not part of the purpose of this chapter to enter into any detailed discussion of the issues relating to accountability. Accountability has many dimensions and many persons to serve. There are many stakeholders, and trying to meet the demands of all of them could lead to contradictions in policy.

As for business ethics teachers, they are accountable to their institution, their business school, and their students. The view taken here is that the first line of accountability is in the classroom. The key question for business schools in teaching business ethics is how can they better serve student learning with the resources they have. Accountability should focus on a determination of whether agreed objectives have been achieved and the action to be taken, if any, if they are not.

WHAT IS OUTCOMES ASSESSMENT?

Assessment is a complex generic skill in use in everyday life. With the increased emphasis on assessment, many business ethics teachers take the view that assessment drives learning, and they therefore design their assessments to have a positive influence on learning. Many also now accept that developing self-assessment skills is valuable. But the idea that there should be mandatory assessment of business ethics teaching efforts is not an idea that is embraced by all business ethics teachers. In my experience, teachers' anxieties about assessment are too often focused on the limitations of assessment and its perceived potential to harm some students rather than on the beneficial effects it could have on learning. Effective assessment in business ethics teaching efforts depends on assessors (i.e., business ethics teachers, administrators, etc.) having a substantial knowledge and comfort level with outcomes assessment and learning.

Assessment is a relatively new word in the context of education generally and business ethics in particular. Traditionally, terms like testing (tests), examining (examinations), and grading (grades) were used. However, early in the 1970s the term assessment came to be generally associated with these activities. Before that the term assessment seems to have been associated with individuals, and it was sometimes specifically associated with judgements about children who had specific learning problems and/or other needs.

For politicians, assessment is about standards, on the one hand, and value for money, on the other. The most significant indicator of performance is the assessment of students made by tests and examinations. For our purposes, outcomes assessment is defined as the systematic basis for making inferences about the learning and development of students. More specifically, outcomes assessment is the process of defining, selecting, designing, collecting, analyzing, interpreting, and using information to increase students' learning and development in business ethics teaching efforts.

OUTCOMES ASSESSMENT IN TEACHING BUSINESS ETHICS

Weber (1990) has noted the importance of determining what the expected impact of an ethics course is, incorporating a longitudinal dimension in assessment designs (pre- and post-course analyses), and going beyond rather simplistic measurement of ethical awareness and reasoning by using Likert scales as a comparison of frequencies and means or using Kohlberg's standard issue scoring method (see Colby and Kohlberg, 1987). Loeb (1991) has also highlighted the importance of similar points—for example, the importance of accounting faculty reaching a consensus on matters that need evaluation, such as at what level or levels should or could ethics education be evaluated (professionwide outcomes and accounting program outcomes) and what possible techniques could be used to measure outcomes (student performance, instructor performance, and course or program assessment).

A variety of methods of assessment have been used in research on teaching ethics (see, for example, The Kohlberg Moral Development Interview and related tests built on the Kohlbergian model such as the Defining Issues Test [Rest, 1979; Thoma, 1994], the Ethical Sensitivity Test [Wittmer, 2000], the Sociomoral Reflection Measure-Short Form [Snarey and Keljo, 1994] and other instruments or formats). As with coming to an agreement on the purpose or goals of teaching business ethics, agreeing upon a common method of assessment for measuring student performance against shared standards or core competencies in business ethics also creates conflicts for teachers. Addressing and resolving such conflict is especially important, since agreement on assessment instruments can ultimately lead to a common objective for business ethics and operationalization of the objective in terms of specific performance indicators.

In many business schools the assessment of outcomes is often equated with measuring performance on examinations. Indeed, if the instructor has presented a highly structured unit on statistics or accounting, for example, a pencil-and-paper test may well be an appropriate choice to assess how well the learning objectives have been met. If, however, the learning objective is to develop the ability to make well-informed ethical judgements, assessment is more complicated than simply measuring the ability to master a body of factual knowledge.

The goal of assessment is to produce reliable data that can be used to aid in the evaluation of efficiency and effectiveness. In much the same manner as an audit, assessment data provide feedback on what has gone before and suggest what should come next. In teaching business ethics the question becomes "Does the incorporation of ethics into the business curriculum make a difference in the ethical behavior of students and business leaders?" (Oddo, 1997).

Loeb (1991) identifies five issues relating to the evaluation of ethics education in business: (1) identifying reasons for evaluating programs, (2) setting goals as a prerequisite to evaluating outcomes, (3) defining broad levels of outcomes, (4) deciding what to evaluate, and (5) measuring outcomes. Training researchers have proposed a number of different criteria and frameworks for assessing training that can be beneficially applied to teaching business ethics (especially in reaching consensus on the areas identified by Loeb). Goldstein (1986) suggests that training be evaluated in terms of whether the change is related to organizational goals and whether similar changes are likely to occur with new participants in the same training program. Kilpatrick (1977) proposes that training programs should be evaluated using four standards: reactions, learning, behavior, and results. First, it is useful to examine reactions to the content and delivery of the training. If individuals see the training as irrelevant or contrary to the prevailing norms, it is unlikely that the training will change their behavior. Second, learning should be evaluated. If individuals never learn or retain critical information in the training programs, they will not be able to apply it. Third, changes in behavior should be examined. It is logical to assess and compare behavior before and after the intervention (see Cascio, 1987; Cook et al., 1990). Finally, the results of training should be examined. For example, faculty can be successful in teaching ethical principles and in changing the behavior of the individuals who receive training, but the results of those changes might not be relevant or worthwhile.

There is evidence that training in ethical principles can be effective. Outcomes assessment is conceptually specified by the four dimensions of reactions, learning, behavior, and results. However, the actual implementation of the outcomes assessment effort must be guided by an action-based model that is designed to assess processes rather than specific outcomes. One model especially well suited to this task is the life cycle approach based on the work of Daft (1989). The five life cycle stages are: entrepreneurial, collectivity, formalization, elaboration, and renewal or decline. Each phase of the life cycle suggests how the educational program can be improved and where there are weaknesses in the process.

The five stages of the life cycle prompt questions such as: What are the purposes or incentives for outcomes assessment in business ethics? Is there consensus about the goals to be achieved and the means to be employed? What type of outcomes assessment data will be collected as part of the evaluation effort? How will outcomes assessment findings be disseminated? And where will we go from here? (See Loeb, 1991 for a more detailed discussion of suggested responses to questions of this type.)

KAIZEN AND OUTCOMES ASSESSMENT IN TEACHING BUSINESS ETHICS

One clear implication growing out of this increased interest in assessing student learning is that teaching in general, and more specifically a teaching topic like business ethics, is coming to be seen more as a collective enterprise for which we as teachers are being held collectively responsible. Note, for example, that the International Association of Management Education (AACSB, 1994) required business schools to integrate the business ethics teaching into their curriculums more than a decade ago. The days are gone when we can go to class, teach our subject, and hope that some our students will "get it." It is no longer possible to avoid probing questions about the amount and quality of student learning. For these reasons, it is important that we conceive of our teaching in terms of student learning and that we organize what we do by employing teaching strategies based on paradigms of learning.

If the impact of teaching of topics like business ethics on student learning is viewed increasingly as a collective enterprise, then the improvement of business ethics teaching efforts is likely to be seen more and more as a collective need of whole faculties and a matter of institutional and business school policy. Business schools must view student outcomes assessment as more than a remedial activity. They must come to view it as a central activity, the vehicle for what the Japanese call *kaizen*—continuous improvement.

Many business schools and business ethics teachers have developed assessment mechanisms to examine basic issues of student quality. It would appear that any business schools and business ethics teachers who are concerned with assessing their effectiveness would begin to ask simple questions such as: What are our educational goals? How are we determining whether we are achieving these goals? And what have we done with the results to improve the educational environment and student learning? Business schools and those business ethics teachers naturally could answers these questions in different ways. Some business schools and business ethics teachers might naturally look towards the business community for guidance. What they would find are several practices and tools that could aid them in undertaking student outcomes assessment. One of these tools is TQM and its *kaizen* philosophy.

Kaizen stresses continuous, gradual improvement to a system or process as opposed to radical change. The concept of *kaizen* thus serves as a link between outcomes assessment and TQM. The following synopsis is offered as a testament to the need for *kaizen* in business schools in general and business ethics teaching efforts in particular: Assessment of student learning in business ethics teaching efforts seems to be most successful when faculty, students, administrators, and staff work together to identify and improve all aspects of the learning process. Such information gathering in a thorough assessment process can and should be used in strategic planning at the department and the business school levels. Gradual changes should occur in the content and structure of the curriculum as well as within the courses themselves. Inevitably, interactions with other faculty and other academic and administrative units have to be addressed because of their impact on students enrolled in business ethics courses. Teamwork is required. Slowly and gradually, the business school culture evolves into one that is more sensitive to better ways of maximizing student learning.

As business ethics teachers begin to pay more serious attention to TQM and its corresponding principles and tools, an effort should be made to adapt those tools and principles to the unique environment that exists at their business schools and their specialized programs.

Thus, the remainder of this chapter focuses not on convincing business ethics teachers that they need to develop and implement student outcomes assessment initiatives or providing guidelines for assessment implementation. The purpose is to show how TQM and its team approach can be used within business schools, and specifically in their business ethics education efforts, to improve student effectiveness and indirectly increase school and educational quality or effectiveness.

OBJECTIVES OF STUDENT OUTCOMES ASSESSMENT IN BUSINESS ETHICS TEACHING EFFORTS

The objectives of student outcomes assessment in business ethics education are numerous. They include providing feedback to help the individual student learn, feedback to help the instructors guide classroom activities; feedback to assist the instructor or department in improving programs;

feedback to support program monitoring at other levels within the business school and larger institution; information to state agencies, donors, alumni, etc. for accountability and funding purposes; feedback for gatekeeping decisions (pass/fail) concerning individual student progress, feedback to accrediting agencies and employers to evaluate programs; and information to assist the public in evaluating business school quality. In this light, the overall objective for using student outcomes assessment in association with TQM in business ethics education efforts is to move from one position on the education continuum to a higher position of quality. This requires a detailed recordkeeping system designed to determine what is working and what needs to be changed in order to move educational quality to a higher point on the quality continuum.

Although Deming's TQM work and its tools have traditionally been applied to companies primarily concerned with the production of goods and services, they can also prove successful for business schools interested in assessing their business ethics education efforts. However, there are some unique barriers that must be overcome in order to adapt TQM to business ethics education.

OVERCOMING FORCES AGAINST TQM/STUDENT ASSESSMENT

As one attempts to implement TQM practices in specialized programs such as student outcomes assessment initiatives, several obstacles immediately present themselves. First, the age-old argument of academic freedom within the classroom emerges. Many business ethics teachers actively resist having their courses scrutinized even if the intention is not to penalize the instructor but rather to improve the educational process. I have found that this resistance may have several faces, ranging from passive behaviors to direct attacks on TQM and assessment. The instructors might argue that TQM is a product of the business sector and thus does not apply to the uniqueness that comes with a topic like business ethics. This especially appears to be the case for those faculty who either come from a philosophy or related department and teach in business schools or those who are actually members of the business school faculty but have a strong philosophical bent in their approach to teaching business ethics. Many will find it difficult to recognize students, alumni, and employers as "customers." This might again be perceived as an impediment to their academic freedom, since according to TQM principles customer preferences should be considered in the design and delivery of academic programs, business ethics courses, and methods of instruction. This fear would serve as a direct attack on TQM and its premise that the driving force for change initiatives rest solely on satisfying customer needs.

A second concern that is closely associated with the need for autonomy in the classroom is the individualistic nature of academician's work. Business school faculty in general and those responsible for teaching business ethics in particular tend to work alone rather than in group settings and sometimes find it difficult to work with others in teams to assess, evaluate, and make revisions in an attempt to improve the processes of student outcomes assessment. This orientation has led to fragmentation of faculty within disciplines, fragmentation between disciplines, and ultimately to in the division of business schools and the university system.

Another force that serves to maintain a quality equilibrium in business ethics education is the "bell curve mentality." "My course has real meat to it," one business ethics teacher said, beaming. "Very few students have ever gotten an A in my course." A college professor I had in a seminar for philosophy majors had put it similarly many years ago as he explained his grading policy on the first day of class: "As are for Plato and Socrates," he declared, pointing to the heavens. "Bs are for scholars such as myself," he proclaimed with an open hand pointing to his chest. He paused for a deep breath. "Cs, Ds, and Fs are for you," he said with his right arm sweeping across the classroom, as he consigned all of us to the depths of mediocrity and worse. Business school administrators, ethics instructors, and oftentimes students themselves have come to believe that the bell curve is the ideal shape for quality business ethics courses and programs.

However, if those responsible for teaching business ethics are to become more effective, they must swiftly move beyond the bell curve mentality by attempting to answer how they know that they are successful. This question can be answered with the simple statement: When all students are continuously improving and feeling good about themselves and their learning.

One final force against using TQM in assessment of business ethics teaching efforts is the length of time that is spent initially in efforts to improve educational processes. One might encounter business school administrators who argue that little time exists to systematically implement incremental change efforts. Their attention is thus focused on dealing with immediate problems rather than on looking farther down the road in an effort to predict unforeseen problems. It is my contention that there is no such thing as an academic crisis and that while an overheated situation may require actions to cool it down, long-term solutions should always be developed using TQM principles. The final section of this chapter also offers some suggestions on improving the likely success of bringing outcomes assessment efforts to fruition in business schools and business ethics teaching efforts.

TEACHING BUSINESS ETHICS: OUTCOMES ASSESSMENT AND CONSTITUENT NEEDS

As business ethics teachers and their schools consider how TQM can benefit their assessment efforts, each business school should take into account its unique market and other special traditions and circumstances that come into play. Emphasis should be placed on identifying the primary and secondary constituents they serve and their needs. In previous years, it may have been argued that the instructor was the primary constituent and thus the center of the educational system. However, this is no longer the case. Over the past 25 years or so, the emphasis has shifted away from the instructor toward the student as the primary constituent or client of the educational process. Thus a new approach to empowering students to be more aggressive in pursuit of their educational progress has emerged. No longer are business instructors expected to simply pass along information. Students are expected to be aggressive seekers of knowledge. Thus, education's role has shifted to helping students learn.

In addition to understanding students' needs and their role as a business school's primary constituents, student assessment in business ethics education efforts must also identify other constituents for their products and discover what their needs, wants, and expectations are. These constituents might include faculty (both in and outside of the business school), staff, parents, alumni, donors, taxpayers, society-at-large, and employers of graduates. Their needs include not only high quality products and services but also reliability of employees, courtesy, and value for the dollar, among others. For example, Chip Mason of the investment firm Legg-Mason once said that he did not want to hire people who would cross any ethical lines. However, although the wants and needs of secondary customers such as employers are important, for the sake of educational improvement, it is important to remember that the overall goals are student satisfaction and development. Thus one could say that student satisfaction and development should be the overall focus of all TQM practices.

THE DEMING CYCLE AND OUTCOME ASSESSMENT IN BUSINESS ETHICS EDUCATION EFFORTS

The outcomes assessment processes in business ethics education efforts must be thoroughly thought out and implemented in order for positive results to be achieved. Assessment efforts should stress a structured approach designed to meet each individual business school's and business ethics teacher's specific objectives for continuous improvement. An often used diagram for guiding TQM processes is the Plan, Do, Study, Act (PDSA) Cycle introduced by Deming in the 1980s (Deming, 1986). This diagram is a variation on Walter Shewhart's Specification-Production-Inspection (SPI) Cycle introduced in the 1920s. This diagram, when applied to outcome assessment in business ethics education efforts, should relate student outcomes objectives to business school needs for improving educational quality. Ethics educational processes and decisions must be directly related to established business school goals for quality improvement.

Deming's PDSA Cycle is a four-stage approach that should be considered as a part of every business ethics education assessment decision. Although each of the four stages is separate and distinct, they operate in a interconnected system. First, a plan for achieving assessment objectives should be developed. Second, this plan should be piloted on a small scale to iron out unforeseen problems (e.g., in a business ethics module or experiential learning exercise). Then, in the third stage, the product is studied to determine if gains have or have not been made in educational quality. The last stage uses information obtained in previous stages to modify the process to improve results in the next assessment cycle or effort.

The entire process is an incremental evolution that leads to constant and continuous improvement of the assessment process in business ethics education. The process continues until one encounters a problem within any given stage. Then, participants must backtrack to the place where the outcomes assessment effort was on track and proceed again using the newly acquired information.

I and others have used several variations of Deming's PDSA Cycle in assessing business ethics and other education efforts. For example, there is the PIAR Cycle—*P*lanning, *I*mplementing, *A*ssessing, and *R*evising. There is also the SIAM Cycle, which stands for *S*tudy current situation; *I*dentify vital problems; *A*ct on problems; and *M*onitor progress. These processes designed to improve business ethics teaching effectiveness are but two examples of how business ethics teachers can revise TQM concepts to fit their purposes. However, because of the simplicity of the terms (Plan, Do, Study, Act) proposed by Deming, they will be used here for further discussion of outcomes assessment in business ethics education.

Planning Stage

Outcomes assessment is an important process for improving teaching business ethics efforts. Thus intense attention should be paid to planning and designing all assessment activities prior to their implementation. This planning stage should include the use of detailed TQM preparatory tools such as flowcharts, checklists, and cause-effect diagrams. Particular attention should also be given to diagramming, and predicting proposed actions should be included and widely disseminated to all participants. Participants should also be made aware of the TQM process, how it evolved and what advantages/disadvantages can be accrued by applying (adapting) it to business ethics education, and particularly to the student outcomes assessment process.

The performance review criteria that will ultimately be used to determine the success or failure of the assessment process should be selected during the planning stage. This performance review criteria should do two things. First, it should define any problems or goals in operational terms (i.e., students completing a business ethics course should be able to apply course learning to an actual work environment or correctly and usefully employ the various conceptual tools provided to assist their moral reasoning/reflection). Second, the improvement objective should be stated in operational terms (i.e., to increase the level of business ethics learned competencies— in ethical reasoning—to parallel work experiences).

A business ethics education needs assessment survey of customers such as faculty, staff, students, alumni, and employers should be conducted to determine what is expected from the entire process. In addition, focus group sessions with customers and open-ended customer interviews are extremely helpful in obtaining customers' ideas and needs. Continuously, monitoring what customers want, their needs, and their expectations should be the top priority for any business school's and ethics teacher's student outcomes/TQM assessment effort.

This needs assessment should include answers to the following questions:

- What is the business school currently doing to determine the quality of the business ethics education processes and student outcomes at the business school?
- What am I currently doing to determine the quality of my business ethics education efforts and student outcomes in my courses?
- Do all individuals involved understand the process?
- Are the business ethics educational process and assessment procedures satisfactory to meet constituents' needs?
- If not, how can the process be improved to meet constituents' needs?
- What is the perceived attitude of administrators, faculty, staff, and students toward this process and potential educational improvements?
- How can we improve ethics education for the students?
- How can we better influence faculty, changes in the curriculum, and administrative processes?

This is just a sample of questions that should be explored and prioritized as those responsible for teaching business ethics plan their outcomes assessment and TQM ventures. They can and should be modified to meet each business school's and ethics teacher's needs and objectives prior to implementing changes, since they serve to identify problem areas. Business ethics teachers must then prioritize these problems and select areas that need immediate attention.

Doing Stage

The doing, or implementation, stage is heavily dependent upon thorough planning and commitment from all involved. It is also the stage where many unforeseen problems can present themselves. These problems might include sabotage by resistant faculty or administrators, or unavailability of resources (both financial and human). Thus, it is important for implementors (i.e., those responsible for undertaking the outcomes assessment) to eliminate as many snags as possible. This can be done by conducting a pilot program (i.e., a business ethics module or experiential learning exercise) designed to identify unforeseen problems. Typically, this means categorizing and displaying relationships through cause-and-effect diagrams, such as the "fishbone" diagram. It is also helpful to make a lists of costs and benefits of the proposed changes. This requires careful attention to study design so that cause-and-effect relationships are more easily recognized.

In this stage, efforts should be focused on determining the quality or baseline of students and business ethics education efforts from several vantage points in the process as suggested by Ozar (1998). The areas to be considered should be selected based on the needs assessment conducted in the planning phase. For the sake of discussion, four general areas can be assessed for quality: entering students, exiting students, alumni, and educational programs.

First, emphasis should be placed on the quality of students entering a business ethics course. Second, emphasis should be placed on the business ethics educational process itself. Third, exiting students should be assessed. And finally, employed students and alumni should be assessed. In doing so, business schools and faculty responsible for teaching business ethics should start with a relatively small part of their educational effort giving emphasis to TQM cycles.

Exiting students should be assessed to determine what they can do as a result of participating in a business ethics course, module, class or experiential learning activity. In most TQM practices this is the final quality control check to determine that all systems function as they should. However, the TQM literature advises that this should not be the sole or primary focus of determining quality, especially for students. Students are multifaceted individuals who display numerous talents. Thus, a one-dimensional test cannot begin to determine how students learn or the effects of educational processes. Final inspection is far less important than some other quality checkpoints because quality must be designed and built into the product or service. It cannot be "inspected in later." Statistical sampling is typically used at this point, as opposed to examining all of the students in a business ethics course or other educational activity or exiting population.

Assessing the quality of students entering a business school or business ethics education effort can begin with identifying the baseline of students (i.e., where the learning begins). That is, what is it that the students can already do to which the business ethics education effort adds and on which it will be built? Responding to this question sets the groundwork for determining the value added once students leave the course.

Developmental psychologist James Rest has distinguished three deficits that moral education strives to help learners overcome and that also serve as the principal explanations for people's inappropriate conduct (Rest, 1983, 1984). The first three deficits are (1) awareness (lack of sensitivity to what is ethically at stake in the situation), (2) reasoning and other reflective skills (leading to incorrect judgements about what ought to be done), and (3) motivation/conviction (deficits in the person's willingness to give over other considerations to the values, principles, or ideals that prompt the action that ought to be done). To these, Ozar (1998) suggests adding implementation (inability to implement the course of action that one has judged ought to be followed).

Given these deficits, one could say that the aim of business ethics education ought to be to help students overcome each of these deficits in relation to a particular situation. As noted above, the first step in identifying outcomes given the four deficits is to identify the baseline—what is it that the students can already do to which the business ethics education effort adds and on which it will be built?

At this point, the business ethics teacher must come to some determination of the background and experience levels of students. For example, at my institution, all of our undergraduate business students enter the business program during their junior year with limited business or work experience. However, most of them have been exposed to a rich, well-rounded liberal education during their first two years at the College of William & Mary and have fulfilled undergraduate distribution requirements. It would be safe to say that most of the students that enter a business ethics course or program have comparable backgrounds. The business ethics teacher should then develop baseline credentials in the four deficit areas: awareness, reasoning/reflective skills, motivation/conviction, and implementation. An example of a baseline characteristic for awareness is "students have a significant (that is conduct-affecting) awareness of such general values as personal autonomy, self-determination, integrity, and social cooperation, together with Rohr's (1989) three 'regime' principles of equality, freedom, and respect for property, and personal ideals consistent with these values and principles" (Ozar, 1998, p. 88).

Ozar (1998) suggests that once the ethics teacher has developed baseline characteristics of the students in the ethics education effort, then specific learning outcomes should be divided into the four categories. For example, the students' awareness of the values, principles, and ideals already indicated as the baseline should grow to be an articulate awareness of these values, principles, and ideals. Additionally, students should be able to identify which of them are at stake in a wide variety of typical cases and issues in a variety of business situations. Students should also become articulately aware that these values, principles, and ideals are often mutually exclusive in concrete situations requiring action (that is, aware of moral/ethical "dimensions), thus becoming aware of the value of moral reflection in addressing such situations. Students' articulate awareness should also include any other values, principles, or ideals that are relevant to any more specific or more specialized role within business for which a particular group of students is specifically preparing (i.e., accounting, marketing, etc.).

Given the baseline characteristic and learning outcomes related to awareness as suggested above, students' achievement of awareness outcomes can be assessed in significant measures by eliciting forms of discourse and evaluating them to see that the desired skills, content, and awareness of cognitive outcomes occurs. This can be done in both oral and written form, individually or in the forum of the class discussion, or by some other mechanism.

For each of the four areas identified for attention (entering students, exiting students, alumni, and educational programs) one should prioritize and select what should be emphasized based on the needs assessment conducted in the planning stage. Attention should then be turned toward identifying ways or means to eliminate or reduce problems. I have found that it helps to list the advantages and disadvantages of each approach.

TQM and its philosophy of continuous improvement serve as a brace for supporting value-added judgements. However, business schools and those responsible for teaching business ethics should start with relatively small parts of their overall system and actively use the feedback gathered in the planning stage from primary (students) and secondary customers (employers, etc.) to constantly modify the process. A second warning should be sounded: If business school administrators and faculty responsible for teaching business ethics are not committed to quality improvements, little will be achieved. Outcomes assessment in business ethics education is a process that cuts across both academic and administrative structures. Business school administrators and faculty must be committed to TQM's basic principles and be willing to maintain the continuous improvement process over time.

After a TQM cycle for business education outcomes assessment program has been established, it should be institutionalized in the business school and in business ethics teaching efforts. However, institutionalization of a process like outcomes assessment in business ethics education's culture requires patience and commitment from all in an attempt to achieve its desired objectives.

Studying Phase

In this stage an open, thorough evaluation is conducted to determine the effects of imposed changes on the business ethics education effort itself. One must be concerned with finding answers to the following questions:

• Were there any new curricula, courses, or materials developed? If so, are they helpful to the outcomes assessment process?

• Has tangible evidence of achievement been cited in connection with each of the stated outcome assessment goals?

It is important for business ethics educators to be sure that achieved results are maintained over time and are not the result of the Hawthorne Effect (temporary performance improvements that are the result of being watched or studied).

Before-and-after comparison techniques such as pre- and post-tests are particularly important TQM tools in this phase. These tools establish the baseline characteristics mentioned earlier and identify what the business ethics education effort enabled students to do once they completed the course. However, one should be warned that the best way to assess the impact of business ethics education efforts is to check with customers to determine if students satisfy their needs.

Acting Phase

Once changes have been evaluated in the assessing phase, they should be incorporated into the day-to-day operations of the business ethics education assessment efforts if they are deemed successful by customers. This may be more easily said than done, depending on the entrenchment of faculty and others directly involved in the process. However, the business ethics education assessment results are more easily implemented when the source for assessment information and the audience for assessment information are the same. Thus, in order to encourage continuous improvement, business school administrators, faculty, students, alumni, and employers should all be involved in the TQM outcomes assessment process. Such involvement increases the likelihood of institutionalizing outcomes assessment in business ethics education. As stated earlier, TQM and outcomes assessment in business ethics education should be a continuous process, which means that new planning initiatives should be developed to continue the improvement process (cycle).

ISSUES AND SUGGESTIONS FOR BRINGING OUTCOMES ASSESSMENT TO FRUITION

Assessment continues to have a special significance for higher education. Indeed, the Latin roots for the word assessment, *ad* and *sedere*, meaning to "sit beside," are well suited to business schools, whose output is so varied, ranging from knowledge of the various aspects of business and other organizations to specific skills for jobs. Many of the job skills can be assessed only by observing actual performance beside the student.

Outcomes assessment helps faculty to think harder and more clearly about educational purposes and expectations. There's a natural logic here:

issues of "outcomes" and "effectiveness" quickly translate into faculty questions: What is it I'm teaching? What knowledge and abilities must students achieve? How do I know when they've achieved them? How good is good enough?

Moreover, with its focus on "larger outcomes" (which both include and transcend the individual course), assessment calls on faculty to pursue these questions not only individually but collectively. For many teachers this may still be a novelty. A member of one business department stated, "We were writing letters of recommendation for each other's students, but it became clear as we talked that we did so with no clear view of each other's expectations or beliefs about learning." It was during discussions of assessment that such issues first arose.

Not surprisingly, such discussions can be stormy. Lengthy, collaborative work on teaching and learning and efforts to create a shared vision are often not what faculty learn to expect in a graduate business school. Nevertheless, the process can be gratifying. One faculty member in another business department noted that assessment has led to "greater integration and coherence for students, helping them see connections between courses and the frameworks of various disciplines."

I have found that great clarity about outcomes is a frequent motif of faculty experience with assessment. An ethics professor at another business school, where assessment is largely "course-embedded," noted "more sense of agreement between students and faculty about goals." The professor went on to note that he used to tell students, " 'This paper should cover this and reflect on that, and, oh yes, it should be well-written, too,' assuming that they knew what that meant. One effect of assessment has been to make me realize that I need to be much more explicit, that students need to know what we mean when we say things like 'well written.' "

"Well-written," "persuasively argued," "sufficiently documented"; these catchwords of assignment-making are, for many faculty, so much a given as to be invisible. The ethics professor's story is both typical and inevitable in its focus on assessment as a prompt to clarify standards and expectations. In the professor's words, "The more explicit I can be, the more students learn."

A related change involves a different way of working with students. A business school colleague of mine observed, "Assessment changes your relationship to the student. I often feel less the evaluator than, in the best tradition of assessment, someone "sitting down beside" her, discussing her strengths and weaknesses, what she's done, what she need to do next. . . . It's a coaching, collegial relationship."

One motif in the faculty experience of assessment, then, is that of clearer, more public articulation of expectations. A related theme is that of higher expectations. For the ethics professor mentioned before, "assessment has meant a higher vision, a greater ambition for students."

In one situation, assessment started when the faculty asked themselves what, ideally, they would like students to learn and be able to do. They did this in a vacuum at first—leaving aside the practical implications of their hopes. Then, they started to understand what it was they needed to be doing to get students up to those levels and what it would mean to hold students to those higher standards. One thing this group of faculty learned through assessment—not just confirmed, but learned—is that if they made greater demands, students would meet them.

Of course, "great demands" are not enough. How can assessment move faculty toward teaching practices that result in more learning? How do clearer, higher expectations affect what faculty *do* with students?

Though assessment is surely not the only force at work, several faculty members have related involvement in assessment to a shift away from lecture methods. One faculty member stated, "I used to feel great after a lecture on the great philosophers that really 'went over.' Yeah, right over their heads." She has turned more and more to active, involving methods, such as group interactions, simulations, and the like. Faced with low student achievement on the GMAT, faculty in one business school looked closely at the test and at their teaching. As a result, they moved away from exercises in recall and recognition toward more applied reasoning items.

An important part of the story to date is that assessment *can* be connected to teaching, deepening the way faculty think about their purposes, raising expectations, and prompting new ways of working with students. *Can* is the operative word, however. External forces continue to drive the assessment movement: more and more states have climbed on the bandwagon and federal guidelines call for all accrediting agencies to require "outcomes" information about student achievement. Not surprisingly, then, on many campuses and business schools assessment stalls at the bureaucratic "we'd better get some numbers together (right now) stage"—far short of the classroom, unconnected to what faculty do with students. What can de done?

CONNECTING ASSESSMENT TO TEACHING

Reform the Issue. A first step toward understanding the implications of assessment for teaching (and vice versa) is to reframe the issue in faculty terms. As many administrators have found, viewing assessment in terms of outcomes, criteria, data, value-added, and instruments is not only foreign but often offensive to many faculty.

Terms more conducive to faculty thinking about student learning are available. One member of a business school cuts through the jargon to what she sees at the heart of assessment: "I need to know if I am teaching what I think I am teaching. I need to know if I am helping them learn." Formulated in these terms, assessment constitutes a recognition of the potential gap between teaching and learning. Patricia Cross, an expert on assessment, sees assessment as a "zipper" for helping to close this gap.

Begin with Questions Faculty Want Answered. Assessment is more likely to be connected to teaching and learning if it answers real faculty questions about students. Many campuses and business schools begin with choices about instruments, looking to technical and administrative features to help make those choices. But a prior question needs to be asked by the faculty: What information would help me deal more effectively with my students? What do I need to know that I don't now?

Adopt Simple, In-Class Methods. In many instances, much of what passes for assessment is top-down research by design, and unwieldy to administer. Involving faculty in assessment means developing an array of methods that are easily used in classrooms with students—methods that are quick, easy to "score," and rich in feedback. Whatever the methods, they should help faculty get a mid-course or end-course reading on what's working and whether "students are learning what I think I'm teaching." In this instance, assessment is not only connected but *integral* to teaching.

Explore Connections between Courses. Over the years, I have found that many faculty report that assessment prompts breakthroughs in teaching because it demands conversations with colleagues and collaboration that would otherwise not occur. What is needed are methods faculty can work at together, beyond the individual classroom, but short of the broadscale outcomes measured by most commercially available, standardized tests. Assessment might involve faculty looking at learning in three interrelated accounting and business policy courses or in a sequence of four management or Business and Society/ethics courses, contexts almost guaranteed to call attention to teaching strategies.

Do What's Good for Students. Assessment needs to be connecting to teaching and also to *learning*—not necessarily the same thing. That means paying attention to students' experience of assessment. As faculty we need to ask: Will it be good for my students? Is this how I want them to spend their time? What does this or that method tell students about what kinds of knowledge and skills I value?

As business faculty we must involve and motivate students who (often correctly) see no personal stake in assessment. We must avoid the temptation of trying to get students to participate in the assessment process (such as showing up for tests) by offering inducements—everything from pizzas to movie tickets to outright cash. Predictably, such efforts have led to limited success.

A different approach to the problem, as suggested by the experience of members of one business school, was to design an assessment for their majors. One member of the department noted that the most gratifying part of the process was seeing the effect of the new instrument on students, who saw it as a rite of passage, a kind of rigorous, tailor-made experience. All but one student returned the following summer, *after* graduation, for a personal feedback session.

The point is that maybe students will be involved in assessment when the quality of the experience is inherently meaningful and engaging and when, in the name of assessing learning, learning occurs.

Link Assessment to Disciplinary Concerns. Assessment in the major is fertile ground for linking assessment to teaching. Though the major is often not really the public bone of contention (the criticism is that students can't write or think critically, not that they don't don't have moral character) within the business school, it is, arguably, the arena where assessment can be most productive. In contrast to studies of the broad effects of assessment within a college, assessment within the business major offers better hope of consensus about outcomes, easier connections to fixable teaching and curriculum features, and a ready client for the information. It is also an arena in which thus-far fuzzy connections between assessment, teaching, and disciplinary subject matter can be explained.

One business ethics professor noted that

What we need are assessment tools that tap the subtle, hard-to-assess, outcomes that faculty care about—the sensibilities that distinguish, say, the accounting major from the management major. We need methods that call forth not only generalized skills but the application of specialized knowledge in specific contexts. We need more integrated, performance-oriented methods (simulations and the like) that allow students to demonstrate what they know and what they can do with what they know.

Get the Big Picture. If, in the name of assessment, business ethics teachers are to look more closely at student learning, they need, as well, to take a closer look at students themselves. What happens in the classroom doesn't happen in a vacuum; student background and preparation, learning styles, efforts, and a range of other factors are relevant, as discussed earlier in this book. This kind of big-picture assessment must involve not only faculty but all other stakeholders as well. It means taking a broader view of college outcomes, including not only cognitive gains but also the development of values, critical thinking, leadership, and civic responsibility—important goals that I have found are often ignored in business school assessment efforts.

Don't Jump to Conclusions. Over and over, one hears that faculty are put off, threatened, and offended by assessment. There are true stories to that effect. There are also self-fulfilling prophecies.

Yes, assessment does ask faculty to think and behave in ways that may be foreign. But in my experience, for many faculty who see themselves first and foremost as teachers, assessment can be career-defining work. It gives faculty something most of them don't get: a signal that teaching matters. That's a big step toward making it better.

CONCLUSION

As business schools and those responsible for teaching business ethics continue to encounter those who suggest that we shouldn't and can't teach business ethics and also wrestle with how best to assess the impact of teaching business ethics, they must continue to perfect their assessment of business ethics education efforts. TQM can prove to be a valuable tool to guide actions and decisions and help teachers with outcomes assessment of their business ethics teaching efforts. TQM is not an all-encompassing answer to the long-term success of continuous improvement in business ethics educational. This can only be achieved by altering business school cultures to emphasize the continuous cycle of improvement. Each business school and faculty member must realize that there is no one best way to implement TQM initiatives. TQM initiatives can be as unique as each individual business school and business ethics course and as unique as each student who participates in the business ethics education process. However, there are four basic areas that each business ethics educator's outcome assessment effort will have in common. They are the stages of the TQM cycle. Those four stages are: (1) thoroughly plan the assessment change initiative; (2) implement the change initiative; (3) assess the effectiveness of the initiative; and (4) revise, if necessary, and then act on the results. Always keep in mind that this is a cyclical, continuous process designed to improve quality, whether for business ethics courses, business ethics programs, or special efforts such as outcomes assessment initiatives in business ethics teaching.

Business school administrators, members of the broader college community, and faculty must attend to those issues that can serve as barriers to bringing outcomes assessment to fruition. The extent to which these issues are successfully addressed increases the likelihood that departments and individual faculty members can help to institutionalize outcomes assessment in business ethics. The next chapter takes a closer look at why and how teachers assess learning and their business ethics teaching efforts.

REFERENCES

AACSB (American Assembly of Collegiate Schools of Business). 1994. *Achieving quality and continuous improvement through self-evaluation and peer review: Standards for accreditation business administration and accounting.* St. Louis, MO: Author.

Adams, J.S., Tashchian, A., & Shore, T.H. 1999. Frequency, recall and usefulness of undergraduate ethics education. *Teaching Business Ethics* 3: 241–253.

Astin, A. 1988. *Achieving educational excellence.* San Francisco: Jossey-Bass.

Astin, A. 1991. *Assessment for excellence.* Phoenix, AZ: American Council on Education and Oryx Press.

Cascio, W.F. 1987. *Costing human resources: The financial impact of behavior in organizations* (2nd ed.). Boston: Kent.

Colby, A., & Kohlberg, L. 1987. *The measurement of moral judgment: Theoretical foundations and research validations, and standard issues scoring manual,* Vols. 1 and 2. Cambridge, MA: Cambridge University Press.

Cook, T.D., Campbell, D.T., & Perrachio, L. Quasi experimentation. In M.D. Dunnette & L.M. Hough (eds.), *Handbook of Industrial and organizational psychology,* Vol. 1 (2nd ed.). Palo Alto, CA: Consulting Psychologists Press.

Daft, R.L. 1989. *Organization theory.* New York: West Publishing Company.

Deming, W.E. 1986. *Out of crisis.* Cambridge, MA: MIT Center for Advanced Engineering Study.

Erwin, T.D. 1991. *Assessing student learning and development: A guide to the principles, goals, and methods of determining college outcomes.* San Francisco: Jossey-Bass.

Goldstein, I.L. 1986. *Training in organizations: Needs assessment, development and evaluation* (2nd ed.). Pacific Grove, CA: Brooke/Cole.

Hosmer, L.T. 2000. Standard format for the case analysis of moral problems. *Teaching Business Ethics* 4: 169–180.

Iyer, G.R. 1998. Integrating business ethics in classroom teaching: Some preliminary considerations. *Teaching Business Ethics* 1: 315–331.

Kilpatrick, D.L. 1977. Evaluating training programs: Evidence vs. proof. *Training and Development Journal* 31: 9–12.

Loeb, J.W. 1992. *Academic standards in higher education.* New York: College Entrance Examination Board.

Loeb, S.E. 1991. The evaluation of outcomes of accounting ethics education. *Journal of Business Ethics* 10: 77–84.

Miller, M.S., & Miller, A.E. 1976. It's too late for ethics courses in business schools. *Business and Society Review* 1: 39–42.

Oddo, A.R. 1997. A framework for teaching business ethics. *Journal of Business Ethics* 16: 293–297.

Ozar, D.T. 1998. An outcomes-centered approach to teaching public-sector ethics. In J. Bowman and D. Menzel (eds.), *Teaching ethics and values in public administration programs.* Albany: State University of New York Press.

Rest, J.R. 1979. *Development in judging moral issues.* Minneapolis: University of Minnesota Press.

Rest, J.R. 1983. Morality. In J. Flavell, E. Markham, & P.H. Mussen (eds.), *Handbook of child psychology: Vol. 3, Cognitive development.* New York: John Wiley & Sons.

Rest, J.R. 1984. The magic components of morality. In W. Kurtines & J. Gewrits (eds.), *Morality, moral behavior, and moral development.* New York: John Wiley & Sons.

Rest, J.R. 1994. Background, theory and research. In J.R. Rest & D. Narváez (eds.), *Moral development in the professions.* Hillsdale, NJ: Lawrence Erlbaum Associates.

Rohr, J.A. 1989. *Ethics for bureaucrats* (2nd ed.). New York: Marcel Dekker.

Schonsheck, J. 1998. A team-taught course in business ethics and its synthesizing capstone assignment. *Teaching Business Ethics* 1: 399–429.

Seymour, D. 1993. *On Q: Causing quality in higher education.* Phoenix, AZ: American Council on Education and Oryx Press.

Sims, R.R. 1990. *An experiential learning approach to employee training systems.* Westport, CT: Greenwood Press.

Sims, S.J. 1992. *Student outcomes assessment: A historical review and guide to program development.* Westport, CT: Greenwood Press.

Snarey, J., & Keljo, J. 1994. Revitalizing the meaning and measurement of moral development. Essay review of "Moral maturity: Measuring the development of sociomoral reflection" by J.C. Gibbs, K.S. Basinger & D. Fuller. *Human Development* 37(3): 181–186.

Thoma, S.J. 1994. Trends and issues in moral judgment research using the defining issues test. *Moral Education Forum* 19(1): 1–7.

Tracey, W.R. 1968. *Evaluating training and development systems.* New York: American Management Association.

Weber, J. 1990. Measuring the impact of teaching ethics to future managers: A review, assessment, and recommendations. *Journal of Business Ethics* 9: 183–190.

Weber, J., & Glyptis, S.M. 2000. Measuring the impact of a business ethics course and community service experience on students' values and opinions. *Teaching Business Ethics* 4: 341–358.

Wittmer, D.P. 2000. Ethical sensitivity in management decisions: Developing and testing a perceptual measure among management and professional student groups. *Teaching Business Ethics* 4: 181–205.

Chapter 13

Outcomes Assessment: Why Evaluate Your Business Ethics Teaching Efforts?

INTRODUCTION

Improving teaching in business ethics is facilitated by feedback. We need ways to find out whether or not we are achieving the learning outcomes of our business ethics teaching efforts. The ultimate criterion for assessing teaching efforts is student learning. John Dewey said, "Teaching is like selling; you can't have a sale unless someone buys. You haven't taught unless someone has learned" (McKeachie, 1994). Student learning is not simply a function of the business ethics teacher. Assessing student learning should therefore be of primary concern to those responsible for teaching business ethics as soon as there is agreement on the goals or purpose of teaching business ethics.

Although it is important for us as business ethics teachers to become more skillful in our teaching and to be able to gain more direct feedback about what learning is occurring as a result of our teaching, the institutions and business schools where we teach are increasingly concerned about providing evidence that teaching has a *cumulative* effect. To put the matter bluntly, business schools, like their host institutions, are being asked to demonstrate that students who study on their campuses are "getting an education." To "get an education" may mean something quite different in a school of arts and sciences than in a business school. But all institutions and business schools today, from the largest to the smallest, are being asked to describe their anticipated educational outcomes for students and to demonstrate that they are making efforts to assess student learning in light of those stated outcomes.

This chapter focuses on the specifics of outcomes assessment in particular business ethics teaching efforts. The chapter first discusses the importance of measuring or evaluating teaching performance. Next, the chapter focuses on selecting evaluation strategies to use in assessing business ethics teaching efforts. Obstacles to introducing outcomes assessment in business ethics teaching efforts are then discussed, followed by a look at assessing learning objectives and satisfaction in interdisciplinary teaching efforts. Before concluding the chapter with a discussion of future concerns, a number of questions designed to adequately evaluate outcomes assessment efforts are highlighted.

The following general definitions of terms encountered in outcomes assessment may be helpful:

- *Assessment*—The collection, synthesis, and interpretation of information to aid in decision making.
- *Testing*—A formal, systematic, usually paper-and-pencil procedure for gathering information.
- *Measurement*—Quantifying or assigning numbers to performance.
- *Evaluation*—Deciding about the quality or goodness of performance or a course of action.

MEASURING YOUR PERFORMANCE

Measuring performance is more important in some situations than others. For instance, if you have just started jogging, you may simply want to go out and run until you're tired and then head for home. After a while, you may become curious and start to look at your watch at the beginning and end of your jog to know about how long you have run. If you decide to train for your first race, you might drive your car along your running route to measure a 10-kilometer course and buy a stopwatch to begin to keep tracking your time. However, if you ever become a competitive athlete, the distance you run will be measured much more accurately and whether you win or lose a race may be a matter of only a few hundredths of a second. In each of these cases, the situation calls for different levels of measurement and a different method of evaluating your progress.

When any one of us sets out to achieve a goal, we use an evaluation process to determine if our goal has been accomplished. Evaluation can also be used to obtain information needed to help us improve our performance in the future. Four key questions related to evaluation in teaching are addressed before moving on to a discussion of outcomes assessment in business ethics education. First, what is the purpose and who is the intended audience for your evaluation? Second what kind of overall strategies should guide your evaluation? Third, what kind of variables should you measure? Fourth, what are the steps in planning an effective evaluation?

What Is Evaluation?

What is an evaluation and why should it be conducted? Lenning (1989) defines the evaluation process as "judgments about value, worth, and ways to improve" (p. 328).

Purpose. Teaching evaluations can be used for many purposes. Evaluations can be used to answer a variety of questions, including: "To what extent is Course X meeting its goals?" "How can the course be improved?" The first step in considering an evaluation is to determine what question you are trying to answer. For example, in one situation you may want to conduct an evaluation simply to give you a rough idea of how you did and give you a few ideas for next time. At the other extreme is a situation in which teaching evaluations must demonstrate effectiveness in order to ensure your ongoing support for offering the course or module. The type of evaluation you conduct will differ depending on its intended use.

Audience. Related to the question of the purpose of an evaluation is the intended audience. For whom is the evaluation being conducted? Who will see the results? How will this information be used? Depending on the context of the course being offered, different stakeholders may have an interest in the results of your evaluation. Andrews (1997) points out that users of evaluative information may include individual learners (students) or interested second parties such as employers, faculty, business school or college administrators, and various government agencies. Herman et al. (1987) point out that "for some evaluations, or courses, the roles of evaluator, sponsor, stakeholder, and user are all played by the same people" (p. 8). This is often the case in teaching business ethics. By clarifying the purpose and audience of these evaluations, you will be more prepared to make decisions about which strategies to employ.

Evaluator. Before you plan your evaluation, you must decide whether you should design and conduct the evaluation yourself or whether you should select an outside evaluator. This decision will be impacted by the breadth and complexity of the evaluation in question, your familiarity with the evaluation process, and the need for objectivity. Although many business school faculty do their own evaluations, there may be situations that call for an outside evaluator who has more expertise or more time and resources to conduct an extensive evaluation. It may also be necessary to use an outside evaluator if you will be reporting your results to stakeholders or decision makers who may have concerns about your ability to evaluate your own business ethics teaching outcomes objectively. For example, it is not unusual for those who endow ethics chairs or programs in business schools to ask for outside evaluations of the impact of business ethics teaching efforts. If you select an outside evaluator, you should choose someone who has experience and expertise appropriate to the evaluation being conducted.

Table 13.1
Characteristics of Formative and Summative Assessments

	Formative	Summative
Purpose	To monitor and guide a process while it is still in progress	To judge the success of a process at its completion
Time of assessment	During the process	At the end of the process
Type of assessment techniques	Informal observation, quizzes, homework, pupil questions, worksheets	Formal tests, projects, and term papers
Use of assessment techniques	Improve and change a process while it is still going on	Judge the overall success of a process; grade, place, promote

DECIDING ON AN EVALUATION STRATEGY

Business ethics teachers must make three choices about evaluation strategies. First, will you use a formative or summative strategy? Second, will you collect quantitative or qualitative data to evaluate your business ethics teaching efforts? Third, will you be conducting a formal or informal evaluation? These decisions will be based on the purpose of evaluation and the audience and will lay a foundation for choosing variables and developing a specific plan. The objectives for the business ethics teaching effort should also be considered when or deciding how it should be evaluated.

Formative or Summative Strategies

The first choice regarding an evaluation strategy is whether to conduct a summative or a formative evaluation (Lenning, 1989). A summative evaluation "looks at the total of a course or program" whereas a "formative evaluation requires collecting and sharing information for course or program improvement" (Sims, 1990; Sims, 1992). In other words, a summative evaluation is most likely to occur at the end of a business ethics course and measure the outcome. A formative evaluation is ongoing, can be either formal or informal, and is more likely to occur in the midst of a course in order to improve it. Table 13.1 provides a closer look at the characteristics of formative and summative strategies.

Quantitative or Qualitative Strategies

The second major choice regarding an evaluation strategy is whether to collect qualitative or quantitative data, or both. Quantitative data give precise numerical measures, while qualitative data provide rich descriptive materials. Traditional methods of evaluation tended to emphasize the need for objective, quantitative data. However, more recent approaches to evaluation recognize the limitations of relying solely on numerical results and, therefore, also include qualitative measures. If your evaluations are simply for your own personal improvement, then you may find qualitative data more helpful. In contrast, if your evaluation will be used by business school administrators to make decisions about the worth and continued support of your teaching efforts, then it may be necessary to provide objective, quantitative measures of outcomes. Many business educators choose to collect both qualitative and quantitative data to take advantage of the strengths of each strategy ("What have you liked most about the course so far?" "How can the remainder of this course be improved to meet your needs better?"). In the end, it is important to remember that with courses that are designed to change behaviors it is often difficult to use quantitative measurements.

Formal or Informal Strategies

The third choice you will make when choosing an evaluation strategy is whether to conduct a formal or informal evaluation. Informal evaluations depend upon casual observation, implicit goals, intuitive norms, and subjective judgement, and formal evaluation is based on controlled comparisons and objective measures. In most business courses, it is helpful to conduct an ongoing informal evaluation even if a formal, summative evaluation is planned. Informal evaluation can be planned by providing time for feedback at choice points during the course or can occur spontaneously. Informal evaluation almost always takes the form of listening to feedback about your course and taking action on what you learn.

Combining Strategies

Of course, business school teachers can combine the various strategies. Most faculty rely on combinations of formative, summative, quantitative, qualitative, formal, and informal evaluation strategies depending on the situation and the intended audience.

Some examples of combinations of strategies and corresponding examples are:

Informal qualitative formative: Midway through a business ethics class, the teacher asks for verbal feedback and presents choices for how to spend time during the remainder of the class.

Informal qualitative summative: At the end of a business ethics module, the teacher leads a discussion about learning activities used, including strengths and weakness of each activity. The teacher takes notes and uses this feedback in designing other modules or classes.

Formal quantitative summative: At the end of the business ethics course, the teacher distributes an evaluation form that asks the students to give numerical rankings regarding the accomplishment of each learning objective.

Formal qualitative summative: At the end of the business course, the teacher distributes an evaluation form that asks students to respond to open-ended questions about each of the learning activities.

DECIDING WHICH VARIABLES TO MEASURE

Once business ethics teachers have decided upon a combination of evaluation strategies, the next step is to determine what variables they want to measure and observe. I have found out that many evaluations attempt to answer the question "How will students be different after participating in the business ethics education effort?" Most evaluations target one of three types of variables: satisfaction, the accomplishment of learning objectives, or behavior change.

Evaluating Satisfaction

The easiest and most frequent evaluation target of business ethics teaching efforts is satisfaction. Evaluating satisfaction answers the questions, "Were students satisfied with the business ethics teaching effort?" and "Did it meet their expectations?" This measures the users' perception of the outcome. In this instance, you are not directly measuring whether students actually changed their behavior after the teaching effort. Although it is often assumed that satisfaction is correlated with more important outcomes like learning or behavior change, this is not necessarily true. Therefore, we should not base our assessments only on satisfaction but also on evaluation of other outcomes. Examples of evaluation items measuring satisfaction are presented below (1 = strongly disagree, 2 = disagree, 3 = neutral, 4 = agree, 5 = strongly agree):

1. The overall quality of this business ethics module was high.
2. This business ethics module met my expectations.
3. I learned a great deal of new information from this business ethics module.
4. The business ethics module effectively used a variety of activities to meet my learning needs.
5. The business ethics teacher was responsive to the needs of students.

These evaluation items are most likely to be used in a formal, quantitative, summative evaluation strategy and would be appropriate for almost any business ethics teaching effort.

Objective-Based Evaluation

Learning objectives set by the business ethics teacher in agreement with other stakeholders are a second type of evaluation variable. In most evaluations, you will want to measure or observe the extent to which the goals of the business ethics teaching effort have been achieved. You must make sure, however, that all the effort's important objectives have been articulated. To evaluate the accomplishment of objectives, you should ask at least one question for each of the learning objectives. Examples of evaluation items measuring the accomplishment of objectives are listed below (1 = strongly disagree, 2 = disagree, 3 = neutral, 4 = agree, 5 = strongly agree):

1. I was encouraged to reflect on and use my own professional experience as a source of learning business ethics.
2. I learned at least three strategies for improving my effectiveness in handling ethical dilemmas (or making ethical decisions).
3. I had an opportunity to experiment actively with and practice at these strategies.
4. I was encouraged to select behaviors and skills that would allow me to enact these strategies in my day-to-day life back in my work or other situations.

The sample items are based on a business ethics teaching module with four objectives based on four types of experiential learning and are most likely to be used in a formal, quantitative, and summative evaluation strategy.

Behavior Change

A third type of evaluation variable is behavior change. (Note: this type of evaluation is offered even though I do not believe that the goal of business ethics teaching efforts should be to bring about behavior change in students.) Evaluating behavior change is often more difficult than evaluating satisfaction or objectives, but it is a more stringent measure of whether a teaching effort actually made an impact. Behavior change can be evaluated either at the conclusion of a teaching effort or some time later. Students can rate their own behavior change, or it can be rated by other students, by the business ethics teacher, or by outside parties such as the colleagues, alumni, or potential employers. It is also possible to have students demonstrate the competencies that the business ethics teaching effort addressed, and the behavior change can be rated to measure the success of the teaching effort.

Behavior change outside the business ethics teaching effort can also be used to evaluate outcome. Performance could be videotaped before and after a teaching effort and this could be rated by experts according to criteria related to the content of the business ethics teaching effort. In many instances, business ethics teachers will need to depend on evaluating satisfaction or student perceptions of the accomplishment of objectives.

DEVELOPING AN EVALUATION PLAN

One cannot understate the importance of carefully planning how to implement an outcomes assessment and how to use the results. An assessment that is thoughtfully conducted but never used is not worth the time and effort required. Therefore, it is important to decide ahead of time how you will use the outcomes assessment data and build utilization into your outcomes assessment plan. One approach to outcomes assessment includes five sequential activities, which include formulating questions and standards, selecting a research design, collecting information, analyzing information, and reporting information. These five steps will be used to address the process of developing an outcomes assessment plan for business ethics teaching and will highlight the choices I have found that you need to make during each step.

Formulating Questions and Standards

The first step in developing and outcomes assessment plan is to specify the question that the assessment is intended to answer. It is important to consider the use of the evaluation and to get input from all the stakeholders who may be looking at the outcome assessment data and conclusion. Your outcomes assessment question may be something like, "Will students be more moral or ethical after the teaching business ethics effort?" or "Will there be a change in ethical decision-making strategies used and students' perceptions of their moral or ethical responsibilities as a result of this business ethics teaching effort?

In addition to clarifying the outcomes assessment question, you will need to decide how you will know whether the answer to the question is affirmative or negative. The answer addresses the issue of standards. Setting outcome assessment standards can be defined as deciding what kind of information will provide convincing evidence of a business ethics teaching effort's success." For example, Kracher (1999) in her article "What Does It Mean When Mitchell Gets an 'A' in Business Ethics? Or the Importance of Service Learning" states that "Mitchell must be able to act responsibly. Thus, a business ethics course must prepare students for ethical business action" (p. 293). Thus, what will Mitchell be able to do with what he learned from the class? The outcomes assessment for Kracher's business ethics teaching effort and for Mitchell would be "Will Mitchell be more prepared for ethical business action?" "Will Mitchell be able to act responsibly and not only give good ethical reasons for acting but actually turn these reasons into right action in tough, fast business situations?"

Basing outcomes assessment standards on experts or other stakeholders, past performance, comparison with other groups or the same group at another time, norms, or the business ethics teacher's course, module, class, or activity description can determine the impact of business ethics teaching efforts. For example, an outcomes assessment that uses a comparison standard might hold as its criterion for success that there is a significant increase in students ethical reasoning/reflection skills between the beginning of the ethics education effort and a point in time three weeks after the ethics education effort. A more specific example can be gleaned from the work of Peppas and Diskin (2000). Peppas and Diskin compared the ethical perspectives of marketing majors to those of other business majors in terms of an ethical practices code. They examined whether taking a course in ethics had an effect on the ethical perspectives of marketing majors. A search of the literature on teaching business ethics suggests that using a comparison standard or method is a favorite among researchers and scholars in this area (see, for example, Cooper & Frank, 1997; Dawson, 1997; Loo, 2001; Sanyal, 2000). Benchmarking with comparable business schools or ethics courses is another way of establishing outcomes assessment standards and making comparisons.

Selecting a Research Design

The second step in developing an outcomes assessment plan is to select a research design. A research design identifies when and from whom measurements will be taken (or data will be collected) and specifies the extent to which certain experimental controls (if any) will be used. Many business ethics modules, classes, or short activities rely exclusively on a post-test design in which data are not collected before the teaching effort and a control group is not used. Although this method may be sufficient for some purposes, using this design makes it difficult to assess whether a business ethics teaching effort had an impact. If you use a pre-test/post-test design, measuring the same group of students before and after a business ethics education effort, you can determine whether a change occurred. McCabe et al. (1994) used a pre- and post-test design to examine changes in students' personal values. Seshardi et al. (1998) also used a pre-test/post-test design in their efforts to assess whether or not formal training in business ethics affected ethical decisions of future executives. Wittmer (2000) suggested using the Ethical Sensitivity Test (EST) as a pre-test for students entering a particular ethics class to assess subjects' (students) awareness (sensitivity) of ethical aspects of problems and analytical abilities in resolving ethical problems. It is important for those who select a pre-test/post-test design to recognize that you cannot conclude that a business ethics teaching education itself was responsible for the change; perhaps the change would have occurred anyway. In order to prove that the teaching effort caused the change, you must use a control group of students and demonstrate that change occurred in the experimental group of students (those who participated in the business ethics teaching effort) but not in the control group (those who did not participate).

Collecting and Analyzing Information

The third step in planning an outcomes assessment is deciding how to collect information related to the outcomes of your business ethics teaching effort. The fourth step is deciding how to analyze your data. Possible methods for collecting information include observations, interviews, questionnaires, tests, product reviews, performance reviews, and journals or portfolios. One way some business ethics teachers collect data from students is through the use of vignettes and questionnaires. For example, in an effort to determine whether or not the same business students would respond to "unfamiliar business ethics dilemmas" as well as more "familiar academic ethical dilemmas," Geiger and O'Connell (1999) used multiple vignettes (10 academic and five accounting/business vignettes) to collect information. After reading each scenario, students indicated on a seven-point semantic differential scale the extent to which they believed the action taken was ethical (1) or unethical (7); the likelihood they would have performed the same action—low (1) to high (7); and their perception of whether their peers would have performed the same action—low (1) to high (7). In other situations, many business ethics teachers require students keep a journal (Kracher, 1999) and write reflection papers (Fort & Zollers, 1999). In completing their journals students are required to make regular entries, which they use to reflect on their experiences (e.g., in a community service learning project). In addition, the business ethics teacher may ask students to produce additional brief papers from time to time as well as a final paper in which they are asked to stand back from the experience and elaborate on what they have learned about business ethics through their service and what they have learned about themselves.

Kracher (1999) offers insight on analyzing outcomes assessment data from her business ethics teaching effort by taking a look at how she assesses or grades service work assignments. She suggests that "because of academic integrity, students cannot achieve an 'A' on a business ethics service assignment only by learning to love service. Students must serve to learn and thus must be graded on what they learn about themselves, business and their community" (pp. 300–301). Kracher assigns grades based on submitted reports using the following objective criteria: organization of the report, description of service experiences, integration of service experiences with academic material, level of personal reflections, and confirmation of service work. She clearly states in her syllabus how to meet each criteria.

To collect and analyze information on their business ethics teaching efforts, Fort and Zollers (1999) rely on: (1) a short reflective paper on the student's model of business ethics; (2) a mid-term exam designed to test the student's moral reasoning process; (3) an assigned final exam topic; and (4) a group research paper. In a business ethics and marketing course Sims and Brinkmann (forthcoming) suggest the following ways to collect and analyze data from a business ethics teaching effort: (1) one individual oral text presentation in class (one-page handout summary/abstract of a book chapter, a journal article, or something similar—pass/fail); (2) case elaboration, analysis and presentation in class with one to three participants (maximum 15-page paper); and (3) individual final essay. (See Loeb & Ostas, 2000 for another example of collecting and analyzing assessment information in teaching business ethics.)

In discussing their use of the guest lecture approach to teaching business ethics Sims and Brinkmann (forthcoming) suggest that the most interesting question for an ethics teacher is how such guest intermezzos cover various ethics teaching objectives, such as furthering moral self-reflection, responsibility awareness, moral judgement, moral sharing, and developing a critical attitude towards frictions and contradictions in relation to the ordinary course content (cf. Brinkmann & Sims 2001). Other interesting questions, according to Sims and Brinkmann (forthcoming), relate to how realistic such a hit-and-run ethics strategy can be and suggest that once business ethics teachers develop the purpose and goals for any business ethics teaching effort they should also identify the specific outcomes they want to achieve. That is, what should students be able to do differently as a result of participating in the teaching business ethics effort? And how will we assess the difference? Table 13.2 offers a simple way to evaluate realistically in five different business ethics courses or courses with ethics components whether students' mind-sets are reached and influenced sufficiently. Empty cells can be filled by criterion-wise teacher and student evaluation, indicated as quantitative grades or qualitative statements (cf. Table 13.2, with a subjective impression of the assumed clearest strengths and weaknesses plotted in as "−" and "+").

In the end, it is not so much which methods business ethics teachers use to collect and analyze information to assess the impact of their business ethics teaching efforts but the fact that they take the time to recognize the importance of doing so. And this recognition must begin as soon as there is consensus on the purpose and goals of teaching business ethics.

Another example of collecting and analyzing data in the assessment of business ethics education is offered by Holt et al. (1998). These authors designed a performance-based assessment of moral reasoning in business ethics, specifically patterned after the essay component of Educational Testing Services' Tasks in Critical Thinking Test—a descendant of the New Jersey General Intelligence Skills Assessment (Livingston, 1994) and a method widely used for the evaluation of writing (White, 1985). Briefly,

Table 13.2
Achievement of Business Ethics Objectives in Different Business Courses or Modules

Teaching business ethics goals (Brinkmann & Sims, 2001)	Courses or Modules				
	Crash Course	Intercultural Communication	Research Methodology	Retail Management	Business and Marketing Ethics
Know thyself	+	+	+	−	+
Responsibility awareness	?	?	?		+
Moral judgement	?	−	−	+	+
Moral sharing	+	+	+	−	+
Criticism of other business courses		−	+	−	+
Moral motivation	+	+	−	?	+
Moral courage		+	?	−	+

students write an extended response to a question or problem, called a prompt, and the results are scored holistically. The "core" in core scoring is a number representing basic proficiency. The assignment of scores is guided by criteria, rubrics, and rangefinders. Criteria specify key components of the skill to be assessed. Rubrics provide general definitions of performance levels in terms of the criteria. Rangefinders are sample papers which display general terms of the criteria.

Holt et al.'s process of constructing an assessment instrument led to a common objective for business ethics—the improvement of ethical reasoning—and operationalized this objective in terms of specific performance indicators. More specifically, Holt et al. identified the essential characteristics of a well-reasoned answer to an ethical issue (i.e., case). It was determined that a well-reasoned answer should be assessed in terms of its relevance, complexity, fairness, argumentation, and depth. That is, students should address a distinctly ethical aspect of the case and not digress from the task at hand. Beyond that, they should be sensitive to the complexities of a case, particularly the different perspectives, interests, and moral principles it might involve; they should acknowledge the relative strengths of alternative approaches; and they should construct a coherent and well-developed argument for their own position. Moral depth takes into account factors such as creative resolution of ethical conflict or development or philosophical considerations underlying choices of moral principles.

Holt et al. provide the following suggestions about how these criteria are to be applied in judging the following performance levels: nonproficient, lower than core proficiency, core proficiency, and higher than core proficiency. To achieve core proficiency, a student must articulate some of the complexities of a case, show an awareness of alternatives, and develop an argument. An essay is less than proficient if it does not clearly contain these elements, and it is rated higher than core proficiency to the extent that these elements are developed more fully or with greater sophistication. An important point to emphasize about the development of the performance-based assessment instrument described by Holt et al. (1998) is that the instrument was the result of interdisciplinary discussions between philosophers, business faculty, and business professionals concerned with the nature of business ethics, the goals of a business ethics course, and the methods available for assessing ethical reasoning abilities.

Schonsheck (1998) also offers a look at how to assess student learning in a team-taught business ethics effort (i.e., the two team members are a business and a philosophy professor) at Le Moyne College's MBA program. In the final capstone assignment students are required to complete a business case analysis and moral philosophy. The capstone assignment (The Grand Synthesis) is a written standard business case analysis of the *SCA Corporation* case, and the format of the paper is composed of the following sections:

Executive summary

Introduction

Problem statement/Analysis of problem (symptoms and causes)

Options/Analysis of options

Recommendations

Implementation plan

Conclusion

The grading criteria for the case are:

Business: show mastery of business strategy; remember to include stakeholder analysis)

Philosophy: identification of philosophically important points of synthesis; accuracy of philosophical treatment

Both: general clarity and coherence

Each student submits two copies of The Grand Synthesis, one to each of the instructors, and they grade them independently. Although each of them tends to concentrate on their own areas of expertise, each feels quite free to comment on anything in the paper. In selecting the case for the capstone assignment, the instructors make sure that there is at least one "natural point of contact" for each of the four philosophers studied in the course: Aristotle, Kant, Mill, and Marx (Schonsheck, 1998). This focus provides the basis for a critique of crucial actions/decisions/policies or points the way toward a morally superior course of action (that is consistent with sound business practices). Thus, when grading the work, the philosophy instructor looks first to those "points of contact." Better papers generally have more points of contact; however, a student could show mastery of the philosophical material of the course by finding but four points of contact: an Aristotelian, a Kantian, a Utilitarian, and Marxian. Students must show mastery of the material by accurately synopsizing the relevant portion of the cited philosopher's position and by using it in a way that improves the analysis of the case by clarifying issues, exposing faulty reasoning, or contributing to the resolution of some ethical issue. Thus, merely finding points of contact is not sufficient.

In less successful papers, students fail to see important points of contact between the philosophical and business issues in the case or fail to develop their argument at points of contact. Papers are also less successful when the account of the philosophical material is flawed—a position is attributed to a philosopher that philosopher does not hold or the account of a philosopher's position contains inaccuracies. Some of the questions the philosophy instructor ask in regard to Aristotle include: Has the student discovered threats to a businessperson's virtue? Has the student identified the vice(s) that tempt? In regard to Kant, questions include: Has the student discovered violations of the Categorical Imperative? Does the student correctly generate the maxims from proposed actions (alternatives) and argue plausibly that he/she could (could not) will those maxims universal law? In regard to Utilitarianism, questions include: Has the student discovered instances in which it is important to maximize utility? Has the student offered a (relatively) complete list of persons affected (i.e., stakeholders)? And in regard to Marx, questions include: Has the student discovered issues where a Marxian analysis yields genuine insight? Does the student show how viewing matters from a Marxian perspective can indicate morally superior courses of action?

Finally, Hosmer (2000) offers a useful assessment tool for collecting and analyzing students' use of ethical principles in analyzing business principles or, more importantly, in achieving the balance between active engagement with the essential issues of a business case and a critical analysis of choices. Hosmer's initial rationale for developing the assessment tool was to improve class discussion. More specifically, Hosmer uses a standardized format that he developed, which he hands out to students each time he assigns a major case. Students are required to thoughtfully complete the fill-in-the-blank responses to 20 questions and hand them back in for grading. A maximum of five points is assigned for each question, and consequently, grading on the familiar scale of 0 to 100 is straightforward and simple.

Each question, or more properly each section that requires a response, comes with a brief description of the issue to be addressed or the principle to be applied. After determining whether or not a moral problem exists in the assigned case, students are expected to proceed through the balance of the steps in the moral reasoning process. The form leads the students through the steps, starting with the identification of the benefits and harms and the rights and wrongs to be received by the different groups of people. The major headings of Hosmer's form are: (1) Identify the benefits; (2) Identify the harms; (3) Identify the rights; (4) Identify the wrongs; (5) State the moral problem; (6) List the major alternatives; (7) Resolve the factual issues; (8) Acknowledge the personal impacts; (9) Self-interests; (10) Personal virtues; (11) Religious injunctions; (12) Government requirements; (13) Utilitarian benefits; (14) Universal duties; (15) Individual rights; (16) Economic efficiency; (17) Distributive justice; (18) Contributive liberty; (19) Reach your moral solution; and (20) Support your moral solution. (See Hosmer, 2000 for a more detailed discussion of each of the categories.)

I have not yet used Hosmer's assessment tool; however, a respected colleague has used the tool twice and highly recommends its use. And as Hosmer (2000) notes, his class discussions have gotten past that "my opinion is just as valid as your opinion" mind block, and students are now clearly working up the hoped-for scale (Rest & Narváez, 1994) of moral sensitivity, moral judgement, moral motivation, and finally, moral character.

Reporting Information

The final step in outcomes assessment planning involves decisions about how to report the results of your assessment. As with other parts of the outcomes assessment process, reporting results can vary in degree of formality. An informal outcomes assessment report may take the form of a discussion of the business ethics teaching effort's strengths and weaknesses with the requester or a written summary of student comments. If you need to write a formal evaluation report, it will probably include the following sections: introduction, method, results, discussion, conclusions, recommendations, and an executive summary. In addition to the written sections of the report, I have found that you should also consider ways to use tables and graphs to present data. Your outcomes assessment report should be a way for you to showcase what you have accomplished in your business ethics teaching effort.

OBSTACLES TO ASSESSING STUDENT LEARNING IN TEACHING BUSINESS ETHICS

When teaching strategies are employed creatively and appropriately and the focus is on learning business ethics, the methods used to assess students will vary with the kind of learning that is taking place through that strategy. This appears to be a simple principle to grasp, but in reality it is not so easy to apply. What are the obstacles?

In the first place, assessment of student learning in business ethics education gets confused with grading in business schools. Indeed, they are often thought of as synonymous. Although as business ethics teachers we cannot turn our backs on the responsibility to produce grades—graduate schools, employers, parents, scholarship administrators, and honors committees need to examine students' grades occasionally—I believe there is a difference between generating grades for a class list and establishing a comprehensive evaluation system that produces useful information about progress in learning both for the student and the business ethics teacher. It is hoped that grades will reflect progress in learning, but a comprehensive evaluation system should produce more than grades. What happens, ironically, is that in the scramble to produce grades, business ethics teachers like myself may fail to gather information that provides knowledge about student learning. In my experience, what typically happens is that a teacher will spell out for the students, usually in the syllabus, what the grade "depends on," and with some variation the following pattern is produced: attendance, 10 percent; group discussion, 15 percent; quizzes, 20 percent; mid-term, 25 percent; final, 30 percent (mid-term and final most often applies to an examination of some type, although in many business ethics courses mid-term and final may refer to a journal or some other form of reflective written assignment). Once this is done, it easy to turn off one's brain and conclude that an evaluation system has been established. But has it?

The second obstacle to developing a more comprehensive approach to the evaluation of student learning in business ethics education is the narrowness of the range of evaluation devices used by a number of teachers in business schools. The tendency in many classrooms is to give tests, quizzes, or exams that require students to select right answers (multiple choice, true-false, matching) or to supply correct answers (completion, short answer, essay) or to respond in writing to case questions. This handful of testing methods often exhausts the repertory of many teachers. Furthermore, most of these methods, though they have the potential for evaluating some fairly complex learning outcomes, are used to test factual recall. Although most tests can be devised to examine more than recall, and although there are some useful suggestions available for how to develop such tests, there is a tendency to stay within the confines of the narrow range of options that many business teachers use. Can alternatives be developed?

Another obstacle to developing a more useful student evaluation system is the natural tendency to focus on end product evaluation as opposed to evaluation that takes place along the way—what is often referred to as "formative evaluation." Although it is important to know if students can reach the objectives of the course (or subunit within a course), it is also useful to know how many students are at what stages along the way. Students need evaluation information to know "how they are doing," and business ethics teachers need that information to make mid-course adjustments or corrections. With the emphasis being placed today on outcomes assessment, it may be important to be reminded that evaluation is most useful as an ongoing process, as opposed to a "terminal experience," about which one may or may not be able to do anything, if the feedback ever arrives. Are there ways to make evaluation continuous?

A final obstacle to designing a more comprehensive evaluation system is our own insecurity with receiving feedback about how students are actually progressing. Sometimes we don't ask because we just don't want to know. While it may not be the best source of information, it could be extremely useful in most business ethics courses to know the answers that students might give to the following questions related to learning outcomes and satisfaction:

- How is the course meeting (or not meeting) your expectations?
- Is this course relevant to you?
- What things do you perceive that you are learning in this course?

- What seems to be too difficult or too easy for you in this course?
- What could be done to make this course more stimulating for you?
- How do you think you are doing in this course?
- How much effort are you devoting to this course?

Knowing what we know about what students could say in response to these questions, it could be rather threatening to hear their answers; nonetheless, knowing what students feel about a business ethics course before it is over could be very useful to the teacher. Is there a way to do this?

Keeping these four things in mind—to think of evaluation as more than grading, to use a broader range of evaluation methods, to do more formative evaluation, and to find out from students how they are feeling about a course before it is over—we can consider the experiential learning teaching strategy, and the examples embedded in the presentation of this strategy, to think more carefully about how to align the system of student evaluation with the experiential learning strategy described earlier in this book.

Experiential learning is concerned with how people learn in a holistic way and that reflection on experience is a major part of this teaching strategy. The learning that occurs is global and personal and is not always easy to measure. It is not unusual for students to be encouraged to establish personal goals for the experience, and these can be used as criteria, or at least a starting point, to examine what learning has occurred. In a sense, the reflection process itself is designed to "bring forth" what learning is taking place, but the reflection process is also part of the learning. For this reason it is important not to make students feel that they are being evaluated or graded during the reflection process, even though this process provides the business ethics teacher some good feedback on what students are actually learning. For evaluation purposes, and for grading, it is probably best to have the students produce some reflective written products, some diaries or journals, some projects associated with their work, or a final paper in which they step back from and describes the learning that occurred. What the business ethics teacher is looking for in the students' work is insight about the experience and growth in self-awareness.

ASSESSING LEARNING OUTCOMES AND SATISFACTION IN INTERDISCIPLINARY BUSINESS ETHICS TEACHING EFFORTS

All the decisions made about issues raised in the previous chapters of this book will determine what can and ought to be done to assess student learning outcomes and satisfaction. If the interdisciplinary team has "done its homework" on the rest of the business ethic teaching effort, the task of assessment becomes much easier. On the other hand, if the teaching effort and desired learning outcomes are unclear, it will be difficult to development a good assessment plan.

Most business courses (including business ethics), discipline-based and interdisciplinary, have built into them some methods of testing students in order to determine grades or learning outcomes. This grading process usually involves quizzes, a mid-term and final exam, and maybe some "research" papers. Faculty often make two mistakes at this point: They usually use only this narrow range of artifacts to determine grades, and they equate the production of these artifacts, for grading purposes, with a system for assessing student learning outcomes and satisfaction. Using this narrow range of artifacts to determine grades and learning outcomes is not wrong, it is just too limited given the existence of so many other options.

The traditional grading and outcomes assessment options are the ones most frequently used for a number of good reasons: long-standing traditions are no accident. They are what most business teachers experienced during their own education, they are relatively easy to use, and they measure certain things traditionally associated with learning—whether students can remember information, whether they can find and draw on sources of information, and whether they can express their ideas in writing. Within this framework, however, the traditional options for assessing learning outcomes and determining grades are often used in incredibly unimaginative ways by business teachers and students. Important questions for business teachers, in general, and business ethics teachers, in particular, are: "Is it possible to be more creative?" "How can assessment of student learning and outcomes satisfaction be enriched in interdisciplinary business ethics education efforts?"

The goal, of course, is not simply to create more interesting and more diverse assessment options (although that is surely desirable), but in doing so, to measure more adequately the desired outcomes of the interdisciplinary business ethics effort. The first step, therefore, in designing more creative assessment options is to return to the basic idea of the business ethics education effort and to the peculiar characteristics of the interdisciplinary business ethics effort that has been generated. With a list of well-conceived learning outcomes for the business ethics education effort in one hand, one might hold in the other hand a menu of assessment options that includes quizzes, exams, and research papers but goes beyond these to include activities that can be especially designed to measure outcomes associated with interdisciplinary teaching and learning of business ethics, such as the following:

- Logs and diaries: Instruments to record systematic daily reflections and responses to ideas, issues, or experiences from various viewpoints.

- Case studies: Written or oral responses to cases that test students' powers of critical analysis, problem-solving abilities, and skill in applying diverse ethical (or moral) perspectives.
- Visual representations: Charts, tables, graphs, outlines, and models to display information, particularly the interrelationships of ethical concepts, ideas, and issues from different disciplines.
- Essays: Narratives in which students must state a point of view and defend it with evidence synthesized from multiple sources.
- Critiques: Thoughtful discussions of the strengths and weaknesses of books, articles, films, concepts, or exhibits, using multiple criteria.
- Team projects: Reports of team projects that require coordination of diverse individual efforts and the synthesis of information from multiple sources.
- Interviews: Reports of interviews with people who have different viewpoints or perspectives on a common theme or problem.
- Panel discussions: Participation on panels where issues are debated and discussed from opposing viewpoints.
- Reflection on experience-based learning: Oral or written reflections on service learning or brief internships.
- Role-plays and simulations: Acting out and then discussing or reporting on situations that can be understood best at a variety of levels or form different perspectives.

The menu can be adapted or lengthened as necessary, but these items give an indication at least of the kinds of things that students can be asked to do to demonstrate some of the desired outcomes of interdisciplinary teaching and learning of business ethics. Not all of the demonstrations of learning need necessarily be graded, but there is no reason why any of the items from the above menu could not be graded, given some carefully thought-out criteria and guidelines for the process.

STUDENT PERCEPTIONS OF INTERDISCIPLINARY APPROACHES TO TEACHING BUSINESS ETHICS

One thing that is useful to know about interdisciplinary team-taught business ethics efforts is what students perceive about the interdisciplinary nature of the efforts. I have found that Likert-scale responses (1–5) similar to the following questions can be used to gather students' perceptions:

1. To what extent would you say there is evidence of collaboration (working together) by faculty in *planning* this business ethics effort?
2. To what extent would you say that faculty have tried to *integrate the content* of this business ethics effort?

3. To what extent would you say that faculty *have been successful* in integrating ethics in the business ethics effort?

4. In describing the classroom teaching in this course (module), to what extent would you say faculty were *collaborating*?

5. To what extent would you say faculty have collaborated in establishing and carrying out *grading and evaluation practices* for this business ethics effort?

It is interesting to note that most of the questions focus on the nature of the business ethics effort as an interdisciplinary initiative in order to see whether students perceive the special values peculiar to interdisciplinary team teaching. If they do not, perhaps the level of collaboration is low or more interpretation needs to be made concerning course goals and learning outcomes. I believe that one of the most important things one might wish to find out about an interdisciplinary team-taught business ethics effort is whether or not, and to what degree, it is perceived as such by students in the course. If students have no perception of this, why are the faculty going to all this trouble?

As noted earlier, assessment data about a business ethics effort can also be gathered through informal means. It may seem odd, but faculty seldom do the most obvious and direct thing to gather feedback about a business ethics education effort: ask students. This can be done in class, through a general discussion, after class with students who linger, at a brown-bag lunch with a representative group of students, or through focus groups, carefully selected to represent all backgrounds. The all-important question for focus groups is: What are we trying to achieve and are we achieving it? If students can't articulate the goals of the business ethics teaching effort or are frustrated in achieving the goals, some modifications may need to be made. If in doubt about how the business ethics education effort is coming across to students, ask them. If you doubt they will tell you, or it may be too painful to listen, get someone else to ask them for you. In whatever manner the conversation with students takes place, it is important to gain feedback from them about their satisfaction as well as their overall perception of the purposes of the business ethics education effort and the way it is functioning.

The ideal interdisciplinary team-taught business ethics effort begins with a willingness to work together by a group of faculty. The team members sometimes face the difficult task of inventing the interdisciplinary business ethics education effort and establishing learning outcomes. Teaching strategies can be identified and modified to take advantage of opportunities for collaboration. Assessment methods can be adapted to measure whether the most-valued learning outcomes are being achieved and whether the business ethics education effort is meeting student expectations.

ENSURING ADEQUATE EVALUATION OF PROGRAM OUTCOMES

Those responsible for planning outcomes assessment of business ethics teaching efforts would do well to address the following questions to ensure adequate evaluation of program outcomes:

1. Does the evaluation design fit the objectives of the outcomes assessment effort?
2. Does the design address important issues such as student, faculty, and department needs and expectations and institutional culture (expectations about authority, how hard to work, etc.)?
3. Does the evaluation method meet standards discussed by the developers of the outcomes assessment program?
4. Does the structure for the program provide a framework where emergent issues can be addressed?
5. Can the design be carried out in the time allotted?
6. Does the design provide a mix of evaluation activities that appeal to different data-gathering methodologies?
7. Is the evaluation logically sequenced?
8. Is there redundancy in information gathered in the evaluation effort? Should there be?
9. Is the design conducive to the ongoing development of outcomes assessment efforts?

Outcomes assessment of business ethics teaching efforts requires a follow-up plan for the improvement of the controllable variables (e.g., student and instructor performance, choice of materials, choice of pedagogy, and course/program assessment). It is important to emphasize the need to continue with those initiatives that are working well. Tracey (1968) points out that little net gain results from a program that stresses deficiencies and at the same time permits strengths to deteriorate. Additionally, overemphasis on improving weak areas, along with failure to recognize strengths, may dampen motivation and commitment to excellence that is essential to improving the outcomes assessment of business ethics teaching efforts.

Faculty involvement and support are critical to the long-term success of the assessment of business ethics teaching initiatives. Business school faculty must develop extensive knowledge that can be used to better assess business ethics education efforts. In addition, if all the key business school stakeholders are not included in the assessment process, they might respond with hostility. This hostility might take the form of open or passive resistance to the process. For example, faculty members might claim there is no need for assessment or refuse to participate in parts of the assessment process (e.g., attending meetings to make sense of assessment findings).

CONCLUSION AND FUTURE CONCERNS

The future of outcomes assessment in business ethics teaching efforts includes increased attention to the usefulness to business schools and their colleges and universities as well as to external stakeholders such as employers, who have a profound interest in outcomes assessment. As outcomes assessment begins to generate both good and bad feedback that may or may not be a positive reflection on the business school, it will be necessary to evaluate the effectiveness of the school's assessment efforts. The goal of such a cost-benefit analysis is to determine whether resources (financial, human, supplies, time, and so forth) have been used both efficiently and effectively at the business school or whether these resources could have been better used elsewhere.

Business schools and the larger institution have to spend more time deciding how their efforts to assess business ethics teaching outcomes will be evaluated from the earliest planning and design of the teaching efforts. This insures that all the needed data is collected at the appropriate time before and during the implementation of the assessment initiative. However, with more and more calls for some type of outcomes assessment information, business schools must avoid the tendency to implement in a crisis-oriented fashion their efforts to determine the impact of teaching business ethics on students. Without evaluation, improvements in our efforts to teach business ethics cannot be made.

Effective outcomes assessment of business ethics teaching occurs by:

- Objective and coordinated evaluation of every aspect of the operation.
- Application of imagination and creative thinking by all stakeholders.
- Deliberate collection of the observations, ideas, and thinking of all stakeholders.
- Critical analysis and synthesis of findings, ideas, and alternatives.
- Systematic, time-phased development and experimentation with policies and procedures as well as identification of resources (people, materials, time, space, and money) needed to carry out plans.

Outcomes assessment of business ethics teaching efforts should be evaluated by business schools, but the process should not end there. As a final step, the evaluation should include a follow-up plan to use the outcomes assessment results to improve efforts to teach business ethics.

In the end, outcomes assessment provides a mechanism for faculty to understand what is and is not working and why. Faculty and other stakeholders must ensure that outcomes assessment begins during their efforts to come to agreement on the goals of business ethics teaching efforts rather than through the lens of a post-course evaluation.

REFERENCES

Andrews, G.J. 1997. Workshop evaluation: Old myths and new wisdom. In J.A. Fleming (ed.), *New directions for adult and continuing education: No. 76, New perspectives on designing and implementing effective workshops.* San Francisco: Jossey-Bass, pp. 71–85.

Brinkmann, J., & Sims, R.R. 2001. Stakeholder-sensitive business ethics teaching. *Teaching Business Ethics* 5: 171–193.

Cooper, R.W., & Frank, G.L. 1997. Helping professionals in business behave ethically: Why business cannot abdicate its responsibility to the profession. *Journal of Business Ethics* 16: 1459–1466.

Dawson, L.M. 1997. Ethical differences between men and women in the sales profession. *Journal of Business Ethics* 16: 1143–1152.

Fort, T.L., & Zollers, F.E. 1999. Teaching business ethics: Theory and practice. *Teaching Business Ethics* 2: 273–290.

Geiger, M.A., & O'Connell, B.T. 1999. Student ethical perceptions and ethical-action propensities: An analysis of situation familiarity. *Teaching Business Ethics* 2: 305–325.

Herman, J.L., Morris, L.L., & Fitz-Gibbons, C.T. 1987. *Evaluator's handbook,* Vol. 1 (2nd ed.). In J.L. Herman (ed.), *Program evaluation kit.* Newbury Park, CA: Sage.

Holt, D., Heischmidt, K., Hill, H.H., Robinson, B., & Wiles, J. 1998. When philosophy and business professors talk: Assessment of ethical reasoning in a cross disciplinary business ethics course. *Teaching Business Ethics* 1: 253–268.

Kracher, B. 1999. What does it mean when Mitchell gets an "A" in business ethics? Or the importance of service learning. *Teaching Business Ethics* 2: 291–303.

Lenning, O.T. 1989. Assessment and evaluation. In U. Delworth & G.R. Hanson (eds.), *Student services: A handbook for the profession.* San Francisco: Jossey-Bass, pp. 327–352.

Livingston, S.A. 1994. *Tasks in critical thinking: Pilot testing the tasks in critical thinking.* Princeton, NJ: Educational Testing Service.

Loeb, S.E., & Ostas, D.T. 2000. The team teaching of business ethics in a weekly semester long format. *Teaching Business Ethics* 4: 225–238.

Loo, R. 2001. Encouraging classroom discussion of ethical dilemmas in research management: Three vignettes. *Teaching Business Ethics* 5: 195–212.

McCabe, D.L., Dukerich, J.M., & Dutton, J.E. 1994. The effects of professional education on values and resolution of ethical dilemmas: Business school vs. law school students. *Journal of Business Ethics* 13: 693–700.

McKeachie, W.J. 1994. *Teaching tips: Strategies, research, and theory for college and university teachers.* Lexington, MA: D.C. Heath and Company.

Peppas, S.C., & Diskin, B.A. 2000. Ethical perspectives: Are future marketers any different? *Teaching Business Ethics* 4: 207–220.

Rest, J., & Narváez, D. 1994. *Moral development in the profession.* Hillsdale, NJ: Lawrence Erlbaum Associates.

Sanyal, R.N. 2000. An experiential approach to teaching business ethics in international business. *Teaching Business Ethics* 4: 137–149.

Schonsheck, J. 1998. A team-taught course in business ethics and its synthesizing capstone assignment. *Teaching Business Ethics* 1: 399–429.

Seshardi, S., Broekemier, G.M., & Nelson, J.W. 1998. Business ethics—to teach or not to teach? *Teaching Business Ethics* 1: 303–313.

Sims, R.R. 1990. *An experiential learning approach to employee training systems.* Westport, CT: Quorum Books.

Sims, R.R., & Brinkmann, J. Forthcoming. Business ethics curriculum design: Issues, premises and experiences. *Teaching Business Ethics.*

Sims, S.J. 1992. *Student outcomes assessment: A historical review and guide to program development.* Westport, CT: Quorum Books.

Tracey, W.R. 1968. *Evaluating training and development systems.* New York: American Management Association.

White, E.M. 1985. *Teaching and assessing writing: Recent advances in understanding, evaluating, and improving student performance.* San Francisco: Jossey-Bass.

Wittmer, D.P. 2000. Ethical sensitivity in management decisions: Developing and testing perceptual measure among management and professional student groups. *Teaching Business Ethics* 4: 181–205.

Chapter 14

Successfully Teaching Business Ethics for Effective Learning

INTRODUCTION

One of the basic premises of this book has been that ethics can be taught (and learned) in business schools, even though it may be difficult in some situations to do so. This concluding chapter is concerned with identifying some of those things that I believe are necessary to successfully teach business ethics. For example, it is important to make sure students are aware that ethical dilemmas exist in the real world. I, like many other writers who believe ethics can be taught, think that its success requires that real-life examples and case studies be used in teaching efforts. Faculty who teach business ethics will have to make sure that students understand that ethics is the basis of good business and that business organizations have social responsibilities to discharge. To do this, they must start by taking the time to come to agreement with other key stakeholders about the purpose and goals of teaching business. In Chapter 2 I suggested seven goal components for teaching business ethics based on my work with Johannes Brinkmann of the Norwegian School of Management. This chapter will first speak about the importance of addressing the relevance challenge in teaching business ethics. The focus then turns to the need to continuously strive to achieve a balance between the active engagement of students with issues and a critical analysis of choices in business ethics teaching efforts. Next, the importance of attending to or managing the learning process in business schools is highlighted as the section revisits the importance of learning styles and experiential learning and explores some reasons why business ethics teachers should not teach to students' learning styles. Some cautionary reflections on using debriefing in teaching business ethics are then introduced. The need to institutionalize outcomes precedes the discussion of some findings gathered from a preliminary study of the aspects of effective and ineffective ethics education. I then offer some suggestions on what is required to deliver ethics education based on interviews in the preliminary study, discussions with colleagues, and my own experience with experimential learning theory.

THE RELEVANCY CHALLENGE

Students and faculty alike complain that textbook and classroom materials are too theoretical and have little or no application in the so-called "real world." This is often especially the case with business ethics. Thus, there should be no surprise that a major criticism of efforts to teach business ethics over the years has been the lack of relevancy for students. Zoellers and Fort (1996) have noted that teaching ethics is different from teaching other courses in a business school. Additionally, some scholars have argued that one has to contend with issues such as ambiguity, credibility, relevance, and effectiveness (McDonald & Donleavy, 1995). The criticism of irrelevance may be intensified during the exposition, for example, of classical moral theory, such as Kant's categorical imperative.

Business school faculty have a responsibility to ensure that students learn how to appreciate and fully engage topics like ethics. Consider the following experience. A few years ago we invited a very successful CEO and principal stockholder of a chemical company to speak to our accounting students. Our speaker was very successful financially and very comfortable with making economic trade-offs between fines for chemical pollution of the environment and business profitability. Also, speaking as an international businessman, he expressed his unhappiness that U.S. legislation imposed criminal sanctions for certain "corrupt" practices that other countries treated as civil problems subject to fines. He argued before the students that on a level playing field the U.S. should not subject him to exposure for "jail time" when other countries would allow him to pay for his premeditated transgressions with fines. Our speaker also identified new international opportunities by naming countries more welcoming to chemical production that would offer greater profit potential because of lax or unenforced environmental restrictions. He ended his remarks by welcoming inquires from interested students. He was, as he said, always on the watch for a few "good accounting students" to add to his staff.

Our guest was controversial. Some students were upset that such a politically incorrect speaker could have slipped through our sensors. How could we expose students to such a pernicious influence? Other students found themselves more interested in the formula for economic success. It was clear that the students were engaged. How was our speaker defining a "good business student?" The theoretical world of ethics had been trans-

lated into a practical question: Do I want to leave a resume with the place-
ment office to get on the interview schedule with this company? To make
the problem more interesting, we can add that our speaker was a member
of the "advisory board" of a business school located in his home city.

The challenge of relevance is to achieve a direct connection between personal choices and real problems and issues. The teaching of business ethics
should provide both a theoretical and experiential framework that students
can apply in evaluating a situation and choosing between conflicting moral
demands. In such a program and/or course, the analysis relies on human
reason to raise important questions of morality and to provide logically
defensible responses.

In 1978, Edmund Pellegrino, then a university president, wrote a classic
paper entitled "Ethics and the Moral Center of the Medieval Enterprise,"
published in the *Bulletin of the New York Academy of Medievalism*. In it,
Pellegrino stated,

Ethics comes into existence, properly speaking, when morality itself becomes problematic, when the validity of beliefs about what is right and good comes into question, or when a conflict between opposing moral systems or obligations must be
resolved. Morality takes its values and beliefs for granted as presuppositions that
apply to all men. (p. 625)

Pellegrino further wrote,

Ethics emerged as a formal discipline when the Sophists and Socrates first began to
question Greek presumptions about the right and the good in political and social
life. Among them, morality for the first time became explicitly problematic and the
history of ethics since then has been an attempt to examine the presuppositions
about what is right and good and what should be normative for human actions.
(p. 626)

In essence, by employing the theories of moral philosophy in conjunction
with a need to inquire about what is right and wrong, business students
will be able to examine their own value systems as well as those operative
in the business environment of the private, public and not-for-profit sectors.
If business schools in general are intended to be liberating experiences designed to develop a student's skills of inquiry, understanding, and expression, then the ethical dimension should serve as a benchmark for a student's
education as well as a foundation upon which to build a successful business
career.

For business students to derive the most from ethics education, faculty
must insure that their efforts reflect those issues that business students need
to realistically understand. That is, ethics education must be geared to the
more immediate and personal issues that students are likely to encounter

throughout their careers. To accomplish this goal, business teachers must continue to avoid the tendency to use pedagogical approaches that reflect a strong bent towards dilemmas that have no direct relevance to the roles that business students will occupy in organizations. What is needed is an emphasis on the real-life situations or actual experiences of practicing managers (Maglagan & Snell, 1992; Sims & Sims, 1991) where students must be able to apply moral reasoning and develop skill in ethical reasoning (Trevino and McCabe, 1994).

Real-life situations reflect the type of challenges students are likely to face and help them bridge the gap between theory and application as case discussions become more relevant and focused on situations that reflect the types of experiences students are likely to face in business. When brief anecdotes are included in textbooks for student discussion, the anecdotes may lack the context necessary for comprehending the ethical dimensions of the situation. These contextual factors include the fact that human beings themselves play highly differentiated roles and have different norms to guide them in different social contexts (Trevino & McCabe, 1994), their organizational culture, and the culture of the society which supports their institutions (Furman, 1990). In addition, students must learn to recognize ethical dilemmas when they are embedded in the complexity of real-life situations. Finally, multiple, and often conflicting, claims are placed on new employees, an issue which must be addressed when teaching ethics, particularly to undergraduates (Furman, 1990). Thus, the classroom experience needs to involve students in discussion that addresses both defining and resolving ethical dilemmas.

In summary, the challenge of relevancy can be expressed in terms of the following operational objectives:

- Create and foster *awareness* of the ethical components of business.
- *Legitimize* the consideration of ethical components as an integral part of business decision making.
- Provide a conceptual framework for *analyzing* the ethical components of business decision making and making choices.
- Help students *apply* ethical analysis to the very real and practical day-to-day business activities.

To achieve the objectives of teaching business ethics, Alam (1999) suggests that the following steps should be taken:

1. Trained staff in multidisciplinary areas should be employed who can relate their discipline(s) with the overall business/decision making.
2. A business-like environment should be created in the class.
3. Workshops to develop different skills and competencies should be organized.

4. Different disciplines should be coordianted through case studies.

5. Consultants from outside should be invited in to provide the broader view of the business.

6. Business people should be involved in designing curricula.

7. Business practices should be analyzed.

8. Different disciplines should be properly coordinated.

9. A fictional company should be developed for study.

10. Courses on business ethics and society should be developed.

11. Role playing should be used to explore ethical problems.

12. Courses relating to social implications of business decision making should be developed.

13. Education should be well-rounded at the lower level and more specialized at the higher level.

14. Student should be provided with workplace experience.

BALANCING PHILOSOPHICAL AND PRACTICAL EXTREMES

Successfully teaching business ethics requires teachers to continuously strive to achieve a balance between the active engagement of students with issues and a critical analysis of choices as mentioned in Chapters 7 and 8. This balancing act is usually the result of faculty having to wrestle with two traditional and conflicting alternatives to teaching business ethics. The first method stresses background knowledge and analytical procedures clearly needed for rigorous moral evaluation. The second method uses cases extensively and focuses much more on the functional and strategic problems of business organizations.

Many teachers are confronted with the situation where it is hard to get students in the classroom to apply specific ethical principles to precise business problems. Students often propose unworkable alternatives to avoid the moral choice and question facts to delay the inevitable decision. And in numerous situations, instead of arguing from the ethical principles the course is attempting to convey, they argue from the personal opinions they have held for years. Two writers recently described this exact problem in their own classes (Fort & Zollers, 1999):

Even an ethics course that requires mastery of a good deal of normative theory is likely to depend upon a high degree of class participation. There thus develops a paradox of, on the one hand, encouraging students to be involved actively in discussion and, on the other hand, avoiding merely superficial sharing of "warm" feelings that avoids critical analysis and dialogue. How does a professor strike a balance whereby students are passionately engaged yet critically analytical, while exploring unfamiliar and challenging material? (p. 274)

One writer has proposed a format for increasing the likely success of achieving the balance between active engagement of students with the issues and a critical analysis of the choices (Hosmer, 2000). Briefly, a standardized format is handed out to students each time a major case is assigned, and students are required to fill in the blanks thoughtfully and hand back the forms for grading. There are 20 questions to be answered and the instructor assigns a maximum of five points for each question. According to Hosmer, "Consequently grading on the familiar scale of 0 to 100 is straightforward and simple." Each question (section) that requires a response comes with a brief description of the issue to be addressed or the principle to be applied. To date, Hosmer notes that the format works remarkably well and has resulted in dramatic improvement in class discussions. Further, Hosmer believes that students are working up the hoped-for scale (Rest & Narváez, 1994) of moral sensitivity, moral judgement, moral motivation, and moral character. I have used a modified version of this standardized format and would highly recommend it as an excellent way of successfully balancing the philosophical and practical approach to teaching business ethics. Those interested in finding out more about this approach should see Hosmer (2000). A copy of the standardized format for case analysis of moral problems can be found in Appendix I of Hosmer's article.

ATTEND TO AND MANAGE THE LEARNING PROCESS

Business ethics teachers like others are aware of the ongoing changes in themselves and students during this period of great change and experimentation in business schools. As they facilitate learning, growth, and development in students during these times of change, faculty responsible for teaching business ethics struggle to improve themselves and to become more effective classroom leaders, planners, presenters, and facilitators. Business school faculty must not only respond to the demands of created by very complex organizational, professional, and technological environments but also reexamine their choice of pedagogy and their assumptions about the learning process. Rather than using only the teaching style with which they may be most comfortable and familiar, those responsible for teaching business ethics must learn to use new techniques and approaches to respond to a variety of educational goals and a variety of student approaches to the learning process.

Kolb and others committed to experiential learning say that adults will learn "no matter what." Learning is as natural as rest or play. With or without books, visual aids, inspiring teachers, or classrooms, adults will manage to learn. Business ethics teachers can, however, make a difference in *what* students learn and in *how well* they learn it. If students know *why* they are learning about ethics, and if the reason fits their needs as they perceive them (the "so what?"), they will learn quickly and deeply. In addition, if business school faculty and administrators take time to manage the learning process through development of business school curricula, student learning will be enhanced.

To conduct the educational process in business schools in a manner that attends to the individual learning styles of students and fosters student development requires management of those aspects of the educational system that influence the learning process. Such a management system must be soundly built on a valid model of the learning process. There has been a great burgeoning of approaches or techniques for teaching business ethics designed to assist the learning process in recent years: computer-aided instruction, experienced-based learning materials, programmed instruction, simulations and games, multimedia curricula, service learning projects, and so on. Although these techniques tend to be highly sophisticated and creative applications, we must constantly ask ourselves if they are enhancing student learning. The weakness of nearly all these techniques is the failure to recognize and explicitly provide for the differences in learning styles that are characteristic of both individuals and subject matters like ethics.

Even though many of these business ethics teaching innovations have been developed in the name of individualized education and self-directed learning, I still believe there has been little attempt to specify along which dimensions individualization is to take place. For example, although computer-aided instruction and programmed learning provide alternative routes or branches for the individual student, these branches tend to be based primarily on various elaborations of the subject matter being taught (i.e., a wrong answer puts the student on a branch giving him or her more information about the question). Little has been done to provide the individual student with branches that provide alternative learning methods (such as those that differ from the faculty member's preferred style or method) based on the student's learning style. In addition, there has been little research to assess how the effectiveness of various approaches to teaching business ethics is contingent on either individual student learning styles or the type of subject matter being taught.

THE CASE FOR NOT TEACHING TO STUDENTS' LEARNING STYLES IN BUSINESS ETHICS EDUCATION

I believe I would be remiss in my responsibilities in offering my views on the value of using learning styles to enhance learning and the teaching of business ethics if I did not note that on the face of it a simple proposition seems to hold the key to effectiveness. If business ethics teachers wish to connect with as many students as possible, all they need to do is to find out about the learning styles these students exhibit and then adjust their teaching exercises and materials to the spread of styles revealed. However, it is important for the business ethics teacher to keep in mind that in determining how someone is going to learn something a number of variables other than an individual's preferred learning style are of equal or greater importance. Chief among these are the nature of the learning task, the student's level of learning readiness, the student's previous experience and knowledge in this area, the student's and the teacher's personalities, the personalities of other learners, the political ethos of the business school and the broader educational institution, and the dominant values and traditions of the culture of which the student is a member. The idea of teaching to easily identifiable learning styles, while superficially simple, is in reality highly complex and this complexity must be taken into consideration by the teacher in any business ethics teaching effort.

In fact, rather than business ethics teachers always adjusting their practice to account for students' preferred learning styles, a good educational case can be made for doing precisely the opposite. In other words, instead of affirming the habitual, comfortable ways our students go about their learning—some of which may involve deeply etched, self-defeating habits—business ethics teachers should think about introducing students to alternative modes of learning.

I have found that the real value in Kolb's experiential learning model is its emphasis on the importance of developing a students' ability to develop learning strengths in each of the four learning modes and not just to teach to a student's preferred learning style. The model recognizes that most learning and life episodes require a variety of learning responses. Thus, it is sometimes important to teach *against* students' preferred learning styles. If the business ethics teacher has students' best interests at heart, the teacher may well decide that the last thing students need is to be confirmed in a comfortable but narrowly focused learning style. Far better to introduce students to a diversity of ways of planning and conducting learning.

The principle of diversity should be engraved on every business ethics teacher's heart. In evaluating the performance of a business ethics teacher (or any teacher for that matter) or in judging the merit of an educational approach, one of the first things I look for is diversity. Are teachers using a range of teaching approaches? Do they use a variety of teaching materials? Do they alternate opportunities for individual study with group collaboration? Do they mix lectures, cases, discussions, and experiential learning pedagogies and techniques? Do they incorporate various philosophical and other ethical theories in their teaching efforts? Do they allow for periods of reflective analysis?

Keeping diversity at the forefront serves two important functions. On the one hand, business ethics teachers stand a good chance of connecting to the preferred learning style of most of their students at some point in their teaching. I have found that at this point students feel comfortable with, and affirmed in, their learning. On the other hand, business ethics teachers probably also introduce most students in their classes to learning modes and orientations that are new to them. Students' repertoire of learning styles will thus be enlarged and they will be more likely to flourish in a greater range of settings outside the academy than would otherwise be the case.

SOME CAUTIONARY REFLECTIONS ON DEBRIEFING

Several cautionary reflections are worth highlighting for those interested in using experiential learning exercises and debriefing in their business ethics teaching efforts. First, you must recognize that not all students will respond favorably to business ethics in general and experiential learning exercises and debriefing in particular. Second, many students are not prepared to take on the active role that is being asked of them as learners nor will they see this as an opportunity for them to develop new and different relationships with faculty members responsible for the course and their fellow classmates. That is, motivation to be involved varies by student. Some exhibit great enthusiasm to experiment with novel situations, while others are reluctant to do so. Third, don't be surprised by differences between students in one class and students in another concerning their willingness to participate in both the experiential learning exercises and the debriefing, which requires students to discuss their attitudes, values, feelings, and behaviors. I have experienced firsthand the difference between students in two sections of a course on Business and Society. One group of students was energetic and open to trying new things and actively participated in the experiential learning activities and the subsequent debriefings throughout the course. Students in the other course appeared to be more resistant to the whole topic of business ethics, experiential learning exercises, and debriefing. On a similar note, the number of international students in a course can also have a profound impact on the dynamics of the course. Some of them, in my experience, are not comfortable with the whole idea of debriefing. It is not unusual for some international students, who may be notorious for proficiency at exams and a deferential attitude towards professors, to view debriefing as strange and even more frightening than it is viewed by students from the United States.

In my more than 20 years of teaching in business schools I have come to believe that skepticism towards and dislike of business ethics, experiential learning exercises, and debriefing is a common denominator among many faculty. Although a good debriefing may look as if it is natural and spontaneous, it does require a different role for faculty who may not be comfortable with a more active student or learning process. Altering one's teaching approach or style, like relying on what may be a new pedagogical approach (i.e., experiential learning exercises), has its costs and is at best an investment of energy and time, with expected return as a key variable. Additionally, using debriefing in teaching ethics can be emotionally more challenging and risky for faculty than teaching other business subjects. Faculty who are interested in using such an approach must be prepared for challenges and risks that may relate to their self-conception, to the communication climate in the classroom, and to their role authority as a function of both.

While there is no clear time frame for becoming proficient with the debriefing approach in teaching business ethics suggested in this book, in my experience, the greatest obstacle is the instructor's fear of personal dissonance and of losing control in the classroom. If being in control at all times and keeping a distance from students is one's preferred style, the ideas offered in this book will not be of much benefit. Finally, perhaps the best advice I can offer to my colleagues to keep two things in mind—"You must know your audience" and "Prepare, be patient, and be flexible." Failure to follow this advice will result in missed opportunities to help students see the value of debriefing and, thus, maximizing their learning about ethics.

INSTITUTIONALIZING OUTCOMES ASSESSMENT

Business schools should make every effort to institutionalize outcomes assessment, and business ethics teachers can take the lead in this area. We can take the lead in finding answers to questions like:

1. What makes for good assessments? Good assessments begin with clear educational purposes, expectations, and learning objectives. I always find it helpful to see if my teaching business ethics goals or objectives pass the SMART model: are they specific, measurable, attainable, results-oriented, and timely.

2. What is good assessment information? The goodness of assessments is determined by their validity and reliability. Validity, the most important characteristic of assessments, is concerned with the collection of information that is most appropriate for making the desired decision. Reliability is concerned with the consistency or typicality of the assessment information collected. Assessment begins when we establish learning objectives for a school, program, course, or activity.

3. Is there an important difference between good teaching and effective teaching? What is good teaching? What is effective teaching? Good teaching refers to the *process of instruction*, while effective teaching refers to the *outcomes of instruction*. Good teaching deals with how we organize and present our instructional activities in order to engage students in the learning process. Effective teaching goes one step beyond good teaching to focus upon what students have actually learned from instruction. Clearly, there is a relationship between good and effective teaching; the better the teaching, the more likely that it will be effective.

Business ethics teachers can also benefit from focusing on these questions as they think about how to measure and evaluate their effectiveness:

- What is it I am teaching?
- What knowledge and abilities must students achieve?
- How do I know when they've achieved them?
- How good is good enough?
- What, ideally, would I/we like students to learn and be able to do?
- Am I teaching what I think I am teaching?
- Am I helping people learn?

THE INTERVIEWS

In order to gain some additional insight into factors contributing to effective ethics education and to validate the challenges it faces as advanced at various points throughout this book, I conducted a very basic study. Twenty-two individuals participated in one-on-one interviews. These individuals were between 30 and 55 years of age and had from two to 16 years of experience as ethics educators. Each person described a peak and a nadir experience of ethics education by responding to the following protocol based on the experiential learning cycle described throughout this book.

The question stated, "Think about a time when you were either a teacher or a student in an ethics education session that was particularly (ineffective or effective) in terms of your learning and the learning of others."

1. *Concrete Experience.* Tell me about the experience—what happened? What were your thoughts, feelings, and perceptions at the time of the experience?
2. *Reflective Observation.* Since the time of the experience, what have been your key reflections how do you make sense of the experience now?
3. *Abstract Conceptualization*: What are your conclusions as a result of reflection and efforts to make sense of the experience?
4. *Active Experimentation*: What rules of thumb and guidelines would you include in any future ethics education designs?

Data were analyzed for recurring comments or themes that are listed in Table 14.1. Findings are presented without interpretation. Factors that contribute to effectiveness in teaching ethics are storytelling, trust and safety, dialogue, gaining personal insight, broadly defining ethics, teaching more than cognition, business ethics education efforts lasting more than one day, clear expectations and goals, and a diverse group of students and teachers. Characteristics of ineffectiveness are negative perceptions of faculty, lack of closure of emotional issues, lack of trust, ethical theories or models as sole foci of the course, feeling unable to be heard, feeling personally attacked or blamed, and the business ethics education effort lasting one day or less.

Females and males were evenly split in identifying storytelling and dia-

Table 14.1
Aspects of Effective and Ineffective Ethics Education

Effective Experiences	Ineffective Experiences
storytelling	negative perceptions of faculty
trust and safety	lack of closure of emotional issues
dialogue	lack of trust
gaining personal insight	ethical theories or models as sole foci of the course
broadly defining ethics	feeling unheard
teaching more than cognition	feeling personally attacked or blamed
business ethics education effort lasting more than one day	insufficient class time—effort lasting one day or less
clear expectations and goals	a diverse group of students and teachers

logue as useful learning tools. The two activities are related. Storytelling, it seems, impacts students in ways that arouse curiosity and a desire to engage in dialogue and often leads to personal insight. Females spoke about trust as a component of effective ethics education, while males associated feeling safe (from attack and blame) with a satisfying experience. Broadly defining ethics positively impacts the experience of males more than females. Expanding the context of ethics creates the opportunity for students to personally relate to others and (work) ethical experiences and positions them for more receptivity to the more controversial aspects of ethics such as racism, sexism, and so forth. This opinion is expressed across the ethnic and gender boundaries of people interviewed. A couple of individuals suggested gradual movement toward the discussion of "hot button" or controversial ethical issues or dilemmas. Ethics is less satisfying for many of the individuals in this study when limited to a focus on either knowledge acquisition or practice.

Ethics educators in this study emphasized that teaching is more important than cognition in a class on ethics. Efficacy in ethics education is unlike competency or skill building where you can be very objective and still do a good job. It touches everyone's feelings. Effectiveness also necessitates more time. Those interviewed felt that two to three days is the minimum time for teaching ethics. Less time often leaves students with unresolved issues. Lack of closure of emotional issues is an aspect of ineffective ethics experiences. One teacher provides individual discussions with students taking classes on ethics. This highlights the importance of debriefing.

Experiences of ethics education were more positive for those interviewed when ground rules and goals were clarified, particularly when this occurred at the beginning of the semester or quarter. One educator is committed to what he refers to as community building in which objectives, ground rules, and roles are explicit and total group as well as subgroup is seen as important. Identifying personal goals for some individuals is just as critical as goal setting for the class in general.

A team or interdisciplinary approach to teaching was preferred by all of the individuals. Having a diverse team of faculty models the complexity and inability to compartmentalize ethics. A multicultural class of students provides richness of discussion and diminishes feelings of isolation and loneliness. Teacher skill was more a concern for males than females. Negative perception of faculty was a key aspect of ineffective ethics education experience. Elements of this theme are perception of faculty as coercive (my way or the highway), lacking in process skills, or unclear about their own inability to listen and be open to new ways of viewing or interpreting ethical or philosophical theories and responses to ethical dilemmas.

Themes from the interviews confirm the challenges confronting ethics education as presented at various points in this book. Interviewees underscore the need for dialogue, psychological safety, and student- or learner-directed education. In singling out a requirement for more than cognition, the usefulness of a more comprehensive method of teaching is also highlighted.

EXPERIENTIAL LEARNING THEORY AND LEARNING STYLES IN ETHICS EDUCATION

If experiental learning theory offers ethics education a framework that integrates personal experience and practical application with perceptive appreciation and understanding of concepts, what then is required to deliver ethics education? I offer some suggestions based on interviews, discussions with colleagues, and my own experience with experiential learning theory in business ethics teaching.

Build Ethics across the Curriculum

Ethics cannot be learned in one course; it must be located in courses across the curriculum. This has increasingly become an important addition to our pedagogical arsenal because it has made us more fully aware that skills build up over time and that practicing them only once or twice does not get us very far. As with writing, what absurdity to think that one can teach ethics in a single course! We know that the principle of continued exposure and practice should not need much advocacy in regard to teaching business ethics and learning to apply ethical principles.

Position Ethics Education as a Holistic Process

It is useful to inform students that an ethics course based on experiential learning might belie some of their assumptions about the teaching process and their role in it. Unlike traditional approaches to learning in which teachers are experts and students are passive recipients of the information that is disseminated, here responsibility for learning is shared by teacher and student. In that a course on ethics is not merely a new content area, it summons all of what students are—their intelligence, their perception, their practicality, and most importantly their emotions. The approach to learning must be guided by a holistic framework and include a range of activities, among them experiential exercises, discussions, readings, and role-plays.

Clarify the Role of the Instructor

Generally, and particularly in ethics education, experiential learning theory requires a different role for the instructor from the one typically seen. That role needs to be clarified. The teacher's role is less one of purveyor of knowledge and more one of managing a classroom as a learning organization. We have stressed that at any given time the instructor could be a role model and colleague, who supports awareness of human experience in the moment; a process consultant who keeps on track an engaging discussion of ethics, ethical behavior, ethical principles, and so forth; an interpreter of knowledge, who does a brief lecture on ethical theories and models; or a coach, who supports the planning of transfer of learnings.

Clarify the Role of the Student

Experiential learning is individualized and self-directed learning. Students who are unaccustomed to this approach may have difficulty with assuming responsibility for achieving their learning objectives. Instructors will need to work with students so that they see value in their own experiences and can apply new knowledge, skills, and attitudes to their life situations.

Assess Learning Styles of Students and Faculty

Learning style immediately creates an alternative view of differences in students that faculty must take into consideration. The Learning Style Inventory (LSI) gives individuals data about which aspects of the learning process they prefer. It also has implications for classroom activities, faculty role, feedback, student engagement in material, and faculty-to-student dynamics. The LSI, when administered in class using the LSI grid, provides data about the learning community that is immediately available to everyone. It is intriguing to watch students act out their learning style during the discussions. Some struggle with feelings they have, others question the pragmatics of the model or challenge the theory behind it, and others just watch and take it all in.

Establish a Psychological Contract

The importance of psychological safety and feelings of trust in ethics education is emphasized in the literature and interviews conducted for this chapter. The concepts of learning environments and dialogue have been presented as constructive mechanisms for creating the ideal climate of learning. The act of negotiating a psychological contract is good for establishing trust and should take place during the first class session. The pinch model introduced earlier in this book captures the dynamic nature of psychological contracts and suggests strategies for renegotiation when "pinches" or disruption of shared expectations occur. It is designed to be a real agreement among members of the learning community—students and teachers alike—that guide their behavior for the entire term.

Identify Guidelines of Behavior

Guidelines complement the contracting process and like the psychological contract should be identified on the first day of class. Identifying guidelines, of course, is a joint activity between students and teachers. Guidelines to consider include honoring confidentiality, affording mutual respect, speaking from personal experience, and engaging in interpersonal conversation. Confidentiality creates a dilemma for students whose learning is supported by discussion outside the classroom, which we encourage and sometimes request. We ask students to refrain from attaching names to opinions or experiences shared by their classmates. Simply put, mutual respect is behavior consistent with the Golden Rule. It is the act of acknowledging that we all hold perspectives of the world which, even when they differ, are valid for each of us.

Encourage Dialogue

Design activities that allow for discussion and processing of experience. Dialogue itself begins with speaking from personal experience and owning experience through the use of first-person language—"I," "my," "me," "mine." First-person language is more engaging in dialogue than the more distant and abstract third person. It lends to "straight talk"—use of clean, clear, direct communication that fosters connections between two parties of equal status. Good conversation requires both speaking and listening and in this regard is not monological. Gestalt principles emphasize calling the other by name as a first step toward good interpersonal contact. Calling someone by name serves to plant a seed for relationship building. Another Gestalt approach to good conversation is to find ways to engage not two or a few but all students in total classroom discussion. Good conversation leads to good moral conversation, and both are key to conversational learning.

Foster Challenge

The insight that students remember as transformative comes from those learning episodes in which some element of challenge was involved. Challenge has a powerful affect on the teaching of business ethics. One of the most laudable characteristics of business ethics teachers is their readiness to affirm and encourage students to learn. In my experience, such affirmation is crucial to strengthening a student's sense of self-regard.

Taken to its extreme, however, affirming students can lead to an educational cul-de-sac in which students feel good about themselves but are never prompted to explore alternative perspectives, to venture into new skill areas, or to scrutinize critically those habitual assumptions underlying their ethical thoughts and actions. To live in a cul-de-sac is quietly comfortable, but it may be self-defeating. Business students are sometimes so enclosed within their narrow frames of reference that they are the last to recognize that these may be self-defeating and harmful. Thus, often the most important thing a business ethics teacher can do for his or her students is to challenge them with alternative perspectives, new activities, and critical reflection.

Use a Variety of Group Structures

It is important to mix groups based on the differences represented in the class (e.g., race, gender, learning style, organization type). It is also advisable to use a variety of structures—pairs, trios, small groups, and total community. I find especially useful the small group structure referred to as "learning teams" that meet during the formal structure of the class as well as outside of class. Time constraints, class size, and other related factors do not always allow for the appropriate and thorough processing/debriefing of student experiences within the classroom setting. Learning teams allow for continued processing/debriefing of experience and serve as support groups for identifying goals and for monitoring progress toward goal achievement. They enrich the learning process, provide a stable reference group, and facilitate trust that spills over into the classroom.

Use Personal Application Assignments

Readings, essays, term papers, thought pieces (a written stream of consciousness in reaction to readings or experiences), and group projects are mechanisms for teaching and learning about ethics and evaluation in ethics education. I like the Personal Application Assignment (PAA) that is used for evaluation of student progress by the student and teacher. The PAA is a paper that corresponds to the experiential learning model, since it is designed to indicate:

- A real situation (concrete experience).
- Understanding of the situation (reflective observation).
- Use of models and concepts to frame understanding of the situation (abstract conceptualization).
- Behavioral plans for similar situations in the future (active experimentation).
- Integration of the four preceding perspectives (synthesis).

The PAA is typically used several times during the course of a semester and is similar to the interview guide of open-ended questions that students respond to as a way of monitoring their development over the course of the class. Used in this manner, the PAA contributes to equalization of power between learner and teacher.

INCREASING THE NUMBER OF FACULTY TEACHING BUSINESS ETHICS

Business schools must also redouble their efforts to increase the number of experienced business ethics faculty. This means that there must be greater training opportunities for faculty interested in teaching business ethics. Although there have been strides made in increasing the number of faculty and improving overall coverage of ethics in business administration programs over the past two decades, faculty development and increased recruitment of faculty to teach business ethics should receive more attention by business schools and accrediting organizations like the International Association of Management Education and other professional associations like the Academy of Management. Each of them should offer assistance through more workshops and conferences. This development must go beyond convening panels and include both financial and other investments. Business schools can begin by asking themselves whether or not they support training and faculty development efforts to improve business ethics education. If they do not, then they can begin by identifying a strategy for rectifying the situation. Verbal encouragement alone is not enough if we are to increase the number of experienced faculty interested in and actually teaching business ethics.

CONCLUSION

The efficacy of business ethics education rests on the degree to which all participants are able to own who they are as individuals, as group members, as citizens of a global community, and as learners seeking knowledge and appreciation of self and other. Experiential learning is a theory of life and learning that celebrates human potential. As a paradigm of business ethics, it appropriately prepares students as learners for life in an ever-changing society.

Perhaps the most important point that I can make in concluding this book is to emphasize that we must deepen our knowledge of students considerably. Some faculty think they know students well enough already. But their views are shaped primarily by appearances, or the masks that students put on in the classroom. We need to acknowledge not only how students learn but also their motivations and aspirations as well as the conditions that inhibit learning or make it impossible, such as a classroom climate not conducive to learning and sharing.

Business school faculty today are overloaded, and their work stretches greatly beyond the canonical 40 hours. However, they must take the time to reorder or change the priorities. If they do not change them, then they should honestly say that making it possible for students to learn ethics and to keep on learning in general is not on the top of their agendas.

We must begin to look at our academic disciplines and ethics in fresh ways. How does our field look at ethics? How do our disciplines and ethics look from the point of view of students? Equally important, we want to build a framework upon which ethics can be taught, and we cannot leave it to the specialists alone, good as they may be. We, the teachers, as those responsible for teaching business ethics, need to articulate what we do. If more professors seriously consider the question of how students learn and the importance of teaching business ethics, we will all help build an effective environment for teaching and learning ethics, and the rewards—for us and for our students—will be exhilarating, with fewer "rabbits" like the one in the opening fable of this book.

REFERENCES

Alam, K.F. 1999. Ethics and accounting education. *Teaching Business Ethics* 2: 261–272.

Fort, T.L., & Zollers, F.E. 1999. Teaching business ethics: Theory and practice. *Teaching Business Ethics* 2: 273–290.

Furman, F.K. 1990. Teaching business ethics: Questioning the assumptions, seeking new directions. *Journal of Business Ethics* 9: 31–38.

Gilbert, J.T. 1992. Teaching business ethics: What, why, who, where, and when. *Journal of Education for Business* 68(1): 5–8.

Hill, A., & Stewart, I.C. 1999. Character education in business schools: Pedagogical strategies. *Teaching Business Ethics* 3: 179–193.

Hosmer, L.T. 2000. Standard format for the cane analysis of moral problems. *Teaching Business Ethics* 2: 169–180.

McDonald, G.M., & Donleavy, G.D. 1995. Objections to the teaching of business ethics. *Journal of Business Ethics* 10: 829–835.

Maglagan, P., & Snell, R. 1992. Some implications for management development research into managers' moral dilemmas. *British Journal of Management* 3: 157–168.

Pellegrino, E.D. 1978. Ethics and the moral center of the medieval enterprise. *Bulletin of the New York Academy of Medievalism* 54: 623–631.

Rest, J.R. 1979. *Development in judging moral issues.* Minneapolis: University of Minnesota Press.

Rest, J. and Narváez, D. (eds.) 1994. *Moral development in the professions.* Hillsdale, NJ: Lawrence Erlbaum Associates.

Sims, R.R., & Sims, S.J. 1991. Increasing applied business ethics courses in business school curricula. *Journal of Business Ethics* 10: 211–219.

Trevino, L.K., & McCabe, D. 1994. Meta-learning about business ethics: Building honorable business school communities. *Journal of Business Ethics* 10: 211–219.

Zoellers, F.E., & Fort, T.L. 1996. Total quality management in the classroom. *Journal of Legal Studies* 14: 1–12.

Index

About the Author

RONALD R. SIMS is the Floyd Dewey Gottwald Senior Professor of Business Administration in the Graduate School of Business at the College of William & Mary, Williamsburg, Virginia. He holds a doctorate in organizational behavior and consults widely with organizations in the private, public, and not-for-profit sectors. Dr. Sims is author or coauthor of more than 75 scholarly and professional articles and more than 20 books. Among his more recent ones are *Organizational Success Through Effective Human Resources Management* (2002), *The Challenge of Front-Line Management* (2000), and *Keys to Employee Success in Coming Decades* (1999, with John G. Veres III).